October 5–8, 2014
Honolulu, HI, USA

Association for Computing Machinery

Advancing Computing as a Science & Profession

UIST'14

Adjunct Publication of the 27th Annual ACM Symposium on
User Interface Software and Technology

Sponsored by:

ACM SIGCHI & ACM SIGGRAPH

Supported by:

University of Toronto, AutoDesk, Microsoft, Marvell, Synaptics, Adobe, GRAND, WaCom, FXPal, Google, University of Hawaii, IBM Research, Tactual Labs, Yahoo! Labs, & Disney Research

Association for Computing Machinery

Advancing Computing as a Science & Profession

The Association for Computing Machinery
2 Penn Plaza, Suite 701
New York, New York 10121-0701

Notice to Past Authors of ACM-Published Articles
ACM intends to create a complete electronic archive of all articles and/or other material previously published by ACM. If you have written a work that has been previously published by ACM in any journal or conference proceedings prior to 1978, or any SIG Newsletter at any time, and you do NOT want this work to appear in the ACM Digital Library, please inform permissions@acm.org, stating the title of the work, the author(s), and where and when published.

ISBN: 978-1-4503-3068-8 (Digital)

ISBN: 978-1-4503-3431-0 (Print)

Additional copies may be ordered prepaid from:

ACM Order Department
PO Box 30777
New York, NY 10087-0777, USA

Phone: 1-800-342-6626 (USA and Canada)
+1-212-626-0500 (Global)
Fax: +1-212-944-1318
E-mail: acmhelp@acm.org
Hours of Operation: 8:30 am – 4:30 pm ET

Printed in the USA

Chairs' Welcome

It is our pleasure to welcome you to the 27th Annual ACM Symposium on User Interface Software and Technology (UIST), held from October 5-8th 2014, in Honolulu, Hawaii, USA.

UIST is the premier forum for the presentation of research innovations in the software and technology of human-computer interfaces. Sponsored by ACM's special interest groups on computer-human interaction (SIGCHI) and computer graphics (SIGGRAPH), UIST brings together researchers and practitioners from many areas, including web and graphical interfaces, input and output devices, information visualization, sensing technologies, interactive displays, tabletop and tangible computing, interaction techniques, augmented and virtual reality, ubiquitous computing, fabrication, wearable and mobile computing, and computer supported cooperative work.

UIST 2014 received a record 333 technical paper submissions from 34 countries. After a thorough review process, the 36-member program committee accepted 74 papers (22.2%). Each anonymous submission was first reviewed by three external reviewers, and a meta-review was provided by a program committee member. If any of the four reviewers deemed a submission to pass a rejection threshold, we asked the authors to submit a short rebuttal addressing the reviewers' concerns, and a second member of the program committee was asked to examine the paper, rebuttal, and reviews, and to provide their own meta-review. The program committee met in person in Toronto, Ontario, Canada, on June 19th and 20th, 2014, to select which papers to invite for the program. Submissions were accepted only after the authors provided a final revision addressing the committee's comments.

In addition to papers submitted directly, the symposium program includes two papers from the ACM Transactions on Computer-Human Interaction journal (TOCHI), as well as 31 posters, 48 demonstrations, and 8 student presentations in the tenth annual Doctoral Symposium. Our program also features the sixth annual Student Innovation Contest. This year, there are 24 teams taking part in the contest, which is focused on household interfaces based on the *Kinoma Create* platform by Marvell. UIST 2014 will feature two keynote presentations. The opening keynote will be given by Mark Bolas (University of Southern California) on designing the user in the user interface. Bret Victor will deliver the closing keynote on the impact of dynamic media on representation of thought.

Our community has been growing tremendously both in the number of submissions as well as attendees. For the first time, this year's program will be held in two parallel tracks. We hope that you will find our program interesting and thought-provoking and that UIST 2014 will provide you with a valuable opportunity to exchange results at the cutting edge of user interfaces research, to meet friends and colleagues, and to forge future collaborations with other researchers and practitioners from institutions around the world.

Hrvoje Benko
UIST'14 General Chair
Microsoft Research, USA

Mira Dontcheva
UIST'14 Program Co-Chair
Adobe, USA

Daniel Wigdor
UIST'14 Program Co-Chair
University of Toronto, Canada

Table of Contents

Doctoral Symposium

Demonstrations

UIST 2014 Symposium Organization

General Chair: Hrvoje Benko *(Microsoft Research, USA)*

Program Chairs: Mira Dontcheva *(Adobe, USA)*
Daniel Wigdor *(University of Toronto, USA)*

Poster Chairs: Daniel Vogel *(University of Waterloo, Canada)*
Gery Casiez *(University of Lille, France)*

Demonstration Chairs: Per Ola Kristensson *(University of St. Andrews, UK)*
Nicolai Marquardt *(University College London, UK)*

Doctoral Symposium Chair: Patrick Baudisch *(Hasso Plattner Institute, Germany)*

Student Contest Chairs: David Kim *(Newcastle University, UK)*
Valkyrie Savage *(University of California Berkeley, USA)*

Video Previews Chairs: Fanny Chevalier *(University of Toronto, Canada)*
Stéphane Huot *(Université Paris-Sud, France)*

Registration Chairs: Jakub Dostal *(University of St. Andrews, UK)*
Siddharth Khullar *(Quanttus Inc., USA)*

Treasurer: Kirstie Magness *(Microsoft Research, USA)*

Sponsorship: Roel Vertegaal *(Queen's University, Canada)*

Proceedings Chair: Clifton Forlines *(Tactual Labs, Canada)*

Local Arrangements Chair: Scott Robertson *(University of Hawaii, USA)*

Student Volunteer Chairs: Stefanie Mueller *(Hasso Plattner Institute, Germany)*
Daniel Leithinger *(MIT Media Lab, USA)*

Web and Social Media Chair: Florian Daiber *(DFKI, Germany)*

Publicity Chairs: Chris Harrison *(Carnegie Mellon University, USA)*
Kentaro Fukuchi *(Meiji University, Japan)*

Keynote Chair: Otmar Hilliges *(ETH Zurich, Switzerland)*

Lasting Impact Award Chair: Ken Hinckley *(Microsoft Research, USA)*

Interactive Program Guide Chairs: Stephen Oney *(Carnegie Mellon University, USA)*
Jason Wiese *(Carnegie Mellon University, USA)*
Eiji Hayashi *(Carnegie Mellon University, USA)*

Design/Signage Chair: Asta Roseway *(Microsoft Research, USA)*

Beach Chair: T. Scott Saponas *(Microsoft Research, USA)*

Program Committee: Maneesh Agrawala *(University of California Berkeley, USA)*
Saleema Amershi *(Microsoft Research, USA)*
Michael Bernstein *(Stanford University, USA)*
Floraine Berthouzoz *(Adobe Research, USA)*
Bernd Bickel *(Disney Research, USA)*
Jeff Bigham *(Carnegie Mellon University, USA)*
Joel Brandt *(Adobe Research, USA)*
Fanny Chevalier *(University of Toronto, Canada)*
Steven Drucker *(Microsoft Research, USA)*
Steve Feiner *(Columbia University, USA)*
Cliff Forlines *(Tactual Labs, Canada)*
Mark Gross *(University of Colorado Boulder, USA)*
Tovi Grossman *(Autodesk, Canada)*
Francois Guimbretiere *(Cornell University, USA)*
Otmar Hilliges *(ETH Zurich, Switzerland)*
Ken Hinckley *(Microsoft Research, USA)*
Eve Hoggan *(Helsinki Institute for Information Technology, Finland)*
Christian Holz *(Yahoo! Labs, USA)*
Pourang Irani *(University of Manitoba, Canada)*
Jun Kato *(AIST, Japan)*
Darren Leigh *(Tactual Labs, Canada)*
Yang Li *(Google Research, USA)*
Kent Lyons *(Yahoo! Labs, USA)*
Wendy MacKay *(INRIA, France)*
Meredith Ringel Morris *(Microsoft Research, USA)*
Tomer Moscovich *(Lab 126, USA)*
Brad Myers *(Carnegie Mellon University, USA)*
Jeff Nichols *(IBM Research, USA)*
Alex Olwal *(Google, USA)*
m.c. schraefel *(University of Southampton, UK)*
Sriram Subramanian *(University of Bristol, UK)*
Bruce Thomas *(University of South Australia, Australia)*
Gina Venolia *(Microsoft Research, USA)*
Daniel Vogel *(University of Waterloo, Canada)*
Jue Wang *(Adobe Research, USA)*
Andy Wilson *(Microsoft Research, USA)*

Doctoral Symposium Committee: Meredith Ringel Morris *(Microsoft Research, USA)*
m.c. schraefel *(University of Southampton, UK)*
Scott Hudson *(Carnegie Mellon University, USA)*

UIST 2014 Reviewers

Konstantin Aal
David Abraham
Mark Ackerman
Aseem Agarwala
Teemu Ahmaniemi
Imeh Akpan
Jason Alexander
Ahmad Aljadaan
Robert Allison
Fraser Anderson
Paul André
Michelle Annett
Alissa Antle
Caroline Appert
Bruno Araujo
Daniel Archambault
Ahmed Arif
Daniel Ashbrook
Ignacio Avellino
Daniel Avrahami
Magnus Axholt
Shiri Azenkot
Ron Azuma
Pierre Bénard
François Bérard
benjamin bach
Seok-Hyung Bae
Ronald Baecker
Brian Bailey
Gilles Bailly
Ravin Balakrishnan
Rafael Ballagas
Nikola Banovic
Jakob Bardram
Connelly Barnes
Sumit Basu
Olivier Bau
Thomas Baudel
Patrick Baudisch
Jean-Charles Bazin
Paul Beardsley
Michel Beaudouin-Lafon
Roman Bednarik
Serge Belongie
Steve Benford
Hrvoje Benko

Edward Benson
Marina Bers
Anastasia Bezerianos
Xiaojun Bi
Jacob Biehl
Eric Bier
Mark Billinghurst
Oliver Bimber
Renaud Blanch
Dan Bohus
David Bonnet
Kellogg Booth
Jan Borchers
Sebastian Boring
Sebastian Boring
Jonathan Botts
Patrick Bourdot
Adrien Bousseau
Doug Bowman
Jordan Boyd-Graber
Erin Brady
Andrew Bragdon
Stacy Branham
Helene Brashear
Karen Brennan
Stephen Brewster
Anke Brock
Eric Brockmeyer
Dave Brown
A.J. Brush
Nick Bryan-Kinns
Leah Buechley
Abdullah Bulbul
Andreas Bulling
Andrea Bunt
Margaret Burnett
D. Alex Butler
Andreas Butz
Bill Buxton
John Canny
Xiang Cao
Thomas Carter
Scott Carter
Géry Casiez
Steven Castellucci
Jessica Cauchard

Amira Chalbi
Liwei Chan
Remco Chang
Kerry Chang
Olivier Chapuis
Duen Horng (Polo) Chau
Siddhartha Chaudhuri
Ciprian Chelba
Alex Qiang Chen
Tao Chen
Nicholas Chen
Hsiang-Ting Chen
Jiawen Chen
Mike Chen
Xiang 'Anthony' Chen
Shiwei Cheng
Lung-Pan Cheng
Erin Cherry
Marshini Chetty
Fanny Chevalier
Pei-Yu Chi
Ed Chi
Lydia Chilton
Alvin Chin
Ming Ki Chong
Philip Chou
Tanzeem Choudhury
Michael Christel
James Clawson
Adrian Clear
Andy Cockburn
Michael Cohen
Gabe Cohn
Andrea Colaco
Sunny Consolvo
Stéphane Conversy
Jeremy Cooperstock
Nikolaus Correll
Dan Cosley
James Coughlan
Céline Coutrix
David Coyle
Michael Crabb
Jácome Cunha
Brian Curless
Allen Cypher

Tanja Döring
Marian Dörk
Laura Dabbish
Raimund Dachselt
Florian Daiber
Nicholas Dalton
Andreea Danielescu
Catalina Danis
Abe Davis
Nicholas Davis
Munmun De Choudhury
Alexander De Luca
David Dearman
Rob DeLine
Nick Demopoulos
Jia Deng
Anind Dey
Nicholas Diakopoulos
Paul Dietz
Danny Dig
Alan Dix
Morgan Dixon
Mingsong Dou
Paul Dourish
Steven Dow
Pierre Dragicevic
Nicolas Ducheneaut
Susan Dumais
Mark Dunlop
Paul Dunphy
Tim Dwyer
James Eagan
Florian Echtler
Keith Edwards
Serge Egelman
Michael Eisenberg
Jacob Eisenstein
Stephen Ellis
Alex Endert
Stephen Fairclough
Shelly Farnham
Ethan Fast
Jean-Daniel Fekete
Adrienne Felt
Ylva Fernaeus
Roland Fernandez

Jennifer Fernquist
Bruce Ferwerda
Rebecca Fiebrink
Leah Findlater
Andrew Fiore
Danyel Fisher
Stephen Fitchett
George Fitzmaurice
Geraldine Fitzpatrick
Morten Fjeld
Scott Fleming
James Fogarty
Sean Follmer
Adam Fourney
Euan Freeman
Dustin Freeman
Adrian Friday
Bernd Froehlich
Jon Froehlich
Hongbo Fu
Jun Fujima
Bill Fulton
Thomas Funkhouser
Krzysztof Gajos
Maribeth Gandy
Jizhou Gao
Jérémie Garcia
Henry Gardner
William Gaver
Hans Gellersen
Aaron Genest
Elizabeth Gerber
Kiel Gilleade
Yotam Gingold
Shiry Ginosar
Andreas Girgensohn
Mike Glaser
Michael Glueck
Mayank Goel
Dan Goldman
Richard Gomer
Liang Gou
Raphael Grasset
Keith Green
Mike Greenberg
Michael Greenberg
Saul Greenberg
Laurent Grisoni

Paul Gross
Jens Grubert
Jonathan Grudin
Jinwei Gu
Yves Guiard
Philip Guo
Sidhant Gupta
Ankit Gupta
Sean Gustafson
Carl Gutwin
Sinem Guven
Tobias Höllerer
Martin Hachet
Alaa Halawani
Michael Haller
Nur Al-huda Hamdan
Tracy Hammond
Jaehyun Han
Mark Hancock
richard harper
Chris Harrison
Björn Hartmann
Khalad Hasan
Jennifer Healey
Marti Hearst
Jeffrey Heer
Kurtis Heimerl
Robert Held
Florian Heller
Nathalie Henry Riche
Christin Henzen
Aaron Hertzmann
Otmar Hilliges
Serena Hillman
Juan David Hincapié-
   Ramos
Uta Hinrichs
Michitaka Hirose
Leanne Hirshfield
Shinsaku Hiura
Steve Hodges
Jeffery Hoehl
James Hollan
Jason Hong
M. Ehsan Hoque
Michael Horn
Kasper Hornbæ
Eva Hornecker

John Horton
Chang Hu
Jeff Huang
Yingdan Huang
Scott Hudson
Matt Huenerfauth
Julie Hui
Jessica Hullman
Seth Hunter
Stephane Huot
Amy Hurst
Takeo Igarashi
Masahiko Inami
Kori Inkpen
Stephen Intille
Shamsi Iqbal
Petra Isenberg
Tobias Isenberg
Edward Ishak
Yoshio Ishiguro
Hiroshi Ishii
Suguru Ishizaki
Poika Isokoski
Ali Israr
Howell Istance
Shahram Izadi
Melody Jackson
Robert Jacob
An Jacobs
Giulio Jacucci
Sushant Jain
Ghita Jalal
Jacek Jankowski
Yvonne Jansen
Alex Jansen
Kenneth Jay
Chandrika Jayant
Haojian Jin
Gabe Johnson
Brett Jones
Ricardo Jota
Wendy Ju
Sasa Junuzovic
Antti Jylhä
Yasuaki Kakehi
Evangelos Kalogerakis
Ece Kamar
Gila Kamhi

Eser Kandogan
Shaun Kane
Emre Karagozler
Karrie Karahalios
Maria Karam
David Karger
Abhijit Karnik
Hirokazu Kato
Danny Kaufman
Joseph 'Jofish' Kaye
Rubaiat Habib Kazi
Daniel Keefe
Caitlin Kelleher
Caitlin Kelleher
Sean Keller
Patrick Gage Kelley
Aisling Kelliher
Wendy Kellogg
Lyndon Kennedy
Andruid Kerne
Cem Keskin
Hamed Ketabdar
Azam Khan
Julie Kientz
Wolf Kienzle
Juho Kim
David Kim
Joy Kim
Jeeeun Kim
Kenrick Kin
Yoshifumi Kitamura
Kris Kitani
Kiyoshi Kiyokawa
Scott Klemmer
Gudrun Klinker
Eric Klopfer
Andrew Ko
Kenneth Koedinger
Jeffrey Tzu Kwan
   Valino Koh
Mark Kohler
Hideki Koike
Johannes Kopf
Jan-Peter Krämer
Antonio Krüger
Sven Kratz
Sivam Krish
Per Ola Kristensson

Ernst Kruijff	Greg Little	Jim McCann	Patrick Olivier
Todd Kulesza	Can Liu	Neil McCurdy	Inah Omoronyia
Alexander Kulik	Zhicheng Liu	Sean McDirmid	Stephen Oney
Chinmay Kulkarni	Shixia Liu	David McGookin	Carol O'Sullivan
Ranjitha Kumar	Yen-Ting Liu	William McGrath	Mai Otsuki
Kai Kunze	Mark Livingston	Michael McGuffin	Antti Oulasvirta
Stacey Kuznetsov	Corinna Loeckenhoff	Andrew McPherson	Tom Ouyang
Irwin Kwan	Benjamin Lok	Amir Meghdadi	Sharon Oviatt
Hyo Sun Kwon	Pedro Lopes	David Mellis	Neri Oxman
Anatole Lécuyer	Fabien Lotte	Nemanja Memarovic	Tim Paek
Markus Löchtefeld	Danielle Lottridge	Sarah Mennicken	Michel Pahud
Ben Lafreniere	Hao Lu	Paul Merrell	Dinesh Pai
Shyong Lam	Zhihan Lu	David Merrill	Aditya Pal
Heidi Lam	Andrés Lucero	Ronald Metoyer	Leysia Palen
James Landay	Paul Lukowicz	Natasa Milic-Frayling	Xueni Pan
Joel Lanir	Aran Lunzer	Robert Miller	Tapan Parikh
Edward Lank	Kurt Luther	Nick Miller	Taiwoo Park
Gierad Laput	Christof Lutteroth	Mark Mine	Andrea Parker
Eric Larson	Kris Luyten	Niloy Mitra	Amanda Parkes
Walter Lasecki	zhihan lv	Neema Moraveji	Kurt Partridge
Celine Latulipe	Max Mühlhäuser	Dan Morris	Kayur Patel
Manfred Lau	Jörg Müller	Martez Mott	Shwetak Patel
Tessa Lau	Blair MacIntyre	Bradford Mott	Fabio Paternò
Joseph LaViola Jr.	Scott MacKenzie	Stefanie Mueller	Donald Patterson
Edith Law	Pattie Maes	Florian Mueller	Neal Patwari
Matthew Lease	Jalal Mahmud	Sean Munson	Reena Pau
Eric Lecolinet	Andrew Maimone	Gail Murphy	Eric Paulos
Bongshin Lee	Aditi Majumder	Roderick Murray-Smith	Amy Pavel
Jinha Lee	Lena Mamykina	Gautham Mysore	Fabrizio Pece
Unseok Lee	Jennifer Mankoff	Mor Naaman	Huaishu Peng
Woohun Lee	Gary Marchionini	Miguel Nacenta	Alex Pentland
Johnny Lee	Adam Marcus	George Nagy	Lucas Pereira
Geehyuk Lee	Anders Markussen	Naoto Nakazato	Charles Perin
Seungyon "Claire" Lee	Jennifer Marlow	Mathieu Nancel	Trevor Pering
Daniel Leithinger	Nicolai Marquardt	Michael Nebeling	Annuska Perkins
Catherine Letondal	Kim Marriott	Carman Neustaedter	Ken Perlin
Golan Levin	Diego Martinez Plasencia	Richard Newcombe	Simon Perrault
Hao Li	Kenji Mase	David Nguyen	Saverio Perugini
Wilmot Li	Michael Massimi	Moira Norrie	Jeffrey Pierce
Wei Li	Toshiyuki Masui	Chris North	James Pierce
Kevin Li	Justin Matejka	Frank Noz	Emmanuel Pietriga
Thomas Lieber	Justin Mathew	Antti Nurminen	Matthew Pike
Daniel Liebling	Noboru Matsuda	Ian Oakley	Clément Pillias
Jialiu Lin	Tara Matthews	Marianna Obrist	Anne Marie Piper
Sharon Lin	Kevin Matzen	Yoichi Ochiai	Pol Pla
Rhema Linder	Nolwenn Maudet	Peter O'Donovan	Henning Pohl
David Lindlbauer	Walterio Mayol-Cuevas	Lora Oehlberg	Franck Poirier
Agnes Lisowska Masson	James McCann	Hyunjoo Oh	Suporn Pongnumkul

Erika Poole
Ivan Poupyrev
John Pruitt
Jie Qi
Yin Qu
John Quarles
John Quarles
Aaron Quigley
Stefan Rüger
Mashfiqui Rabbi
Emilee Rader
Hayes Raffle
Nitendra Rajput
Raf Ramakers
Gonzalo Ramos
Roberto Ranon
Jussi Rantala
Ramesh Raskar
Majken Kirkegaard
  Rasmussen
Kyle Rector
David Redmiles
Colorado Reed
Holger Regenbrecht
Derek Reilly
Steven Reiss
Jun Rekimoto
Xiangshi Ren
Philippe Renevier Gonin
Alexander Repenning
Mitchel Resnick
Penny Rheingans
Stephan Richter
Julie Rico
Alec Rivers
Tom Rodden
Daniel Roggen
Michael Rohs
Jannick Rolland
Ilya Rosenberg
Anne Roudaut
Thijs Roumen
Nicolas Roussel
Steve Rubin
Jaime Ruiz
Enrico Rukzio
Bryan Russell
Daniel Russell

Kimiko Ryokai
Jeffrey Rzeszotarski
Gábor Sörös
Daniel Saakes
Ramik Sadana
Adam Sadilek
Daisuke Sakamoto
Christian Sandor
T. Saponas
Sayan Sarcar
Arvind Satyanarayan
Greg Saul
Valkyrie Savage
Lauri Savioja
Manolis Savva
Christopher Scaffidi
Johannes Schöning
Florian Schaub
Dieter Schmalstieg
Chris Schmandt
Dominik Schmidt
Ryan Schmidt
Ryan Schubert
Julia Schwarz
James Scott
Stacey Scott
Sue Ann Seah
Julian Seifert
Kate Sellen
Abigail Sellen
Marcos Serrano
Peter Sestoft
Orit Shaer
Chirag Shah
Ariel Shamir
David Shamma
Ryan Benjamin Shapiro
Ehud Sharlin
Aaron Shaw
Eli Shechtman
Chia Shen
Karthik Sheshadri
Buntarou Shizuki
Ben Shneiderman
Garth Shoemaker
Mike Sinclair
Ronit Slyper
Mark Smith

Ross Smith
Brian Smith
Boris Smus
Noah Snavely
Kiley Sobel
Rajinder Sodhi
Erin Solovey
Jie Song
Hyunyoung Song
Alexander Sorkine-
  Hornung
Michiel Sovijärvi-Spape
Daniel Spelmezan
Robert St. Amant
Kay Stanney
Thad Starner
John Stasko
Anthony Steed
Jürgen Steimle
Frank Steinicke
Sophie Stellmach
Craig Stewart
James Stewart
Maureen Stone
Daniel Strazzulla
Daniel Strazzulla
Wolfgang Stuerzlinger
Simone Stumpf
Simon Stusak
Oezge Subasi
Ozge Subasi
Maki Sugimoto
Yuta Sugiura
Mengu Sukan
Sudeep Sundaram
Leila Takayama
Kentaro Takemura
Desney Tan
John Tang
Anthony Tang
Steven Tanimoto
Alex Taylor
Robert Teather
Jaime Teevan
Alexandru Telea
Michael Terry
Anuj Tewari
William Thies

James Tompkin
Cesar Torres
Melanie Tory
Caroline Traube
Adrien Treuille
Khai Truong
Theophanis Tsandilas
Nicolas Tsingos
Kathleen Tuite
Jayson Turner
George Tzanetakis
Brygg Ullmer
Marynel Vázquez
Kaisa Väänänen-Vainio-
  Mattila
Daniel Västfjäll
Rajan Vaish
Dimitar Valkov
Jan Van den Bergh
Kristof Van Laerhoven
Brad Vander Zanden
Lucy Vanderwende
Giovanni Vannucci
Aditya Vashistha
Radu-Daniel Vatavu
Ansh Verma
Arnold Vermeeren
Frederic Vernier
Roel Vertegaal
Chi Vi
Nicolas Villar
Simon Voelker
Juergen Vogel
Stephen Voida
Romain Vuillemot
Chat Wacharamanotham
Julie Wagner
Daniel Wagner
Ron Wakkary
James Wallace
Jagoda Walny
Yan Wang
Jingtao Wang
Feng Wang
Hao-Chuan Wang
Yi Wang
Roy Want
Jamie Ward

Peter Wardrip

Junji Watanabe

Martin Wattenberg

Jenny Waycott

Andrew Webb

Gerhard Weber

Carolyn Wei

Christian Weichel

Malte Weiss

Gregory Welch

Michael Weller

Stephan Wenger

Jonathan Westhues

reto wettach

Gordon Wetzstein

Sean White

Emily Whiting

Steve Whittaker

Alexander Wiethoff

Daniel Wigdor

Wesley Willett

John Williamson

Karl Willis

Graham Wilson

Max Wilson

Raphael Wimmer

Holger Winnemoeller

Jason Wither

Jacob Wobbrock

Kanit Wongsuphasawat

Woontack Woo

Allison Woodruff

Charles Woodward

Leslie Wu

Robert Xiao

Jianxiong Xiao

Cheng Xu

Xing-Dong Yang

Angela Yao

Lining Yao

Koji Yatani

Tom Yeh

William Yerazunis

Sai-Kit Yeung

Chuang-wen You

James Young

Massimo Zancanaro

Klaus-peter Zauner

Shumin Zhai

Haoqi Zhang

Hao (Richard) Zhang

Zhengyou Zhang

Yanxia Zhang

Haimo Zhang

Shengdong Zhao

Jian Zhao

Mianwei Zhou

Jamie Zigelbaum

John Zimmerman

Oleksandr Zinenko

Amit Zoran

Vinayak

UIST 2014 Sponsors & Supporters

UIST 2014 gratefully acknowledges our sponsoring SIGs and the support of the following organizations:

Sponsors

Program Committee Meeting Sponsor

Platinum Supporters

Gold Supporters

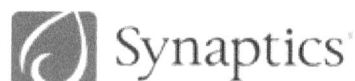

Silver Supporters

Bronze Supporters

Bronze Supporters (Continued)

IBM Research  YAHOO! LABS

Friend of UIST

Scalable Methods to Collect and Visualize Sidewalk Accessibility Data for People with Mobility Impairments

Kotaro Hara

HCIL | Makeability Lab

University of Maryland, College Park

kotaro@cs.umd.edu

Figure 2: Our proposed data collection methods will provide unprecedented levels of street-level accessibility information. I will use the information to develop map-based accessibility tools such as RouteAssist (mockup shown above), a mobile-phone based tool that personalizes route suggestions based on a user's reported mobility-levels.

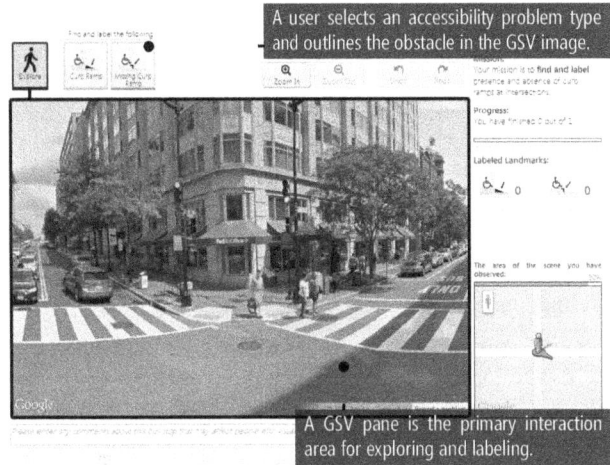

Figure 1: I design, develop, and evaluate tools to locate, identify and assess sidewalk accessibility features in GSV (The latest version of the interface shown above).

ABSTRACT

Poorly maintained sidewalks pose considerable accessibility challenges for mobility impaired persons; however, there are currently few, if any, mechanisms to determine accessible areas of a city *a priori*. In this paper, I introduce four threads of research that I will conduct for my Ph.D. thesis aimed at creating new methods and tools to provide unprecedented levels of information on the accessibility of streets and sidewalk. Namely, I will (i) conduct a formative study to better understand accessibility problems, (ii) develop and evaluate scalable map-based data collection methods, (iii) integrate computer vision algorithms to increase the scalability of the methods, and (iv) develop accessible-aware map-based tools that demonstrate the utility of our data (Figure 1 and 6).

KEYWORDS

Crowdsourcing accessibility; Computer Vision; Accessible Urban Navigation; Google Street View

UIST'14 Adjunct, October 5–8, 2014, Honolulu, HI, USA.
ACM 978-1-4503-3068-8/14/10.
http://dx.doi.org/10.1145/2658779.2661163

ACM CLASSIFICATION KEYWORDS

H5.m. Information interfaces and presentation

INTRODUCTION

According to the most recent US Census (2010), roughly 30.6 million adults have physical disabilities that affect their ambulatory activities. Of these, nearly half report using an assistive aid such as a wheelchair (3.6 million), cane, crutches, or walker (11.6 million) [11]. Despite comprehensive civil rights legislation for Americans with disabilities many city streets and sidewalks in the US remain inaccessible. The problem is not just that sidewalk accessibility fundamentally affects where and how people travel in cities but also that there are few, if any, mechanisms to determine accessible areas a priori.

The overarching goal of my thesis is to create new methods and tools to provide unprecedented levels of information on the accessibility of streets and sidewalks (Figure 2). Using a combination of crowdsourcing, computer vision (CV), and online map imagery such as Google Street View (GSV), I will design, develop, and evaluate methods and tools to collect and visualize street-level accessibility information (Figure 1, 2, 3, 5, and 6).

BACKGROUND AND RELATED WORK

There are three primary components related to my thesis: (i) taxonomy of street-level accessibility features and existing

Figure 3: The labeling tool allows users to remotely identify sidewalk accessibility features by inspecting GSV images and drawing labels on them. These labels are useful both as raw data for my proposed accessibility applications as well as for training computer vision (CV) algorithms.

Figure 4: Our research team conducted semi-structured interviews with three wheelchair users (two males with spinal cord injury and one male with cerebral palsy). Each wheelchair user also took part in an image labeling session. They were asked to "think-aloud" during the session so that we could better understand the rationale behind their labeling decisions.

accessibility audit methods; (ii) crowdsourcing image labeling; and (iii) CV techniques.

Sidewalk Accessibility Factors and Audit Methods

As I develop the novel methods and tools to collect sidewalk accessibility information, it is crucial to understand how the design aspects of streets and sidewalks can limit the access of people with mobility impairments. A list of common accessibility problems include: lack of sidewalks, missing curb ramps, poor walking surfaces, blocked pathways, difficult street crossings, and narrow sidewalks [10].

In the US, state and federal departments conduct and encourage the use of street audits to find and assess the aforementioned deficiencies. But audits are often time-consuming and expensive, thus more efficient auditing methods have been explored including the use of GSV to audit characteristics of neighborhoods [8]. Reported benefits of these remote methods include time-savings and the ability to monitor cities from a central location. In contrast, applications such as *SeeClickFix.com* allow citizens to report accessibility problems directly via their mobile phone. While I focus on remote, virtual methods for auditing, mobile phone data-collection techniques could be integrated as well.

Crowdsourcing Image Labeling Tasks

Our image labeling task is analogous to that often performed in training CV systems (Figure 1 and Figure 3). For example, *LabelMe* [9] provides granular segmentation by allowing users to draw polygonal outlines around objects that are publically viewable and editable. Our proposed image labeling work is different not only in focus (accessibility) but also in the unique integration of both crowdsourcing and CV to increase scalability and control for quality. In addition, our labels do not just identify features, they also describe their quality.

Computer Vision

Work in analyzing outdoor scenes via CV algorithms is also relevant. For example, [3] use edge-based cues to trigger rectangular objects in man-made environments. I will apply and adapt these methods towards our aims, primarily (i) automatically detecting accessibility features in GSV images and (ii) triaging scenes and adapting crowd workflows.

RESEARCH GOALS AND METHODS

My thesis is comprised of four primary threads of research: (i) a formative study to better understand the accessibility problems via interviews and surveys; (ii) the development and evaluation of scalable map-based data collection methods and interactive labeling tools to acquire street-level accessibility data; (iii) the integration and use of CV algorithms to further increase the scalability of the data collection methods; and finally, (iv) the design, development, and evaluation of two accessible-aware map-based tools that demonstrate the utility of our data.

i. Formative Inquiry

To inform our designs, I will conduct three formative inquiries. First, I will interview sidewalk design experts to understand current practices around accessible design. Second, I will interview mobility impaired persons to gain deeper insight into how street-level accessibility affects their lives. I will also interview caregivers to understand their perspective on managing travel and what technologies they use for determining accessible routes.

In the summer of 2012, our research team conducted semi-structured interviews with three wheelchair users (Figure 4) [5]. Using this as a foundation for future interview studies, I will turn to a grounded theory approach to categorize, group, and contextualize the interview results.

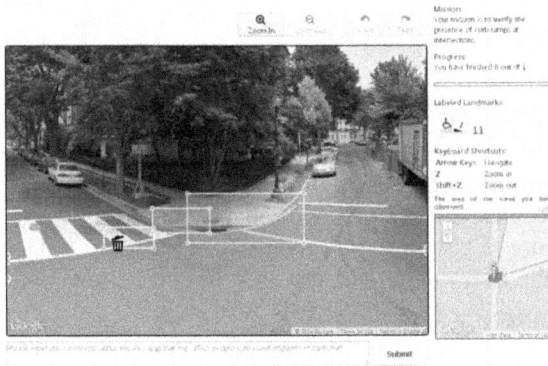

Figure 5: I explored initial approaches to scalably detect accessibility problems in GSV images by combining automated approaches and crowdsourcing. Green boxes in the image show automatically detected curb ramp labels. A user of this validation interface can delete automatically detected labels by clicking the ones that are not on curb ramps.

ii. Crowdsourcing Accessibility Data Collection

The primary goal of my thesis is to design scalable methods and interactive tools to collect street-level accessibility information from GSV. Ultimately, I will create a volunteer-based crowdsourcing system similar to *SnapshotSerengeti.org* where any online user can contribute to collecting accessibility information. As a starting point, however, I have been developing and deploying interactive tools on Amazon Mechanical Turk.

I have conducted three preliminary studies centered on exploring new data collection methods using GSV. First, because inspecting sidewalk accessibility in streetscape imagery is a potentially ambiguous task, I investigated its feasibility with six motivated and diligent labelers, and showed that the labeling approach is reliable [5]. Second, I piloted a range of labeling interfaces and examined the effect of three different labeling interfaces on task performance including labeling time and accuracy [4]. Third, I performed preliminary experiments using a manually curated database of 229 GSV images demonstrating that minimally trained crowd workers could correctly determine the presence of accessibility problems with 81% accuracy. With simple quality control methods, this accuracy increased to 93% [5].

The follow-up study that were submitted to UIST2014 complemented the previous study; I addressed some of the limitations by improving the labeling interface and analyzing the effect of images' age [7]. The new interface queries images from GSV API instead of using manually curated street scape imagery and allows users to pan around the 360-degree view (Figure 1). I investigated workers' labeling performance with a new labeling interface, where the tasks involved identifying the presence and absence of curb ramps—an important sidewalk accessibility attribute [1]. To provide feedback to workers about their performance, I included some scenes with ground truth. If a worker makes mistakes at a ground truth scene, after hitting

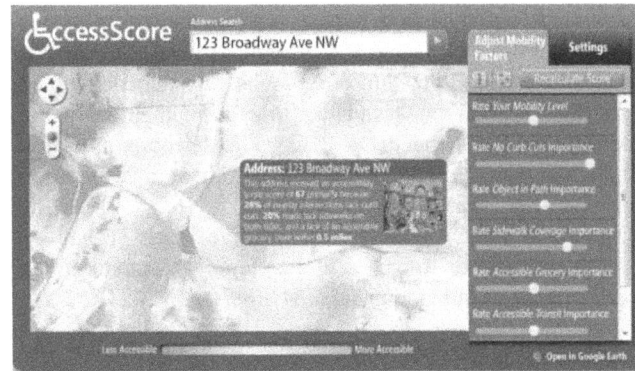

Figure 6: I will design, develop, and evaluate two applications that utilize the collected data: *RouteAccess* (Figure 1) and *AccessibilityScore* (mockup shown above). AccessibilityScore is an easy-to-understand visualization of the accessibility of cities that will be available via a computer or mobile device. Red areas are least accessible and green areas are most accessible.

the submit button, the interface provides visual feedback about the error and show the proper corrective action. We observed, even with the increased task complexity, workers were capable of identifying accessibility attributes in GSV.

GSV images' age is a potential issue as what we find could be obsolete. However, I found that there was high concordance between curb ramp infrastructure in GSV and physical world through in person audit described in [7]. Future work should extend this study to other types of accessibility attributes.

III. Increasing Scalability with Computer Vision

Crowdsourcing accessibility data collection is labor intensive, and is not readily scalable to large areas. At the same time, automatic methods are unlikely to identify accessibility problems with a sufficiently high level of accuracy to create a useful system. I will therefore explore methods of combining the two. I plan to use CV to produce improved labeling in several distinct ways. First, I will design methods and tools for humans to *verify* and *fix* computer detection results (rather than provide the raw labels themselves). Second, I will use CV algorithms to automatically scan large regions for potential accessibility problems. The goal is to focus human efforts on a small set of streets that are most likely to contain problems (*i.e.,* scene triaging). Finally, I will propose methods to increase human labeling efficiency and accuracy using automated methods. For example, CV can play roles in locating and positioning the GSV camera in geographic space and selecting an optimal viewpoint, and estimate "scene complexity" to smartly allocate workers to different workflows.

Thus far, I have developed a preliminary accessibility feature detector using state-of-the-art CV techniques, and proposed a method of controlling a workflow to allocate workers to increase time-efficiency. As a starting point, I have focused solely on detecting curb ramps because of their visual salience in images as well as their significance to accessibility [1]. Our research team has explored various object detection algorithms [6,7]. The one that performed best in internal assessments was implemented using Deformable Part Model (DMP) [2]. The detection precision and recall were 29% and 67%. Although human verification can increase the detection precision to 68% (2.3x the original) as humans reject false positive labels (Figure 5), our false positive rate is still too high compared to the performance of human labelers (84%) [7].

To overcome insufficient performance of current CV and human verification approach, I have designed and developed a "smart" system, Tohme, that combines machine learning, CV, and custom labeling/verification interfaces to find curb ramps [7]. Tohme consists of two workflows, a human labeling pipeline and a CV pipeline with human verification, which are scheduled dynamically based on predicted performance. I showed that Tohme could provide curb ramp detection accuracy comparable to manual labeling approach at a 13% reduction in cost. This figure will only increase as the performance of automated methods improve. Future work includes improving the performance of the detector by, for example, taking contextual cues into account, and using the detector for triaging. In addition, we will examine how CV can be used to speed up the labeling task itself (*e.g.,* via smart labeling where the outline "pen" sticks to edges).

IV. Proof of Concept Accessibility Applications

There will be multiple ways to incorporate the collected accessibility information. As a proof of concept, I will design: *AccessibilityScore* (Figure 6) and *RouteAccess* (Figure 2). For both applications, the key research question is how to incorporate new data related to mobility access. Employing a user-centered design process, I will design the tools to allow end-users to easily discover both areas of high accessibility in cities as well as areas that are particularly inaccessible.

RESEARCH SITUATION AND DISSERTATION STATUS

In the fall of 2014, I will be a fifth year Ph.D. student in the Department of Computer Science at the University of Maryland, College Park. Although I have not proposed my dissertation, I have been committed to this project over two years and am well into the dissertation stage. I plan to propose my dissertation this fall based on feedback from the UIST doctoral symposium. I expect the remaining proposed work to take 1-2 years.

EXPECTED CONTRIBUTIONS TO UIST/CHI COMMUNITY

This research will contribute to the UIST/CHI community by: (i) extending the knowledge of how people with mobility impairment interact with technology to navigate through cities; (ii) introducing the first work that demonstrates that GSV is a viable source for learning about the accessibility of the physical world; (iii) introducing scalable methods that combine crowdsourcing and CV to collect accessibility information; and (iv) presenting and evaluating tools that empower people with mobility impairments as well as city governments.

ACKNOWLEDGEMENTS

I thank my advisor, Prof. Jon Froehlich for his guidance. Though this paper carries only one name, it represents the work and efforts of my collaborators. This work is supported by an NSF grant (IIS-1302338), a Google Faculty Research Award, and an IBM PhD Fellowship.

REFERENCES

1. 3rd Circuit, C. of A. *Kinney v. Yerusalim, 1993 No. 93-1168.* 1993.

2. Felzenszwalb, P., McAllester, D., and Ramaman, D. A Discriminatively Trained, Multiscale, Deformable Part Model. *CVPR,* (2008).

3. Han, F. and Zhu, S.C. Bottom-Up/Top-Down Image Parsing with Attribute Grammar. *IEEE PAMI. 31,* 1 (2009), 59–73.

4. Hara, K., Le, V., and Froehlich, J. A Feasibility Study of Crowdsourcing and Google Street View to Determine Sidewalk Accessibility. *Proc. of ASSETS'12, Poster Session,* ACM (2012), 273–274.

5. Hara, K., Le, V., and Froehlich, J. Combining Crowdsourcing and Google Street View to Identify Street-level Accessibility Problems. *Proc. of CHI'13,* ACM (2013)

6. Hara, K., Sun, J., Chazan, J., Jacobs, D., and Froehlich, J. An Initial Study of Automatic Curb Ramp Detection with Crowdsourced Verification using Google Street View Images. *Proc. of HCOMP'13, Work-in-Progress,* (2013).

7. Hara, K., Sun, J., Jacobs, D.W., and Froehlich, J.E. Tohme: Detecting Curb Ramps in Google Street View Using Crowdsourcing, Computer Vision, and Machine Learning. *Proc. of UIST,* (2014), TBD.

8. Rundle, A.G., Bader, M.D.M., Richards, C.A., Neckerman, K.M., and Teitler, J.O. Using Google Street View to audit neighborhood environments. *Ame. J. of Prev. Med. 40,* 1 (2011), 94–100.

9. Russell, B., Torralba, A., Murphy, K.P., and Freeman, W.T. LabelMe: a database and web-based tool for image annotation. *IJCV. 77,* 1-3 (2007), 157–173.

10. Sandt, L., Schneider, R., Nabors, D., Thomas, L., Mitchell, C., and Eldridge, R. *A Resident's Guide for Creating a Safe and Walkable Communities.* 2008.

11. U.S. Census Bureau. *Americans with Disabilities: 2010 Household Economic Studies.* 2012.

Depth Based Interaction and Field of View Manipulation for Augmented Reality

Jason Orlosky
Osaka University
Osaka, Japan
orlosky@lab.ime.cmc.osaka-u.ac.jp

ABSTRACT

In recent years, the market for portable devices has seen a large increase in the development of head mounted displays. While these displays provide many benefits to users, safety is still a concern. In particular, ensuring that content does not interfere with everyday activities and that users have adequate peripheral vision is very important for situational awareness. In this paper, I address these issues through the use of two novel display prototypes. The first is an optical see-through multi-focal plane display combined with an eye tracking interface. Through eye tracking and knowledge of the focal plane distances, I can calculate whether a user is looking at the environment or at a focal plane in the display. Any distracting text can then be quickly removed so that he or she has a clear view of the environment. The second prototype is a video see-through display which expands a user's environmental view through the use of 238° ultra wide field of view fisheye lenses. Based on the results of several initial evaluations, these new interfaces have the potential help users improve environmental awareness.

Author Keywords

Augmented reality; eye tracking; wide field of view; multi-focal plane; spatial interaction; fisheye vision.

ACM Classification Keywords

H.5.2 [**User Interfaces**]: Prototyping

INTRODUCTION

In mobile augmented reality, users should ideally have a clear view of both content in the real world and virtual viewing space, regardless of the type of display. Optical see-through displays such as the Google Glass or Epson Moverio provide some transparency, but still suffer from occlusion and can be distracting. Additionally, immersive video see-through displays such as the Augmented Reality Oculus Rift often suffer from a narrow field of view.

Multiple Focal Plane Prototype

In order to deal with distracting content in monoscopic optical see-through displays, I propose a combination of eye tracking with a multi-focal plane head mounted display (HMD), as shown on the left of Figure 1. By taking advantage of users' natural tendencies to focus on objects of attention at different depths, the need for physical button presses or other manual interaction can be reduced [10]. 3D gaze has been proposed as a form of interaction, but to date has only been implemented with static displays [4]. Most other gaze based methods only show the direction a user is looking, but not depth. Using focal depth, I can calculate whether the user is looking at content on the display or at an object in his or her environment. Content can then be automatically dimmed or closed when necessary. This provides a more natural and robust interface for quickly interacting with virtual content.

Fisheye Display Prototype

In the case of video see-through displays, expanding the field of view (FOV) is very important for user safety in everyday augmented reality (AR) applications, especially when navigating or checking for oncoming traffic. Current solutions to this problem include a number of prototypes designed to provide a wide FOV, but many are bulky [1, 3, 7] or do not provide good binocular vision [2]. In my system, shown on the right of Figure 1, pixels in the binocular region are undistorted and viewed as normal. However, in contrast to other vision expansion methods, the images in the display's peripheral regions are presented to the user as if viewed through a fisheye lens. This allows users to notice potentially dangerous objects outside of the display's inherent FOV. Wide angle lens distortion in the binocular field would introduce a number of problems such as reduced depth perception and skewed direction estimation. However, visual acuity in the periphery is low and does not have a binocular component, so a peripheral fisheye view can escape many of these problems.

UIST'14 Adjunct, October 5–8, 2014, Honolulu, HI, USA.
ACM 978-1-4503-3068-8/14/10.
http://dx.doi.org/10.1145/2658779.2661164

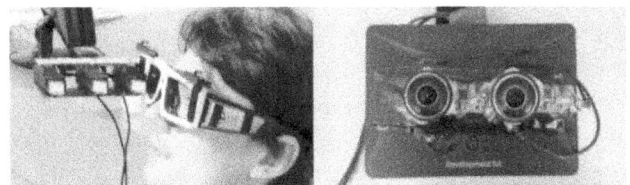

Figure 1. Images showing prototypes of the combined monoscopic multi-focal plane display and eye tracker (left) and the stereoscopic fisheye FOV expansion display (right).

EYE TRACKING IN A MULTI-FOCAL PLANE DISPLAY

In order to address some of the previously mentioned challenges for monoscopic displays, I set out to build a multi-focal plane prototype and test its potential for focus based interaction. This included the combination of a 3D gaze tracking system with a multi-focal plane HMD. Additionally, I propose a framework to facilitate more natural interaction with elements at varying focal distances and various methods for safely managing virtual content.

Display Construction

The prototype consists of an array of three 800 by 600 pixel AirScouter displays, each with its own input and depth control. The three displays are lined up so that three separate images can be viewed simultaneously. The number of planes and their corresponding distances were selected via pilot experiments, and focal distances are set at 30cm, approximately 1m, and 10m, resembling other 3D display setups [5, 6]. In general, these distances allow for the easiest separation of focal planes, though other combinations are possible for different application needs.

Secondly, in order for focal depth to be measured appropriately, a user's eye convergence must be consistent and eye tracking hardware must provide enough accuracy to correctly select a target icon in the proper focal plane. To ensure these conditions, I propose the use of SMI's Eye Tracking Glasses and a 3D printed fastener that can affix the distance between the prototype HMD and the eye tracker as shown on the left of Figure 2. Though the system still needs to be adjusted slightly for height and width of a user's eyes, the distance between tracker and HMD remains constant, allowing for more accurate tracking.

Plane discretization and Tracking

From the eye tracker, a 3D vector of the direction of each eye is first extracted, and then a regression model of focal depths is trained based on the x-value of both gaze vectors. In short, by comparing the current gaze vectors to a number of previously saved gaze vectors for each focal plane, we can achieve a more accurate depth estimate. This regression model functions similarly to methods that find the intersection of two vectors, but accounts for gaze vectors that may be parallel, obtuse, or non-intersecting.

Though regression can be used to calculate a depth for any given gaze data, the estimation may still be inaccurate. If the task is only to discretize the plane at which the user is currently looking at, this can be considered a classification problem, and the calculation can be simplified. In other words, even if noisy gaze data is taken or if calculated depth varies between users, the plane in the prototype on which a user is focused can still be calculated.

Towards Natural Interaction

As a user looks away from virtual content and at the environment, physical objects of interest, or oncoming traffic, virtual content should automatically be removed from the field of view to reduce distraction. To accomplish this, focal depth can be used since the eyes start refocusing soon after switching gaze to a new location. As soon as a user's focus leaves the focal plane containing virtual content, text is removed from the screen. For example, if a user changes his or her focus from virtual text at 1m away to a car that is approaching at 10m away, content would be dimmed as soon as the user's gaze leaves the focal range of the virtual text. This will occur as soon as the user's calculated gaze depth exceeds the limit of the current focal plane discretization. In the case of a user walking through a city gazing at building annotations at 30m, text would be dimmed if he or she were to change focus to pedestrians or obstacles on a sidewalk at 1m away.

Experiments

In order to determine whether the automated dim/close method would be feasible, I conducted an experiment where users were tasked with viewing a number of different icons through the HMD at different focal depths. This allows us to go a step beyond typical depth perception studies and learn about the physical behavior of the eye.

A total of 14 users, 9 male and 5 female, participated in the experiment, and were presented with 9 sets of 3 different icons, including a number of different depth cues such as relative size, texture gradient, defocus blur, and a combination of all three. Three different colors were also presented, including bright green, fuchsia, and white to test whether certain colors are better focal targets at different depths. The most important result from this set of experiments was that we achieved a high degree of accuracy for focal plane identification. Out of all samples taken for all users, 98.63% of points were classified into the correct focal plane. Relative depth and plane classifications for several trials are shown in Figure 3. Even in the worst case scenario (Figure 3, center), 85.6% accuracy was achieved [10].

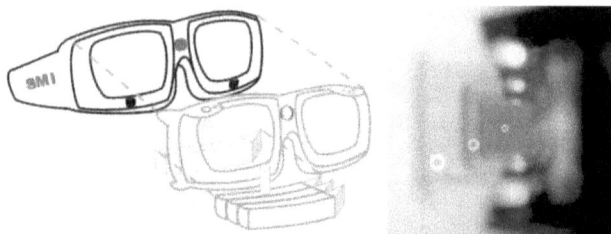

Figure 2. 2D model of the eye tracker, 3D printed attachment, and multi-focal display prototype (left) and the view through the display screen (right).

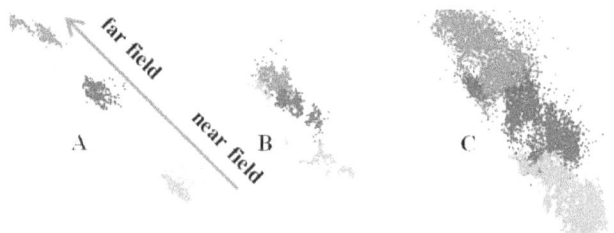

Figure 3. Classified gaze samples for A) a trial with high plane classification accuracy (left), B) the trial with the worst accuracy (center) and C) all trials for a single user (right), where green is 30cm, blue is 1m, and red is 2+m [10].

SPATIAL COMPRESSION PROTOTYPE DESIGN

To build a usable prototype that could expand effective peripheral vision, I needed a lightweight, portable display that had at least an 80° horizontal field of view. Secondly, stereo cameras had to have an appropriate frame rate and wide enough field of view to match the opening of the fisheye lenses. To provide a decent initial FOV, I selected the Oculus Rift, primarily for its 90° horizontal viewing angle. This allows for the use of 60° of binocular vision and the remaining 30° of peripheral vision for each eye. It is in these remaining 30° sections that approximately 60° of peripheral vision per eye is compressed. Two 238° wide FOV lenses are then affixed to two Logicool C310 web cameras. Each of the cameras is then individually aligned for stereoscopy. Next, the central portion of each camera image must be undistorted, and the peripheral image must effectively fit 180° worth of content into the virtual FOV.

Peripheral Space Manipulation

The initial methods I use for undistortion and compression can be summarized in three distinct steps, including binocular undistortion, peripheral partial compression, and misalignment correction. The binocular view of 60° is corrected using standard OpenCV functionality. A camera image through the fisheye lens is first faced toward a checkerboard to obtain camera parameters. The imageundistort function is then applied to both video streams for all pixels within the display's binocular FOV, as shown on the right hand side of each image in Figure 4.

The more complex part of the design lies in the manipulation of the peripheral FOV. Here, over 60° of environmental FOV must be compressed into 30° or less of virtual FOV. First, I tried leaving a portion of the virtual image untouched, as if viewed through the fisheye lens. Unfortunately, this results in a very obvious line where the compressed and non-compressed images meet, which is visible on the left image of Figure 4. So, I was left with an interesting problem: How can the pixels in the periphery be compressed, yet remain smoothly connected to the undistorted binocular image? After considering a number of image-stitching and mosaic algorithms to merge the misaligned portion, I found a much more efficient solution, which also provides a more natural view for the user. Instead of running a time consuming alignment algorithm, the undistortion is computed using only the y values of the coordinate map.

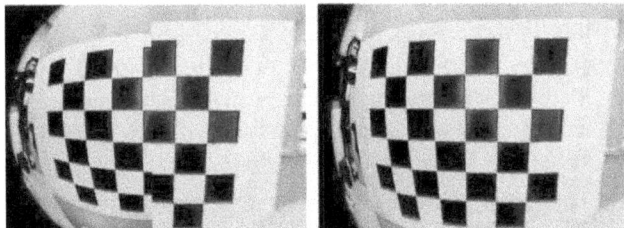

Figure 4. Screenshots from the left-eye camera showing the misalignment problem (left), and my solution for smoothly merging the compressed and binocular images (right).

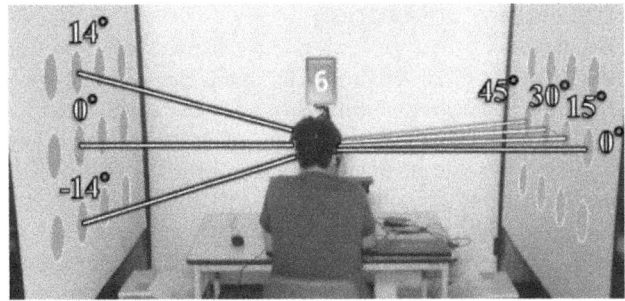

Figure 5. Experiment setup showing projector screens and numbers displayed on a tablet for the reading task. Angles and large icons at every position are overlaid for reference.

This provides a relatively clean alignment and a less distorted perspective in the vertical domain. As a result, the virtual peripheral view still compresses objects horizontally, the vertical ratio of real objects to virtual objects becomes closer to one, and the peripheral and binocular images align, as shown in on the right of Figure 4.

Experiments

To test how the display's FOV compared to the naked eye, an experiment with a total of 10 volunteers, 3 female, 7 male was carried out. The experiment task was to press a button when an icon came into view, and I recorded accuracy and reaction time for correctly detected icons for both the fisheye display and the naked eye. The setup is shown in Figure 5, with simulated large icons and angles overlaid for reference. Two projector screens were stationed at 105 centimeters (cm) to the left and right of the user and a headrest was centered at 104 cm above the floor. Directly in front of the participant at a distance of 140 cm was a tablet PC, which displayed random numbers between 0 and 9 every three seconds. Participants read these numbers aloud to ensure concentration on their central field of view.

To clearly show significant tendencies regarding acuity, accuracy of the display versus eye according to icon size is shown in Figure 6. A two way analysis of variance (ANOVA) showed a main effect of device ($F(1,9)=204.4$, $P<.01$), and a slight interaction of size and angle conditions ($F(9,180)=2.28$, $P<.02$). Although there is a relatively large difference between eye and display for small icons, the difference decreases as object size increases. For objects over 5.8° of FOV, the difference was only 15.8%. This means that pedestrians would likely notice a peripheral car or bicycle at 10 meters, but might not see a tennis ball.

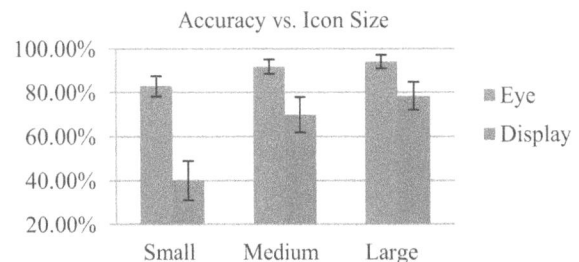

Figure 6. Graph showing accuracy (correctly discovered icons) according to icon size and standard deviation.

INTELLIGENT INTERACTION

Though these prototypes can provide a user with a better view of his or her environment, managing content that needs to be present at all times can still pose a problem [8]. Ideally, notifications, labels, or other mobile virtual information should be placed in a nonintrusive, easy to see location. In an attempt to address this issue, I have also developed a system that can manage text in a user's field of view. By automatically detecting the most visible locations in a user's immediate environment, the system can smoothly migrate text to new locations in real time. Experiments show that the locations chosen by my algorithm resemble human choices in about 70% of cases in both static and mobile situations [9].

PLAN FOR COMPLETION

One last challenge that needs to be overcome to thoroughly test these devices is accurate, real time registration of digital objects in the real world. For example, if I want to test whether or not someone will notice peripheral objects while trying to read map information in the central field of view, both the map and periphery must appear as if they are part of the real world. Several tracking and mapping methods are available to do this, but I must develop a modified system that is efficient enough to be run simultaneously with any eye-tracking, text management, or FOV compression algorithms. In the remaining 18 months of my PhD, I will experiment with combinations of these designs, which will be important for creating practical, real-world applications.

Once an appropriate tracking method has been developed, I intend to test a variety of off-screen visualization methods. For example, in the multi-focal display, I would compare the use of arrows, leader lines, and damage indicators, all at different focal depths. This can provide insights into which focal depths are the most appropriate for showing navigation or indicative information. In the case of the Fisheye Vision display, I intent to explore the use of different regions of the compressed periphery for showing items such as labels or traffic indicators. Ideally this type of view management can provide users with a more encompassing view of virtual information, without having to overlay content onto regions within binocular vision.

DISCUSSION AND CONCLUSION

In conclusion, my goal is to develop more natural interfaces for interaction with and viewing of augmented and virtual elements. To do so, I have prototyped a hybrid multi-focal plane HMD and eye tracking interface, which facilitates methods to automatically close, remove, or dim distracting content from a user's field of view. Through experimentation, I found that users can accurately focus on virtual content displayed on different focal planes in this prototype. More importantly, distracting text can be quickly dimmed or removed in situations that require immediate attention.

Secondly, I introduce the fisheye vision display prototype, which expands a user's effective field of view in see-through displays using fisheye lenses. The prototype takes advantage of the compressed nature of the lenses, but only in the periphery, allowing users a wider field of view without sacrificing binocular vision. Experiments show that users can effectively see up to 180°, and that the larger the object, the smaller the difference between the display and the naked eye in terms of visual acuity. This method can not only be used to expand a user's virtual field of view, but can be used to improve the development and study of new peripheral spatial compression functions and applications.

Though more testing is necessary, I am confident that these displays and methods for interaction can help improve safety for users of mobile augmented reality devices.

REFERENCES

1. Ardouin, J., Lécuyer, A., Marchal, M., Riant, C., & Marchand, E. FlyVIZ: a novel display device to provide humans with 360° vision by coupling catadioptric camera with hmd. *Proc. VRST,* 2012 (pp. 41-44).

2. Fan, K., Huber, J., Nanayakkara, S., & Inami, M. SpiderVision: extending the human field of view for augmented awareness. *Proc. AH,* 2014 (p. 49).

3. Kiyokawa, K. A wide field-of-view head mounted projective display using hyperbolic half-silvered mirrors. *Proc ISMAR,* 2007 (pp. 1-4).

4. Kwon, Y. M., Jeon, K. W., Ki, J., Shahab, Q. M., Jo, S., & Kim, S. K. (2006). 3D Gaze Estimation and Interaction to Stereo Display. *In IJVR,* 5(3), (pp 41-45).

5. Liu, S., Hua, H., & Cheng, D. A novel prototype for an optical see-through head-mounted display with addressable focus cues. *In TVCG,* 2010. 16(3), 381-393.

6. Maimone, A., & Fuchs, H. (2013, October). Computational augmented reality eyeglasses. *Proc. ISMAR,* 2013 (pp. 29-38).

7. Nagahara, H., Yagi, Y., & Yachida, M. A wide ‐ field ‐ of ‐ view catadioptrical head ‐ mounted display. *Electronics and Communications in Japan (Part II: Electronics),* 2006. 89(9), (pp 33-43).

8. Orlosky, J., Kiyokawa, K., & Takemura, H. Managing mobile text in head mounted displays: studies on visual preference and text placement. *In MCCR,* 2014. 18(2), (pp. 20-31).

9. Orlosky, J., Kiyokawa, K., & Takemura, H. (2013, March). Dynamic text management for see-through wearable and heads-up display systems. *Proc. IUI,* 2013. (pp. 363-370). ACM.

10. Toyama, T., Orlosky, J., Sonntag, D. & Kiyokawa, K. (2014, May). A natural interface for multi-focal plane head mounted displays using 3D gaze. *Proc. AVI,* 2014. (pp. 25-32). ACM.

Leveraging Physical Human Actions
in Large Interaction Spaces

Can Liu
can.liu@lri.fr

| Univ Paris-Sud & CNRS (LRI) | INRIA | Telecom ParisTech & CNRS (LTCI) |
| F-91405 Orsay, France | F-91405 Orsay, France | F-75013 Paris, France |

ABSTRACT

Large interaction spaces such as wall-size displays allow users to interact not only with their hands, like traditional desktop environment, but also with their whole body by, e.g. walking or moving their head orientation. While this is particularly suitable for tasks where users need to navigate large amounts of data and manipulate them at the same time, we still lack a deep understanding of the advantages of large displays for such tasks. My dissertation begins with a set of studies to understand the benefits and drawbacks of a high-resolution wall-size display vs. a desktop environments. The results show strong benefits of the former due to the flexibility of "physical navigation" involving the whole body when compared with mouse input. From whole-body interaction to human-to-human interaction, my current work seeks to leverage natural human actions to collaborative contexts and to design interaction techniques that detects gestural interactions between users to support collaborative data exchange.

Author Keywords

Wall-sized displays; data manipulation; multiuser interaction.

ACM Classification Keywords

H.5.2 [Information Interfaces and Presentation]: User Interfaces - Interaction styles

INTRODUCTION

High resolution wall-sized displays are designed to display large amounts of data. I started my PhD by observing real users performing tasks on a ultra-high resolution wall display (5.5m×1.8m with 20480×6400 pixels). Our users are mostly professionals working with large data sets, such as neuroanatomists comparing many brain scans on the wall display to classify them or organizers of the CHI 2013 conference fine-tuning the 200+ sessions according to various criteria (Figure 1). We observed users' needs when moving items

around and grouping them in a way that was meaningful to their task.

Previous research has studied the usability of large displays for various tasks. Ball et al [1] show that larger displays promote physical navigation and improve user performance for search, navigation and pattern finding tasks. However, most previous research has addressed search, visualization and sense-making tasks [2, 1] while data manipulation tasks have been mostly ignored. When users need to navigate large amounts of data and manipulate data items at the same time, the task becomes harder to perform in traditional desktop setups because the combination of data manipulation, e.g. using pick-and-drop, and navigation, e.g. with pan-and-zoom increases the complexity of interaction. Using the wall-sized display seems easier because users can navigate by walking around and manipulate data with their hands. Users can physically "zoom in" the data by approaching the display and get an overview by stepping back. In order to analyze and understand the benefits and drawbacks of using such a wall-sized display for data manipulation and navigation tasks, my dissertation first presents a set of experiments involving both single-user and multi-user classification tasks.

Among the large body of research on gestural input, some work has focused on tracking full human body movement in collaborative settings. For example, Shadow Reaching [9] facilitates interaction at a distance by projecting a virtual shadow of the user while Sparsh [7] uses the human body as a medium to transfer data. Collocated social interaction involves not only verbal communication but also gestures and relative positions that can be detected by tracking systems to support between-user interactions, such as exchanging data. Pass-Them-Around [5] lets users share photos by throwing them towards another mobile phone. Proxemic interaction takes into account the physical distances between users and displays to improve interaction [3, 6].

Existing techniques that let users exchange digital data rely mainly on traditional user interfaces: Often times, people discuss face-to-face about some content then send emails to each other to exchange the actual data. Tabletop or public displays facilitate such digital exchanges by providing graphical representations or territories for each user. Why not support a more direct way to exchange information when users are physically present in social or collaborative environments? My dissertation proposes to augment human-to-human interactions by

Figure 1. Observation of a real task - researchers working on the CHI13 program (left) and a participant performing the controlled experiment with an abstract classification task (right)

designing new techniques that support fluid and natural cross-user interactions. To our knowledge, this approach has not received much attention in the literature.

BENEFITS OF WALL-SIZED DISPLAYS FOR NAVIGATION

While users can physically navigate a large data set in front of a wall-sized display, they can perform the same task on a computer desktop using virtual navigation techniques. We conducted a first experiment to study the trade-offs between these two types of navigation [4].

In order to compare performance of wall vs. display, we designed an abstract task that captures important aspects of real classification tasks. The task consists of moving disks to containers according to a label located in their center. It operationalizes two important factors: information density, operationalized as the text size of the labels, and task difficulty, operationalized as the number of categories. The results showed strong effects: the wall display outperformed the desktop when information density was higher and the tasks were more difficult, and the desktop performed slightly better in the opposite condition.

We performed quantitative data analysis to explain the performance gain in the wall-sized display condition. Both the wall and desktop screens displayed the exact same scene so that the exact same pixels were displayed on the wall and on the desktop when participants zoomed in to the maximum level of detail. Both physical and virtual trajectories of navigation were tracked and logged throughout the experiment. This includes the physical head movements in front of the wall and to the virtual trajectories of the view point when panning and zooming on the desktop. We computed and compared several measures to look for differences between the conditions.

The analysis of the trajectories suggested that participants operated in a larger area of the scene in front of the wall-sized display than on the desktop. This is probably due to the advantage of moving the head freely, while the monitor window constrains the view in the desktop condition. This may also explain the more qualitative differences that we observed: head trajectories follow smooth curves while virtual view-point trajectories feature sharp turns (see [4] for details.)

This experiment revealed a surprisingly strong benefit of leveraging users' natural movements for interaction. Physical navigation allows users to "zoom and pan" by walking and moving their head while performing pick-and-drop interactions with an input device. On the desktop, pan, zoom and pick-and-drop actions are performed more sequentially since the mouse is the only input device. Physical navigation therefore lets users parallelize interactions naturally.

This study raises new research questions and can inspire new interaction techniques. For example: can we design a better navigation technique when data manipulation is needed, such as a novel bi-manual interaction technique or the use of eye-tracking to improve performance on the desktop? We plan to work on this subject in the future. Another important outcome of this work is our abstract task, which can be used as a test bed for the evaluation of other techniques.

Support of Collaboration

Large interaction spaces are well suited for collaborative tasks. Previous work has studied collaborative behaviors extensively for tabletops [8]. While part of this work may apply to wall-sized displays, there are key differences due to the higher mobility of users and the fact that they are not always close to the display. We are conducting a second study with the same classification task to find out if and how a wall-sized display can support collaboration effectively.

Participants pick and drop data items with cursors on the wall that are controlled by VICON-tracked pointing devices. They perform classification tasks in pairs with three strategies: (1) *Divide and conquer:* the two participants are not allowed to talk to or help each other; (2) *Collaboration with Even Control:* participants are instructed to speak out the label they are looking for and they are encouraged to collaborate while keeping the goal of being as fast as possible. The amount of collaboration is estimated by counting the number of pick-and-drop operations done collaboratively; (3) *Collaboration with Dominant Control:* only one participant has an input device so that the other one can help but not operate. By comparing these conditions we expect to understand the gain and cost of collaboration at the interaction level on a wall display.

For a deeper understanding, we assess collaboration efficiency of wall-sized displays with a secondary factor: the *Locality* of the data layout. Locality refers to the distance between a picked item and the closest target container it can be dropped into. We expect more *local* layouts to reduce the advantage of collaboration. Locality is a relative concept that depends on the distance of the user to the wall (the layout becomes less local if the user comes closer to the display). In the previous experiment, this had a major influence on the difference in performance between wall-sized and desktop displays. We are therefore interested in finding out how locality affects collaboration. After gaining insights about the benefit and cost of collaboration on the wall, we will compare it to remote collaboration with multiple desktop.

We are currently conducting a few pilot studies. Interestingly, they seem to show lower performance in the *Collaboration with Even Control* condition when compared with *Divide and Conquer*, while *Collaboration with Dominate Control* performs better than we expected. If this result stands, it might suggest that collaboration involves a coordination cost, whereas dominant control might make collaboration more effective because users are more focused on either operating or searching. The full study will therefore hopefully help us design more effective collaborative interfaces.

LEVERAGING NATURAL ACTIONS BETWEEN USERS

When users work on a task collaboratively in front of a wall-sized display, a user who needs to deliver information or delegate a task to another user typically needs to notify this user verbally or move virtual artifacts close to them, hence disrupting them. The other user will have to process the requested task at a later time if she is not ready to perform it right away, which is time consuming and error prone. While it is important for collaborators to be aware of the task in progress while working in parallel on different subtasks [10], the overhead of managing these coordination actions and maintaining awareness of the division of labor can be significant.

I am exploring the idea of supporting data exchange by taking advantage of the users' physical presence in the same space and their natural gestural interactions in a co-located environment. This extends the concept of leveraging body movements to multi-user contexts by augmenting human-to-human interaction with digital power.

PoPle Prototype

To instantiate the concept, I designed PoPle - an interaction technique for multiple users to exchange data and delegate tasks (Figure. 2). This project is still in an early stage. The first design has been created and I have implemented a working prototype with the key functionalities.

Figure 3a) shows a sending user (left, in blue) who picks an item on the wall using her mobile device, then points to the target user (in green) and sends him the selected item. As feedback, the mobile device vibrates when a user is in the line of sight of the device. The sending user can then tap a button to transfer the item. The action is confirmed by a "drop" sound on the sender's device. The receiving user gets a different notification sound on his device.

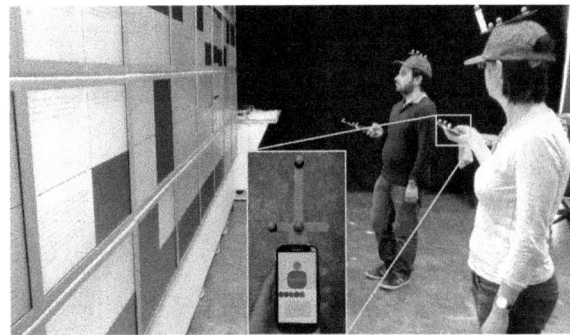

Figure 2. PoPle technique. One user(orange head) points to another user with a pointer to send him data. The pointer vibrates and shows a blue person icon (for blue head user) as well as his task load. The owner's task queue is displayed in the middle of the interface, with color-coded items to indicate the sender.

In order to minimize interruptions, items received while the receiving user is not available are buffered on their mobile device. The queue is displayed on the device and the user can pick an item by tapping it (Fig. 2). Users can choose among three levels of availability. *Immediate* mode is for users working in tight collaboration: The transfered item appears directly on the wall display and is attached to the receiving user's cursor so that he does not have to pick it up. If the receiving user already has an item attached to the cursor, the received item is added to the queue. Buffered items are automatically retrieved and attached to the cursor (one by one, in receiving order) as soon as the user releases the item attached to the cursor. *Queue* mode is intended for loose collaboration: Items are always buffered and must be manually retrieved by tapping the desired item in the queue. This makes it possible to process items in a different order than the receiving order. Finally, *Busy* mode prevents receiving items from other users.

Gestures in human-to-human communication often have subtle social meanings and implications for coordination. The current prototype highlights the items in the queue on the receiver's mobile device if the users are face-to-face when transmitting data. This way the receiver can retrieve the item easily. A common use case is when a user delegates an urgent task and talks to the other user to prioritize it. It is implemented by tracking the orientations of users to detect the face-to-face configuration.

Users can retrieve real-time information about other users' tasks in order to provide awareness of the progress of each user. Such information is important to help users monitor and equalize their workload. When pointing to a user, the sending user's mobile device shows the receiver's ID and the number of tasks on his queue (Fig. 2). Activity data related to that user can also be displayed on the wall-sized display (Fig. 3b). The system can also highlight relevant items when co-workers are close to each other (Fig. 3c).

When using raycasting to point at users, several people may be in or near the line of sight of the target user's device. To disambiguate among pointed people, we display the icons of the pointed users by increasing distance, with the selected one highlighted (Fig. 3d). The user can change the selection by moving the device closer or further away from him.

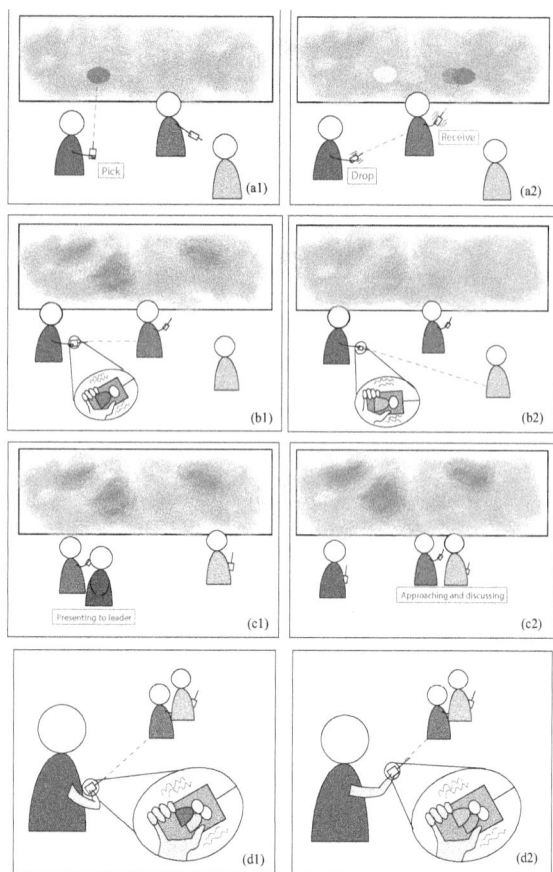

Figure 3. PoPle Techniques: Sending information (a), Highlighting related data by aiming (b) or by proximity (c), disambiguating users (d).

Design Choices

The current prototype is a starting point to explore the concept of pointing at people in collaborative settings. I plan to define a design space of such techniques that emphasizes the design and implementation choices and their effects.

For example, *directness of interaction* captures how direct, and therefore how potentially disrupting, the designation of a target user can be. It ranges from interacting with the name or icon of the person, to approaching or touching the person to sticking a physical document in their hand. The current design of PoPle is relatively direct, taking advantage of users physical presence, while providing a queuing mechanism to make it less disrupting.

Feedback and *notification* of user actions can be designed in many different ways in terms of their location, e.g. personal device of shared display, and modality, e.g. audio, tactile or visual. These choices can affect the awareness and privacy between users, as well as the availability of background information, which are known to be very important factors in collaborative tasks [10].

Finally, while the current design targets collocated collaborative interactions, the concept can be generalized to other multi-user environments. It could be used for example in an office environment or in meeting rooms to provide a more di-

rect way to share documents among co-workers. If advanced tracking technology is not available, it could use the compass available on many smartphones, or augmented reality.

CONTRIBUTION AND CONCLUSION

My dissertation will contribute to the state of the art in two main areas. First, the more fundamental research will provide a deeper understanding of the benefits of high-resolution wall-sized displays compared to desktop screens. In particular, it will show the power of leveraging human body movements for interaction. Second, the more design-oriented work will investigate the concept of augmenting human-to-human interaction with interaction techniques that detect natural social interactions to support fluid interactions among users.

I hope that this doctoral symposium will be an opportunity to discuss this work and inspire new ideas, such as: Which other human-to-human actions can be recognized and augmented with technology? How can we design systems that leverage social interactions without disrupting users?

ACKNOWLEDGEMENTS

I thank my advisors Olivier Chapuis, Michel Beaudouin-Lafon and Eric Lecolinet for their help and guidance. This research was partially supported by Labex DigiCosme (project Idex Paris-Saclay ANR-11-IDEX-0003-02 operated by ANR as part of the program "Investissement d'Avenir").

REFERENCES

1. Ball R., North C. & Bowman D. A. Move to improve: Promoting physical navigation to increase user performance with large displays. *CHI '07*, ACM (2007).
2. Bradel L., Endert A., Koch K., Andrews C. & North C. Large high resolution displays for co-located collaborative sensemaking: Display usage and territoriality. *IJHCS 71*, 11 (2013).
3. Greenberg S., Marquardt N., Ballendat T., Diaz-Marino R. & Wang M. Proxemic interactions: The new ubicomp? *Interactions 18*, 1 (2011).
4. Liu C., Chapuis O., Beaudouin-Lafon M., Lecolinet E. & Mackay W. E. Effects of display size and navigation type on a classification task. *CHI '14*, ACM (2014).
5. Lucero A., Holopainen J. & Jokela T. Pass-them-around: Collaborative use of mobile phones for photo sharing. *CHI '11*, ACM (2011).
6. Marquardt N., Hinckley K. & Greenberg S. Cross-device interaction via micro-mobility and f-formations. *UIST '12*, ACM (2012).
7. Mistry P., Nanayakkara S. & Maes P. Sparsh: Passing data using the body as a medium. *CSCW '11*, ACM (2011).
8. Scott S. D., Carpendale M. S. T. & Inkpen K. M. Territoriality in collaborative tabletop workspaces. *CSCW '04*, ACM (2004).
9. Shoemaker G., Tang A. & Booth K. S. Shadow reaching: A new perspective on interaction for large displays. *UIST '07*, ACM (2007).
10. Yuill N. & Rogers Y. Mechanisms for collaboration: A design and evaluation framework for multi-user interfaces. *ACM ToCHI 19*, 1 (2012).

Using Brain-Computer Interfaces for Implicit Input

Daniel Afergan

Tufts University

afergan@cs.tufts.edu

ABSTRACT

Passive brain-computer interfaces, in which implicit input is derived from a user's changing brain activity without conscious effort from the user, may be one of the most promising applications of brain-computer interfaces because they can improve user performance without additional effort on the user's part. I seek to use physiological signals that correlate to particular brain states in order to adapt an interface while the user behaves normally. My research aims to develop strategies to adapt the interface to the user and the user's cognitive state using functional near-infrared spectroscopy (fNIRS), a non-invasive, lightweight brain-sensing technique. While passive brain-computer interfaces are currently being developed and researchers have shown their utility, there has been little effort to develop a framework or hierarchy for adaptation strategies.

ACM Classification Keywords

H.5.m. Information Interfaces and Presentation (e.g. HCI): Miscellaneous

INTRODUCTION

I propose a framework and taxonomy to consider implicit interfaces, which use brain data as input to interactive systems, along with the design principles and patterns I have developed from my previous work with them. I discuss considerations specific to designing implicit user interfaces based on functional near-infrared spectroscopy (fNIRS) brain data. Based on these considerations, I present an overview of examples of brain-based adaptive systems that we have built and studied, which illustrate these principles and patterns, and demonstrate effective use of brain data in human-computer interaction. My research focuses specifically on signals coming from the brain, but these principles and strategies can be applied broadly to other physiological sensor data, and this work has applications in many domains of data analysis involving multitasking or varying cognitive workload.

Using brain, body, behavioral, and environmental sensors, it is possible to capture subtle changes in the user's cognitive state in real time. This opens new doors in human-computer

interaction research. This information can be used as continuous input to interactive visualization systems, making the systems more in sync with the user, providing appropriate help and support when needed. However, brain, body, and other sensor data are different from most existing input modalities. To achieve this goal, the interactive system must be carefully designed to take advantage of this more subtle new class of input, leading to *implicit interfaces*. Implicit inputs are user actions or situational contexts that the system understands as input, but that were not actively chosen by the user to interact with the system. For interfaces that incorporate these, the properties of the sensor data must be considered as well as the user states that can be classified successfully from the data. While the design principles and strategies are generalizable and could apply to any type of physiological sensor, I propose that fNIRS is especially useful for implicit input because it is lightweight and non-invasive, and allows users to interact with a system in a natural manner without influencing the signal.

BACKGROUND

Implicit Input

Most human-computer interaction techniques use explicit input, in which the user consciously manipulates a device (e.g., mouse or keyboard) to indicate a desired command or action in the system. In contrast, passive brain-computer interfaces (BCIs) are based on "reactive states of the user's cognition automatically induced while interacting in the surrounding system" [16]. Passive inputs assess user state and use that to help control interaction without direct or intentional effort from the user. These systems supplement direct input with implicit input, typically derived from physiological sensors attached to the user, in order to adjust application parameters based on user state. Driven by more efficient monitors and the computational power and algorithms to process large quantities of data in real time, modern technology can more affordably integrate passive systems and has spawned research into passive biocybernetic adaptation [5]. Such implicit input is fundamental to the fields of ubiquitous computing and context-aware systems, but mainly focuses on situational and environmental context, and not on cognitive state as context. Interactive visualizations can be improved by using the state of the user as an input to the system, and adapting subtle aspects of the interface appropriately.

Adaptations triggered by passive input face two primary challenges: to accurately model the user's cognitive state and to sensibly adjust the system based on this model. BCI

UIST'14 Adjunct, October 5–8, 2014, Honolulu, HI, USA.
ACM 978-1-4503-3068-8/14/10.
http://dx.doi.org/10.1145/2658779.2661166

helps solve the first challenge of passive systems by providing user models that more directly tap into the source of user state. Cutrell and Tan suggest that the implicit commands inferred from a user's changing brain activity may be the most promising, universal application of BCI [4]. Explicit brain-issued commands suffer disproportionally from errors and have a limited range of input, whereas implicit commands offer purely additional information without the user's deliberate attention, and the user does not see misclassifactions, nor have to spend additional cognitive resources recovering from these errors.

fNIRS and Prefrontal Cortex

fNIRS uses near-infrared light to detect levels of oxygenated and deoxygenated hemoglobin on the surface of the prefrontal cortex. Light at this wavelength penetrates biological tissue and bone but is absorbed by hemoglobin in the bloodstream, and has similar vascular sensitivity to fMRI [10]. Since neural activity is accompanied by increased oxygen demands in order to metabolize glucose, much like fMRI, fNIRS can detect activation at localized areas of the brain. For a more in depth validation of fNIRS signals in comparison to fMRI, we refer to Strangman et al. [15]. fNIRS detects slow trends of hemodynamic changes, and is thus more appropriate to detect overall state rather than event-related responses.

Recently, fNIRS has increasingly been leveraged to research users because it is considered to be safe, comfortable, relatively robust to movement artifacts, and can be designed for portability. In addition, it is resilient to head movement, facial movement, ambient noise, heartbeat, and muscle movement [7, 13]. This is critical for complex environments where the user must be able to function freely and normally.

Predictive models have been used to differentiate the fNIRS signal between levels of workload [12], verbal and spatial working memory [9], and to determine periods of cognitive multitasking [14] and levels of expertise [3].

DESIGN PRINCIPLES

Regardless the type of sensor, implicit user interfaces that utilize brain and body sensor data share important characteristics, and together define a new class of user interfaces. First, by definition, implicit input is passively obtained from the user. In addition, sensor data is often noisy, is constantly changing, and is continuous, unlike a discrete menu selection or mouse click. Further, the machine learning classification algorithms only provide estimates of cognitive state, with some inherent level of uncertainty. The nature of this input requires careful consideration to ensure successful user interface design. I outline high level principles that can guide development of interfaces that can take advantage of implicit input channels such as those coming from brain and body sensors. Many of these principles could also apply to other similar input channels.

For non-disabled users, passive channels of input are most useful when augmenting other input devices and providing a supplemental channel that indicates user state, instead of being the primary source of input in a system. In addition, because physiological data can be noisy, the adaptations must

be resilient to misclassifications. One way to help prevent this is to provide a confidence value for predictions, in order to influence the interface only when the system is certain of state. Because the prediction might not always be correct, a visualization designer should avoid irreversible or mission-critical adaptations. Instead, the adaptations must be used in a paradigm where the benefits outweigh the costs, and where a high number of correct adaptations can improve performance more than the damages from incorrect classifications.

The adaptation should make subtle, helpful changes to the interface that would not be too disruptive if the user's state is misinterpreted. For example, cognitive state information may be used to change future interactions rather than to make prominent changes directly to the current display. Other potential types of interfaces would be those with multiple views or with limited screen real estate. The brain data could be used to make tradeoffs based on the user's cognitive state. Interface adaptations, which run the risk of causing confusion and adding to the user's workload, must be designed carefully to avoid performance decrements. In particular, care must be taken to avoid surprising or confusing the user by making unexpected changes to the interface.

ADAPTIVE STRATEGIES

I propose a novel taxonomy, still in progress, in which adaptations are categorized by their target functional level and immediacy. Specifically, adaptations can affect the semantic or syntactic levels of a system [6], and can be implemented as either immediate or future changes. From combining these levels and timing, I propose a 2x2 model of four different adaptive strategies.

The semantic level of a system refers to the functions performed and the system's internal values and parameters, while the syntactic level of a system refers to the sequence of inputs and outputs, but not the values of these operations [6, 11]. Thus, we can think of the semantic changes as ones that affect the behavior of the system and the goals and actions of a user, whereas syntactic changes are based on the user interface and do not modify the content of the application.

These system changes can be adjusted in two different levels of immediacy. Immediate changes affect the elements currently on screen or being interacted with, while future changes adjust variables and elements that have not yet appeared. Immediate adjustments have the advantage of mapping directly to the user's experience and having a direct effect. However, they need to be done subtly in order to not disrupt user experience. Future changes can be effective because stronger changes to the system may occur without surprising the user. However, future changes to the state of the system may be difficult to implement and evaluate.

I propose that these strategies can be implemented in conjunction with each other to produce four distinct adaptive strategies for interactive systems: immediate semantic adaptations, future semantic adaptations, immediate syntactic adaptations, and future syntactic adaptations. Below, I outline how each of these adaptations affects a system and then illustrate these principles through descriptions of several systems that I have either built or am currently building.

In **immediate semantic adaptations**, the main display stays consistent; however, actions triggered by interaction with on-screen elements change according to implicit cognitive state input. The system may take control of elements such as timing, or actions of elements that are currently displayed, change the effects of input devices, or even adapt autonomy levels.

As in the previous category, in **future semantic adaptations** the display does not change, but over time the underlying functionality may change based on the implicit cognitive state input. An example of this might be search results, where information can vary in content. Physiological sensors could monitor user state during interaction with the information, and map visual designs with metrics such as engagement or preference. Over time, an intelligent system could compare the user's state across different information delivery mechanisms, and slowly gravitate towards personalized interfaces that elicit better performance and cognitive measures.

In **immediate syntactic adaptations**, information on-screen is modified, filtered, or emphasized according to a user's cognitive state. This can be done via methods such as changing the peripheral data or layering of information on a display, and may aid the focus of the user by making critical information more salient at critical moments. Constant updates across the entire interface or changes in the display format may be jarring and unsettling for users, and disrupt their ability to form cohesive mental models of the system. Instead, subtle modifications to inactive elements on screen may clarify the display for the user. Here, we can leverage the high temporal resolution of physiological sensors. Rather than evaluating the entire interface as one cohesive entity, we can evaluate individual interface elements and personalize them in a way that they might best serve the user.

In **future syntactic adaptations**, we change the upcoming layout of a system based on cognitive state. Combining user state with predictions of how the user will react to user interface elements, the system can decide how to appropriately present information to the user. We can modify the type of visualization or stimuli, level of detail, number of options initially visible in a menu, or size of visual elements to provide what might be most suitable for the user.

IMPLEMENTATION AND USER STUDIES

Real-Time Classification

To explore these interactions, I use and built upon a platform to study brain-based adaptive, implicit user interfaces. It focuses on capturing brain activity from functional near-infrared spectroscopy sensors, but the main components can be used for other brain and body sensors as well. This platform expands the functionality of our Online fNIRS Analysis and Classification (OFAC) system [7] and Brainput system [14]. The system learns to identify brain activity patterns occurring as a user experiences various cognitive states. It provides a continuous, supplemental input stream to an interactive system, which uses this information to modify its

behavior to provide better support for the user. Thus, I can use non-invasive methods to detect signals coming from the brain that users naturally and effortlessly generate while using a computer system.

The main principle of the system is that I calibrate a user model based on a validated cognitive task known to induce specific cognitive states (e.g., high workload vs. low workload or multitasking vs. non-multitasking). By performing these known tasks repeatedly, we generate a dataset of labeled data. This data set is used in the modeling phase to build a machine learning model that finds specific patterns in this data that indicate one cognitive state or another in future, unlabeled data. I have implemented feature detection, which decreased the computational complexity of the system, and improved the runtime and accuracy of the model (as measured by cross-validation accuracy) using better models and parameter searching. One of my other additions to the system is that it also returns confidence values of the classification, so that we can assess the certainty of the model's predictions and only make adaptations when we have high levels of confidence.

UAV Operation

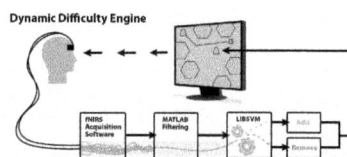

Figure 1. Diagram of our closed-loop dynamic difficulty adaptation engine for UAV adaptation. Raw signals acquired the fNIRS device are filtered, then used to classify user workload. When we are confident that the user is in a suboptimal state, we appropriately add or remove UAVs in order to provide the right amount of work.

I provide an example of *immediate syntactic adaptation*, where we directly add or remove work for the user, in a system for unmanned aerial vehicle (UAV) path planning. We [1] hypothesized that avoiding extended periods of too low or too high workload in this task may lead to flow, a state of immersion and increased engagement. To demonstrate this idea, we ran a laboratory study in which participants performed path planning for multiple UAVs in a simulation. We calibrated a machine learning model on their signals of low and high workload and then varied the difficulty of the task by adding or removing UAVs when we deemed it appropriate. We found that we were able to decrease errors by 35% over a baseline condition of random additions and removals. Our results show that we can use fNIRS brain sensing to detect task difficulty in real time and construct an interface that improves user performance through dynamic difficulty adjustment.

Brain-Based Target Expansion

To show an *immediate syntactic adaptation*, in which physiological signals change how the user interacts with elements on screen, I introduce a brain-based target expansion system [2]. This system improves the efficacy of bubble cursor [8] by increasing the expansion of high importance targets at the optimal time based on brain measurements correlated to a particular type of multitasking. We demonstrate through controlled experiments that brain-based target expansion can deliver a graded and continuous level of assistance to a user according to their cognitive state, thereby improving task and speed-accuracy metrics, even without explicit visual changes to the system. Participants performed a primary audio task (audio recall n-back) while also performing a visual search task with targets of high and low priority. Participants performed best on both tasks, earning the most points, and clicked on targets faster when using a dynamic expansion that reacted to brain input compared to no expansion or static (always full) expansion. Such an adaptation is ideal for use in complex systems to steer users toward higher priority goals during times of increased demand.

Future Research: Phylter for Google Glass

As wearable computing becomes more mainstream, it holds the promise of delivering timely, relevant data to the user. However, these devices can potentially inundate the user, distracting them at the wrong times and providing the wrong amount of information. This can disrupt work or social interactions, and exacerbate the very problems that wearables such as Google Glass might solve. Can we use this for future semantic changes, in which we change the information that we show the user, or future syntactic changes, in which we only change the visual form of graphics or data shown to the user?

To solve this, I am building a system *Phylter* that uses physiological sensing to modulate notifications to the user. Phylter receives streaming data about a user's cognitive state (in the form of machine learning classifications), and receives potential information for the user. It then bases its decision on whether to deliver the message on the message's specified importance and prediction about the user's interruptibility. The current software is calibrated to receive physiological input from the fNIRS-based classification system but is generalizable to other input and output devices. It displays and logs when it receives notifications so that when a system utilizes the service it knows whether or not the user has received a message.

I am currently exploring how to best use this system. In a proof-of-concept pilot, I demonstrated that the software indeed sends the notifications at the right time. I am in the process of conducting an experiment that proves the system modifications can be meaningful, as well as developing additional features.

REFERENCES

1. Afergan, D., Peck, E. M., Solovey, E. T., Jenkins, A., Hincks, S. W., Brown, E. T., Chang, R., and Jacob, R. J. Dynamic difficulty using brain metrics of workload. In *Proc. CHI 2014*, ACM Press (2014).

2. Afergan, D., Shibata, T., Hincks, S. W., Peck, E. M., Yuksel, B. F., Chang, R., and Jacob, R. J. Brain-based target expansion. In *Proc. UIST 2014* (2014).

3. Bunce, S. C., Izzetoglu, K., Ayaz, H., Shewokis, P., Izzetoglu, M., Pourrezaei, K., and Onaral, B. Implementation of fNIRS for monitoring levels of expertise and mental workload. In *Foundations of Augmented Cognition. Directing the Future of Adaptive Systems*. Springer Berlin Heidelberg, 2011, 13–22.

4. Cutrell, E., and Tan, D. BCI for passive input in HCI. In *Proc. CHI 2008*, ACM Press (2008).

5. Fairclough, S., Gilleade, K., Ewing, K. C., and Roberts, J. Capturing user engagement via psychophysiology: measures and mechanisms for biocybernetic adaptation. *International Journal of Autonomous and Adaptive Communications Systems 6*, 1 (2013), 63–79.

6. Foley, J. D., and Van Dam, A. Fundamentals of interactive computer graphics. *Addison-Wesley Systems Programming Series, Reading, Mass.: Addison-Wesley, 1982 1* (1982).

7. Girouard, A., Solovey, E. T., and Hirshfield, L. M. Distinguishing Difficulty Levels with Non-invasive Brain Activity Measurements. *INTERACT 2009* (2009), 440–452.

8. Grossman, T., and Balakrishnan, R. The bubble cursor: enhancing target acquisition by dynamic resizing of the cursor's activation area. In *Proc. CHI 2005*, ACM Press (2005).

9. Hirshfield, L., Gulotta, R., and Hirshfield, S. This is your brain on interfaces: enhancing usability testing with functional near-infrared spectroscopy. In *Proc. CHI 2011*, ACM Press (2011).

10. Huppert, T., and Hoge, R. A temporal comparison of BOLD, ASL, and NIRS hemodynamic responses to motor stimuli in adult humans. *NeuroImage 29*, 2 (2006), 368–382.

11. Jacob, R. J. K. Using formal specifications in the design of a human-computer interface. *Communications of the ACM 26*, 4 (1983), 259–264.

12. Peck, E. M., Afergan, D., and Jacob, R. J. K. Investigation of fNIRS brain sensing as input to information filtering systems. *Augmented Human 2013* (2013).

13. Solovey, E. T., Girouard, A., Chauncey, K., Hirshfield, L. M., Sassaroli, A., Zheng, F., Fantini, S., and Jacob, R. J. K. Using fNIRS Brain Sensing in Realistic HCI Settings: Experiments and Guidelines. In *Proc. UIST 2009*, ACM Press (2009).

14. Solovey, E. T., Schermerhorn, P., Scheutz, M., Sassaroli, A., Fantini, S., and Jacob, R. Brainput: Enhancing Interactive Systems with Streaming fNIRS Brain Input. In *Proc. CHI 2012*, ACM Press (2012).

15. Strangman, G., Culver, J. P., Thompson, J. H., and Boas, D. A. A Quantitative Comparison of Simultaneous BOLD fMRI and NIRS Recordings during Functional Brain Activation. *NeuroImage 17*, 2 (2002), 719–731.

16. Zander, T. O., Kothe, C., Welke, S., and Rötting, M. Utilizing secondary input from passive brain-computer interfaces for enhancing human-machine interaction. In *Foundations of Augmented Cognition, Neuroergonomics and Operational Neuroscience*, Springer Berlin Heidelberg (2009), 759–771.

Interacting with Massive Numbers of Student Solutions

Elena Leah Glassman
MIT CSAIL
elg@mit.edu

ABSTRACT

When teaching programming or hardware design, it is pedagogically valuable for students to generate examples of functions, circuits, or system designs. Teachers can be overwhelmed by these types of student submissions when running large residential or recently released massive online courses. The underlying distribution of student solutions submitted in response to a particular assignment may be complex, but the newly available volume of student solutions represents a denser sampling of that distribution. Working with large datasets of students' solutions, I am building systems with user interfaces that allow teachers to explore the variety of their students' correct and incorrect solutions. Forum posts, grading rubrics, and automatic graders can be based on student solution data, and turn massive engineering and computer science classrooms into useful insight and feedback for teachers. In the development process, I hope to describe essential design principles for such systems.

Author Keywords

data mining; programming exercises; MOOCs

ACM Classification Keywords

H.5.m. Information Interfaces and Presentation (e.g. HCI): Miscellaneous

INTRODUCTION

When teaching programming or hardware design, it is pedagogically valuable for students to generate examples of functions, circuits, or system designs. However, when running large residential or massive online courses, teachers can be overwhelmed by these types of student submissions. Summarizing, exploring, and assessing these types of solutions to assigned problems, even those that can be run through a battery of test cases, involve unsolved challenges.

This work focuses on engineering course assignments that have a behavioral specification students must meet, and allow for a broad range of internal designs. There may be several distinct, correct solutions, some of which may be unanticipated by teachers.

UIST'14 Adjunct, October 5–8, 2014, Honolulu, HI, USA.
ACM 978-1-4503-3068-8/14/10.
http://dx.doi.org/10.1145/2658779.2661167

The underlying distribution of student solutions to a particular assignment may be complex, but the newly available volume of student solutions represents a denser sampling of the distribution. The increasing scale of the classroom creates a research opportunity. For example, if we attempt to classify solutions with a Support Vector Machine (SVM), the volume of labeled training data (solutions labeled by teachers) is key to its performance. Such classifiers could be incorporated into the user interfaces I am designing for teachers to explore students' solutions, and could even be trained further based on teachers' interactions with the interfaces.

I am guided by the following questions:

1. How do we help teachers understand the space of solutions generated by students? What features of solutions, and user interface designs, are useful for visualizing and clustering alternative solutions?

2. How do we help teachers understand whether students absorbed a particular lesson or principle relevant to the internal design of their solutions? How do we help teachers respond to common problems, improve a specific assignment, or refine a grading rubric?

3. As a side-effect of discovering common variations of solutions, as well as bugs and misunderstandings, how can peer-to-peer teaching and assistance be enhanced by this knowledge?

Thesis Statement A system that empowers teachers to explore the variety of their students' correct and incorrect solutions will enable data-driven refinements to teaching materials. Forum posts, grading rubrics, and automatic graders can be based on student solution data, and turn massive engineering and computer science classrooms into useful insight and feedback for teachers.

RELATED WORK

There is a growing body of work on both the front end and back end required to manage and present the large volumes of solutions gathered from MOOCs, intelligent tutors, online learning platforms, and large residential classes. The back end necessary to analyze solutions expressed as code has followed from prior work in fields such as program analysis, compilers, and machine learning. A common goal of this prior work is to help teachers monitor the state of their class, or provide solution-specific feedback to many students. However, there has not been much work on developing interactive user interfaces that enable an instructor to navigate the large space of student solutions.

Huang et al. [7] worked with short Matlab/Octave functions submitted online by students enrolled in a machine learning MOOC. The authors generate an abstract syntax tree (AST) for each solution to a programming problem, and calculate the tree edit distance between all pairs of ASTs, using the dynamic programming edit distance algorithm presented by Shasha et al. [13]. Based on these computed edit distances, clusters of syntactically similar solutions are formed. The algorithm is *quadratic* in both the number of solutions and the size of the ASTs. Using a *computing cluster*, the Shasha algorithm was applied to just over a million solutions.

Codewebs [11] created an index of "code phrases" for over a million submissions from the same MOOC and semi-automatically identified equivalence classes across these phrases, using a data-driven, probabilistic approach. The Codewebs search engine accepts queries in the form of sub-trees, subforests, and contexts that are subgraphs of an AST. A teacher labels a set of AST subtrees considered semantically meaningful, and then queries the search engine to extract all equivalent subtrees from the dataset.

Both Codewebs [11] and Huang et al. [7] use unit test results and AST edit distance to identify clusters of submissions that could potentially receive the same feedback from a teacher. These are non-interactive systems that require hand-labeling in the case of Codewebs, or a computing cluster in the case of Huang et al.

Several user interfaces have been designed for providing grades or feedback to students at scale, and for browsing large collections in general, not just student solutions. Basu et al. [1] provide a novel user interface for *powergrading* short-answer questions. Powergrading means assigning grades or writing feedback to many similar answers at once. The back end uses machine learning that is trained to cluster answers, and the front end allows teachers to read, grade or provide feedback to those groups of similar answers simultaneously. Teachers can also discover common misunderstandings. The value of the interface was verified in a study of 25 teachers looking at their visual interface with clustered answers. When compared against a baseline interface, the teachers assigned grades to students substantially faster, gave more feedback to students, and developed a "high-level view of students' understanding and misconceptions" [3].

At the intersection of information visualization and program analysis is an interactive visualization embedded in the MathWorks' Cody[1], an informal learning environment for the Matlab programming language. The Cody programming challenge does not have any teaching staff associated with it but does have the interactive *solution map* visualization to help participants discover alternative ways to solve the programming problem, after they submit at least one function that passes all test cases. A solution's parse tree size is the arbitrary metric by which solutions are ranked. Some participants try to race others to the solution with the smallest parse tree, through both their own ingenuity and the mining of alternative code snippets from other solutions revealed in the

solution map. The solution map plots each solution as a point against two axes: time of submission on the horizontal axis, and parse tree size on the vertical axis. Despite the simplicity of this metric, solution maps can provide quick and valuable insight when assessing large numbers of solutions [4].

This work has also been inspired by information visualization projects like WordSeer [9, 10] and CrowdScape [12]. WordSeer helps literary analysts navigate and explore texts, using query words and phrases [8]. CrowdScape gives users an overview of crowdworkers' performance on tasks. An overview of crowdworkers each performing on a task, and an overview of submitted code, each executing a test case, are not so different, from an information presentation point of view.

VISUALIZING, CLUSTERING, AND EXPLORING CODE

I led the development of OverCode, an interactive visualization for the many code solutions submitted to a programming exercise in a massive online course [5]. Without tool support, a teacher may not read more than 50-100 solutions before growing frustrated with the tedium of the task. In the MOOC datasets we tested the tool on, there were at least a thousand solutions per programming problem. Given a relatively small sample size of the spectrum of solutions, teachers cannot be expected to develop a thorough understanding of the variety of strategies used to solve the programming problem, or produce instructive feedback that is relevant to a large proportion of learners. They are also less likely to discover unexpected, interesting solutions.

With OverCode, teachers can explore the variation in hundreds or thousands of programming solutions generated by students attempting a set of Python programming exercises in a large university course or MOOC. Understanding the wide variation in students' solutions is important for providing appropriate, tailored feedback, refining evaluation rubrics, and exposing corner cases in automatic grading tests.

Implementation

OverCode's novel back end cleans up student solutions for easier visualization by renaming variables. The back end tracks each solution's local variables during execution on the same test case. During renaming, variables that behave 'the same' across different solutions are automatically given the same name, as a function of the students' original naming choices.

With lightweight static analysis after renaming variables, the back end creates clusters of functionally identical solutions. The cleaned solutions are readable, executable, and describe every solution in their cluster. The algorithm's running time is *linear* in both the number of solutions and the size of each solution. In contrast to CodeWebs [11] and Huang et al. [7], OverCode's pipeline does not require hand-labeling and runs in *minutes on a laptop*, then presents the results in an interactive user interface.

OverCode's front end presents the cleaned solutions as each cluster's unique descriptor, which otherwise would be difficult to automatically generate. In Fig. 1, (a), (b), and (c) are

---

[1]`mathworks.com/matlabcentral/cody`

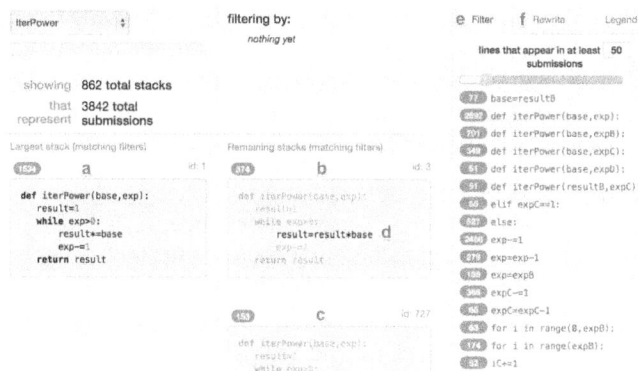

Figure 1. OverCode user interface.

cleaned solutions with renamed variables representing clusters of 1534, 374, and 153 solutions, respectively. The differences between clusters (d) are highlighted. Given those initial clusters, OverCode lets teachers further filter (e) and merge (f) clusters based on rewrite rules.

Value for Teachers

The value of OverCode for teachers comes in the form of confidence and improved feedback to students. Compared to a non-clustering baseline, OverCode allowed teachers to more quickly develop a high-level view of students' understanding and misconceptions, and plan course forum posts with feedback that is relevant to more students. We are currently extending OverCode's pipeline to include other languages, such as Java and hardware description languages, and more complex coding assignments. I hope OverCode will help teaching staff continue to gain a deeper insight into their students' design choices.

Value for Students

While in the role of the 'teacher' working with OverCode, I learned new Python syntax. With modification to the interface, students may also learn from interacting directly with OverCode. This model of learning echoes the interactive solution maps in Cody, the MathWorks' programming game, which has no teaching staff. In future work, I can investigate what changes to OverCode are necessary to create a visualization of fellow students' solutions that is beneficial for students' learning, instead of teachers' understanding. This may also address the question of how students can help each other explore alternative designs.

HELPING STUDENTS GUIDE EACH OTHER

Teaching peers, also called peer learning, is pedagogically valuable [2]. I am currently pilot testing various systems for matching students, keeping in mind that different students may be working on different, but equally valid, correct solutions to the same problem. The following prototypes motivate further systematic data collection, on which more theoretical models could be based.

Evaluating Alternative Solutions

In MIT's Computation Structures course, students create digital circuits in a hardware description language. Through exploration of hundreds of previous student solutions to an early, basic lab assignment, I found that the space of alternative correct circuit designs is nearly completely separable by the number of device primitives, i.e., transistors, in each design. Picking from previous student designs, I was able to automatically present current students with design alternatives that were better or worse than their own. Students were asked to give advice to a future student about how to improve the poorer of the two designs. Their explanations gave a rich window into their understanding. Students in the Spring '14 offering of the course gave strikingly cogent advice to future students. A question I plan to further explore is: how best do we close this loop, so that students benefit from the design alternatives and advice generated by classmates?

Pairing Students Based on Their Solutions

In another assignment in the same course, students are asked to create a Turing machine that determines whether a string of parentheses is balanced, i.e., has a closing parenthesis for every open one. I visualized the dynamic behavior of over a hundred students' Turing machines, and found that there were two distinct common designs. Several fellow teachers were only aware of one. At least one teacher admitted steering students away from designs that, in retrospect, may have been the 'other' common solution they did not know about. In addition to better preparing teachers, can we automatically recognize which design a student is working on? When they need help, should we pair them with another student who is working on, or has already finished, the same design? How do we support, or at least not interfere with, students working toward novel designs? I hope to address these questions by integrating a program analysis-based user interface like OverCode with systems for social hint-giving and receiving between students.

Debugging Advice Based on Test Cases

In the same course, students ultimately build entire simulated processors composed of logic gate primitives. These solutions, expressed as pages' worth of an in-house declarative programming language, can become so complex as to be very challenging to debug even with the one-on-one help of a seasoned teaching staff member. Students who have previously resolved a bug can be in a better position than a staff member to help a fellow student with the same bug, if the staff member has never encountered that bug before.

"Dear Beta" is a website I built so that students can post explanations of their own resolved bugs, indexed by the failed test cases the bug caused. Providing the explanation is pedagogically useful, and students struggling with a bug can reference it for advice. When students sought help and found one of their fellow students' hints helpful, they had the option of upvoting it. Both website usage statistics and anecdotal evidence suggest that students find the website to be helpful. What are the necessary factors to consider when generalizing this peer-helping framework to additional software design courses?

USING SYSTEM INTERACTIONS TO TRAIN MACHINE LEARNING ALGORITHMS

In a domain as complex as student solutions to engineering and programming assignments, traditional machine learning may fail. Teachers each have their own internal metrics for what is and is not important when sorting through student solutions. For example, when a small sample of introductory programming course teaching assistants were consulted about how to cluster students' solutions to simple programming assignments, their clusterings often disagreed with each other on how to group and explain student variation.

From the prototypes that culminated in OverCode, two things are clear. First, program analysis can do rigorously what was not possible with unsupervised clustering techniques running on student solution feature vectors [6]. Second, program analysis and manually specified rewrite rules can only get teachers so far. Teachers' ability to interrogate the thousands of student solutions available to them in our datasets was limited by their patience to specify what they believed to be irrelevant differences between clusters of solutions.

This is an application ideally suited to interactive machine learning (IML) techniques. By logging teachers' interactions with the data, IML techniques could suggest or predict additional helpful feature equivalences and rewrite rules, rather than requiring teachers to specify each one by hand. These decisions can become the subject of staff and classroom discussions, and be incorporated into teaching materials and automated grading rubrics.

IML techniques may also 'learn' from student-to-student interaction logs gathered from the social systems described in the previous section. If students are each working on debugging their own distinct solutions, and a group of students all mark a debugging hint, provided by another student, as helpful, then those solutions are related by the relevance of that particular hint. IML techniques may be able to suggest merging particular clusters of solutions in OverCode, based on shared hint relevance.

SUMMARY

At the conclusion of my graduate work, I hope to have built systems that help both teachers and students in large-scale engineering and programming courses. In the development process, I hope to describe essential design principles for such systems, and show that teachers using the systems gain deeper insight into their students' thoughts and designs, allowing richer conversations with students about their design choices. To better support learners when teachers are vastly outnumbered by students, or when teachers are simply not present, I hope that these systems help students discuss their solutions and guide each other.

ACKNOWLEDGMENTS

I am grateful for the support and guidance of my thesis advisor, Rob Miller, Professor of EECS in MIT's Computer Science and Artificial Intelligence Lab. This material is based, in part, upon work supported by the National Science Foundation Graduate Research Fellowship (grant 1122374), the Microsoft Research Fellowship, the Bose Foundation Fellowship, and by Quanta Computer as part of the Qmulus Project. Any opinions, findings, conclusions, or recommendations in this paper are the author's, and do not necessarily reflect the views of the sponsors.

REFERENCES

1. Basu, S., Jacobs, C., and Vanderwende, L. Powergrading: a clustering approach to amplify human effort for short answer grading. *TACL 1* (2013), 391–402.

2. Boud, D., Cohen, R., and Sampson, J. *Peer learning in higher education: Learning from and with each other.* Routledge, 2014.

3. Brooks, M., Basu, S., Jacobs, C., and Vanderwende, L. Divide and correct: using clusters to grade short answers at scale. In *Learning at Scale* (2014), 89–98.

4. Glassman, E. L., Gulley, N., and Miller, R. C. Toward facilitating assistance to students attempting engineering design problems. In *Proceedings of the Tenth Annual International Conference on International Computing Education Research*, ICER '13, ACM (New York, NY, USA, 2013).

5. Glassman, E. L., Scott, J., Singh, R., Guo, P. J., and Miller, R. C. Overcode: Visualizing variation in student solutions to programming problems at scale (in submission). *ACM Trans. Comput.-Hum. Interact.* (2014).

6. Glassman, E. L., Singh, R., Gulley, N., and Miller, R. C. Feature engineering for clustering student solutions. CHI 2014 Learning Innovations at Scale Workshop, 2014.

7. Huang, J., Piech, C., Nguyen, A., and Guibas, L. J. Syntactic and functional variability of a million code submissions in a machine learning mooc. In *AIED Workshops* (2013).

8. Muralidharan, A., and Hearst, M. Wordseer: Exploring language use in literary text. *Fifth Workshop on Human-Computer Interaction and Information Retrieval* (2011).

9. Muralidharan, A., and Hearst, M. A. Supporting exploratory text analysis in literature study. *Literary and linguistic computing 28*, 2 (2013), 283–295.

10. Muralidharan, A. S., Hearst, M. A., and Fan, C. Wordseer: a knowledge synthesis environment for textual data. In *CIKM* (2013), 2533–2536.

11. Nguyen, A., Piech, C., Huang, J., and Guibas, L. J. Codewebs: scalable homework search for massive open online programming courses. In *WWW* (2014), 491–502.

12. Rzeszotarski, J. M., and Kittur, A. Crowdscape: interactively visualizing user behavior and output. In *UIST* (2012), 55–62.

13. Shasha, D., Wang, J.-L., Zhang, K., and Shih, F. Y. Exact and approximate algorithms for unordered tree matching. *IEEE Transactions on Systems, Man and Cybernetics 24*, 4 (1994), 668–678.

Powering Interactive Intelligent Systems with the Crowd

Walter S. Lasecki

Computer Science Department, University of Rochester

wlasecki@cs.rochester.edu

ABSTRACT

Creating intelligent systems that are able to recognize a user's behavior, understand unrestricted spoken natural language, complete complex tasks, and respond fluently could change the way computers are used in daily life. But fully-automated intelligent systems are a far-off goal – currently, machines struggle in many real-world settings because problems can be almost entirely unconstrained and can vary greatly between instances. Human computation has been shown to be effective in many of these settings, but is traditionally applied in an offline, batch-processing fashion. My work focuses on a new model of continuous, real-time crowdsourcing that enables *interactive* crowd-powered systems.

Author Keywords

Crowdsourcing; human computation; intelligent systems

ACM Classification Keywords

H.5.m. Information Interfaces and Presentation: Misc.

INTRODUCTION

Intelligent systems make it easier for users to find and access information, complete tasks, and get feedback. However, current computational systems are limited by the abilities of machines to perceive and reason about the world. My work explores how to create systems that overcome these barriers by integrating human intelligence from dynamic groups (crowds) of people who can be recruited on-demand to quickly contribute small units of work. These people might be volunteers, full-time employees, or micro-task workers. Underlying these systems is a novel class of workflows and interfaces that allow people and machines to build on one anothers abilities [15]. My work is the first to explore crowd-powered systems that can provide real-time responses *continuously* over the course of multiple interactions.

I will outline some of the systems that I have created which exemplify key algorithms and design principles for systems that combine human and machine intelligence in ways that yield better performance than either one alone (Figure 1). My work has three main focuses: access technologies for users with disabilities, general intelligence systems that go beyond what AI can do alone, and crowdsourcing workflows that optimize for response speed and consistency.

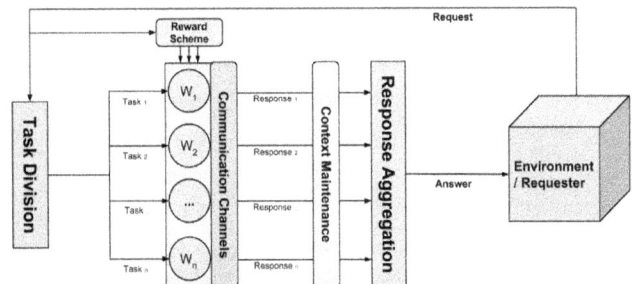

Figure 1. The architecture of a real-time crowd-powered system.

Access Technology

Access technology provides users with cheaper, more readily available, and more easy-to-use tools for perceiving, understanding, and interacting with the world around them. However, classic (machine) computation often struggles most in exactly those domains that are most needed by users with disabilities, such as vision, natural language processing, and recognizing speech [3].

I have created systems that provide deaf and hard of hearing users with real-time captions [8], recognize real-word activities to help older adults and people with certain cognitive impairments live more independently [11, 13], and make getting answers to visual questions much more efficient and usable for blind and low vision users [12]. The potential for creating systems that have a transformative effect on people's daily lives drives me to not only develop approaches that can satisfy access needs, but also to build and deploy them so that people can use these tools.

General Intelligent Systems

Using the same principles that make it possible to support access technologies using the crowd, we can also develop general-purpose intelligent systems that are able to interact with people more naturally than automated systems alone. For example, Chorus [14] is a crowd-powered conversational assistant that is able to answer arbitrary user questions in natural language over multiple turns of conversation, and Glance [9] allows researchers and other analysts to code video using natural language descriptions in minutes instead of days.

Crowd Agent Framework

All of the work I will describe in this paper fits into a framework for interactive crowdsourcing called *crowd agents*. This new class of intelligent system (see Chapter 1 of [17]) views a machine and workflow moderated collective as a single intelligent entity, but to achieve this, crowdsourcing workflows

Scribe
System Overview

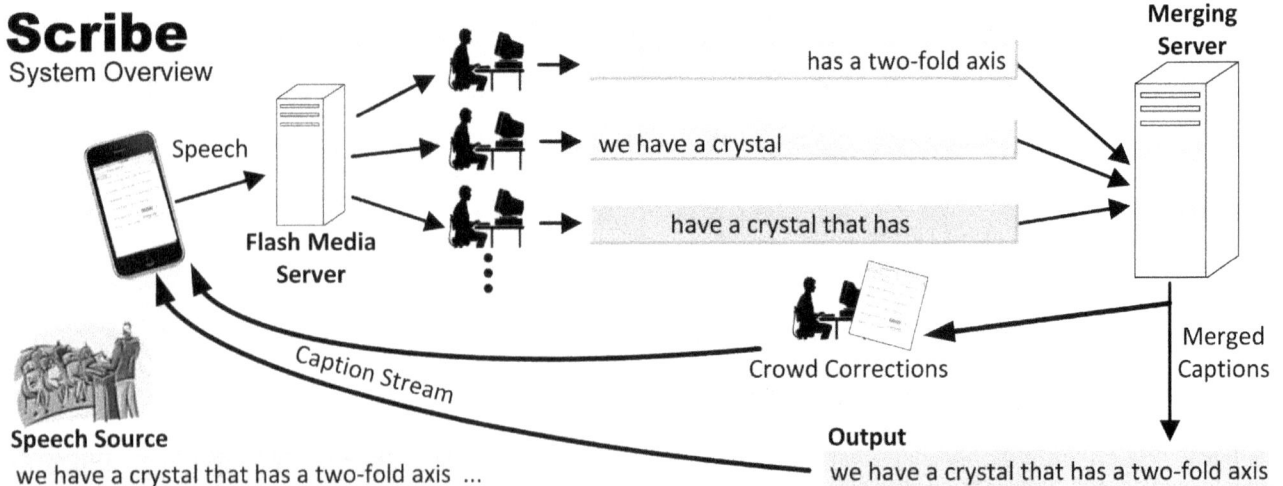

Figure 2. Scribe allows users to caption audio on their mobile device. The audio is sent to multiple amateur captionists who use Scribe's web-based interface to caption as much of the audio as they can in real-time. These partial captions are sent to our server to be merged into a final output stream, which is then forwarded back to the user's mobile device. Crowd workers are optionally recruited to edit the captions after they have been merged.

must be focused on ensuring quick, consistent, and reliable output. These ideas are developed throughout this paper.

SYSTEMS

To demonstrate the power and generalizability of interactive crowd-powered systems, we have developed several systems that explore different key approaches to organizing collective intelligence processes in real-time.

Legion

Legion [10] is a system that enables groups of crowd workers to collectively control an existing user interface in real-time with no modification needed to the interface itself. This work was the first to introduce the continuous real-time crowd-sourcing model. Prior work had investigated real-time crowd-sourcing in the context of being able to quickly recruit members of the crowd to perform a single discrete task [1, 2]. However, in many cases this limits the amount of feedback that workers can get regarding their inputs effect on the task itself. We expect that this leads to a decreased task learning rate for workers. Furthermore, for time-sensitive tasks that involve performing several small tasks, the overhead incurred by each worker having to accept a new task at every step might exceed the actual work provided.

Workers were asked to perform an interactive control task (such as driving a robot), so we need a model that would allow each worker to get feedback from the environment, while also leveraging the wisdom of the crowd. Legion does this by binning time into small windows (roughly 0.5-1 seconds), then implicitly using each workers input as a vote for a given action. The most effective strategy across the tasks we tested turned out to be weighting workers based on their current and past agreement with the rest of the crowd, then electing a leader for each time window. This avoided cases where vote splitting in the crowd caused the average decision to be incorrect. For example, when half the crowd wanting to drive a robot left to avoid an obstacle, and the other half wanting to drive to the right.

Legions use of input from different workers selected at different times allowed the final result to be a single, coherent control stream that could be forwarded to an existing interface. In effect, all of the workers collectively acted as a single worker, allowing the interface to be controlled without needing any special modification. Legion handles a diverse range of tasks, and has been tested in a variety of different interfaces and domains using tasks such as robot navigation through a physical maze, powering an intelligent assistive keyboard for motor impaired users, data-entry in a spreadsheet, OCR from an image of text, and games.

Scribe

Legion:Scribe [8] provides real-time captions of speech using non-expert workers who each type part of what they hear. Currently, the two most common approaches to collecting real-time captions are professional stenographers who can cost as much as $200/hour, and automatic speech recognition, which does not provide usable captions in real-world settings.

Scribe aims to solve that by allowing multiple non-expert captionists to collaboratively caption speech in real-time (Figure 2). Professional stenographers train for years to be able to keep up with natural speaking rates that average about 150 words per minute. Non-expert workers are generally only able to caption about a third of this rate. However, Scribe is able to merge multiple non-expert captionists into a single reconstruction of the original speech by using an online multiple sequence alignment algorithm [16]. This differs from the original model presented in Legion since instead of the final output being a selection of different worker inputs, Scribe actually merges the captions together to outperform what an constituent worker could do alone.

Glance

Behavioral researchers spend considerable amount of time coding video data to systematically extract meaning from subtle human actions and emotions [5]. We introduced Glance to improve this process. Glance is a tool that allows researchers to rapidly query, sample, and analyze large video datasets for behavioral events that are hard to detect automatically [9]. Glance takes advantage of the parallelism available in paid online crowds to interpret natural language queries and then aggregates responses in a summary view of the video data. Glance provides analysts with rapid responses when initially exploring a dataset, and reliable codings when refining an analysis.

Our experiments have shown that Glance can code nearly 50 minutes of video in 5 minutes by recruiting over 60 workers simultaneously, and can get initial feedback to analysts in under 10 seconds for most clips. We present and compare new methods for accurately aggregating the input of multiple workers marking the spans of events in video data, and for measuring the quality of their coding in real-time before a baseline is established by measuring the variance between workers. Glance's rapid responses to natural language queries, feedback regarding question ambiguity and anomalies in the data, and ability to build on prior context in follow-up queries allows users to have a conversation-like interaction with their data – opening up new possibilities for naturally exploring video data.

Chorus

Legion allowed an interface to be autonomously controlled by the crowd using natural language, but didn't allow the workers to respond to the user if the problem was underspecified, or if the crowd wanted to know which valid option to select. While many other previous crowdsourcing systems also provide end-users with the ability to make natural language requests to the crowd, most do not allow for multiple inputs in a turn, and none allowed for a dialogue with the crowd. Chorus was developed to allow users to hold a conversation with the crowd using an instant messenger style interface, and encourages workers to respond as if the crowd were a single consistent conversational partner.

This consistency is a product of two main components. The first is a propose-and-filter step in which workers are asked to both propose responses to a workers input then see what others have proposed and vote for those answers they think are the most appropriate. The second component that Chorus uses to maintain consistent conversations is a working memory. A highlights window shows facts that workers think are the most important to the current task. The ability of the crowd to remember as a group, by passing on knowledge to future workers points to potential applications of this model for other organizations.

Chorus:View

Chorus:View [12] uses Chorus's conversational interaction paradigm to answer visual questions about the world around them. Conceptually, this work extends VizWiz [2], a system for nearly real-time (within roughly 30 seconds to 1 minute) visual question answering from photographs. In VizWiz, the single-photograph requirement (that often results in difficultly for blind users when framing information), in conjunction with the delayed response time, meant that asking for a

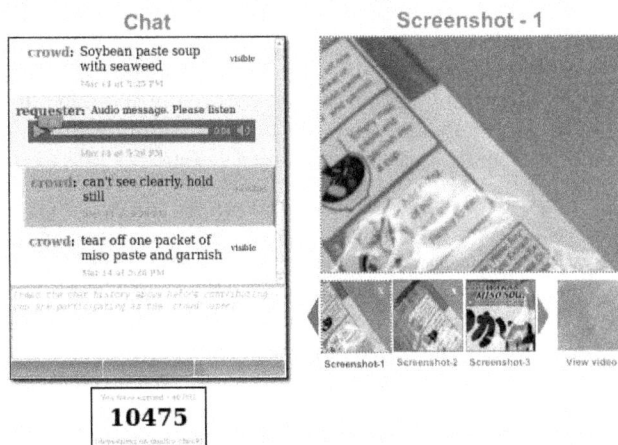

Figure 3. View's worker interface. Workers are shown a video streamed from the user's phone, and asked to reply to spoken queries using the chat interface. In this example, the recorded message asks workers "How do I cook this?" a question that often involves multiple image-framing steps and was often challenging using VizWiz.

series of answers, such as when navigating in an unfamiliar area where visual cues might be the only guidance.

View lets users stream audio and video to crowd workers who are presented with a Chorus-like interface for responding to the users questions in a more natural, conversational style (Figure 3). While workers reply in text, a screen reader on the users phone uses text to speech conversion to make the responses accessible. View allows very rapid successions of answers to complex or multi-stage questions, and can even let workers give feedback to users on how to frame the required information. Our studies showed that blind users can get answers in a fraction of the time of VizWiz in settings where multiple questions are needed. Users were also extremely excited to get the chance to use the prototype. Our release version is in progress and will allow the thousands of VizWiz users to better access the world around them.

Legion:AR

Legion:AR [11] uses the collaborative content generation that unpins Scribe to make it possible for people to supply an activity recognition system with action labels as actions occur in a video stream. Activity recognition provides automated systems with the context behind user interactions [6]. We focus this work on monitoring settings where prompting systems can help people in their daily lives, such as helping older adults or cognitively impaired individuals live more independently, or monitoring public spaces for emergencies.

Legion:AR combines human intelligence and machine learning approaches in this labeling process. It uses a Hidden Markov Model (HMM) to learn activities from the labels provided by workers, then uses an active learning approach to ask the crowd for labels for the activities or actions the system cannot yet identify with high confidence. When asking the crowd for labels, Legion:AR can also contribute its best guess. When this guess is correct it significantly reduces the time that workers must spend on their labeling task, reducing the cost and latency of the system overall.

Even with the ability to get assistance from the crowd when needed, training an automated system takes many examples to reliably learn to identify patterns appropriately. Unfortunately, video training data is often very costly and difficult to collect because of the need to either stage a set of events, or wait for them to occur in an observed setting.

ARchitect [13] is a system that asks simple queries to crowd workers to extract information about structural dependencies between the actions in an activity. By doing this, our experiments showed we were able to collect over 7x as much training data from each activity video, allowing automated systems to be trained faster than using label-only approaches. Eventually, my goal is to leverage human understanding to approach near one-off learning in machines by exploring how people can transfer their knowledge to computers effectively.

Apparition

Prototyping allows designers to quickly iterate and gather feedback, but the time it takes to create even a Wizard-of-Oz prototype restricts the effectiveness of this process [7, 4]. In on-going work, we are creating an infrastructure and techniques for prototyping interactive systems in the time it takes to simply describe the idea visually and verbally.

Apparition is a system that uses paid crowds to make even hard-to-automate functions work immediately, allowing more fluid prototyping of interfaces that contain interactive elements or complex behaviors. As users sketch their interface and describe it aloud in natural language, crowd workers translate the sketch into traditional interface elements, add animations, and provide Wizard-of-Oz control to the prototype. This crowd- powered prototype can be used immediately by the design team for iteration or user study. Our approach can be combined with existing tools, and how, over time, the prototypes we develop can scale towards fully implemented versions of the systems they simulate.

CONCLUSIONS AND FUTURE WORK

My work focuses on creating robust intelligent systems that are capable of working now, even in real-world settings where artificial intelligence is not reliable. These systems provide a way to create novel systems, as well as a means of collecting realistic training data that would not be possible without deploying these systems.

My future work will focus on crowdsourcing workflows that not only minimize response time and worker effort while allowing situational context to be maintained, but also account for how machines can best learn from the human work being contributed. In this way, crowd-powered systems can act as a scaffold for artificial intelligence, creating a way for intelligent systems to be deployed, trained in situ, and then fully automated over time to yield faster, cheaper, and more reliable systems than have been possible before.

ACKNOWLEDGEMENTS

My work is supported by a Microsoft Research Ph.D. Fellowship, Google, and the National Science Foundation. I would also like to thank all of my collaborators on these projects.

REFERENCES

1. Bernstein, M. S., Brandt, J., Miller, R. C., and Karger, D. R. Crowds in two seconds: Enabling realtime crowd-powered interfaces. In *UIST* (2010).

2. Bigham, J. P., Jayant, C., Ji, H., Little, G., Miller, A., Miller, R. C., Miller, R., Tatarowicz, A., White, B., White, S., and Yeh, T. Vizwiz: Nearly real-time answers to visual questions. In *UIST* (2010).

3. Bigham, J. P., and Ladner, R. E. What the disability community can teach us about interactive crowdsourcing. *Interactions 18*, 4 (July 2011).

4. Davis, R. C., Saponas, T. S., Shilman, M., and Landay, J. A. Sketchwizard: Wizard of oz prototyping of pen-based user interfaces. In *UIST* (2007).

5. Heyman, R. E., Lorber, M. F., Eddy, J. M., West, T., Reis, E. H. T., and Judd, C. M. *Handbook of Research Methods in Social and Personality Psychology*. Pending, 2014, ch. Behavioral observation and coding.

6. Kautz, H. A., and Allen, J. F. Generalized plan recognition. *AAAI 86* (1986).

7. Landay, J. A., and Myers, B. A. Interactive sketching for the early stages of user interface design. In *CHI* (1995).

8. Lasecki, W., Miller, C., Sadilek, A., Abumoussa, A., Borrello, D., Kushalnagar, R., and Bigham, J. Real-time captioning by groups of non-experts. In *UIST* (2012).

9. Lasecki, W. S., Gordon, M., Koutra, D., Jung, M., Dow, S. P., and Bigham, J. P. Glance: Rapidly coding behavioral video with the crowd. In *UIST* (2014).

10. Lasecki, W. S., Murray, K. I., White, S., Miller, R. C., and Bigham, J. P. Real-time crowd control of existing interfaces. In *UIST* (2011).

11. Lasecki, W. S., Song, Y. C., Kautz, H., and Bigham, J. P. Real-time crowd labeling for deployable activity recognition. In *CSCW* (2013).

12. Lasecki, W. S., Thiha, P., Zhong, Y., Brady, E., and Bigham, J. P. Answering visual questions with conversational crowd assistants. In *ASSETS* (2013).

13. Lasecki, W. S., Weingard, L., Ferguson, G., and Bigham, J. P. Finding dependencies between actions using the crowd. In *CHI* (2014).

14. Lasecki, W. S., Wesley, R., Nichols, J., Kulkarni, A., Allen, J. F., and Bigham, J. P. Chorus: A crowd-powered conversational assistant. In *UIST* (2013).

15. Little, G., Chilton, L. B., Goldman, M., and Miller, R. C. Turkit: Human computation algorithms on mechanical turk. In *UIST* (2010).

16. Naim, I., Gildea, D., Lasecki, W. S., and Bigham, J. P. Text alignment for real-time crowd captioning. In *HLT-NAACL* (2013).

17. Russell, S., and Norvig, P. *Artificial intelligence: a modern approach*. Prentice Hall.

Making Distance Matter: Leveraging Scale and Diversity in Massive Online Classes

Chinmay Kulkarni
Stanford University
353 Serra Mall, Stanford CA 94305
chinmay@cs.stanford.edu

ABSTRACT

The large scale of online classes and the diversity of the students that participate in them can enable new educational systems. This massive scale and diversity can enable always-available systems that help students share diverse ideas, and inspire and learn from each other. We introduce systems for two core educational processes at scale: discussion and assessment. To date, several thousand students in a dozen online classes have used our discussion system. Controlled experiments suggest that participants in more diverse discussions perform better on tests and that discussion improves engagement. Similarly, more than 100,000 students have reviewed peer work for both summative assessment and feedback. Through these systems, we argue that to create new educational experiences at scale, pedagogical strategies and software that leverage scale and diversity must be co-developed. More broadly, we suggest the key to creating new educational experiences online lies in leveraging massive networks of peers.

Author Keywords

Peer assessment, discussion, online education, MOOC, social computing

PEER OPPORTUNITIES FOR LEARNING AT SCALE

Massive online classrooms bring together students from around the world in one connected classroom. This educational setup starkly contrasts how students have traditionally learned in small groups. For instance, design education has relied on small studio groups since the École des Beaux-Arts in Paris introduced the studio model in 1819 [13]. Similarly, other disciplines have relied on models such as seminars, which at best can scale to a few hundred students. Online classes have orders of magnitude more students.

Separated from our traditional techniques, the temptation is to view education at scale as fundamentally inferior to in-person learning. We instead ask: could we transform scale

UIST '14 Adjunct, Oct 05-08 2014, Honolulu, HI, USA
ACM 978-1-4503-3068-8/14/10.
http://dx.doi.org/10.1145/2658779.2661169

into an opportunity? Could we go beyond being there [9], and design social computing technologies to enable education that is impossible at smaller scales?

This dissertation proposes to achieve this goal by leveraging interactions amongst students at scale. Our research in this area is inspired by the powerful role peers play in traditional classrooms. They motivate students by setting norms and expectations, and they help students learn by acting as mediators between students and instructors [2]. Peer interactions shift students from 'automatic' thinking to more 'active, effortful, conscious' thinking, which aids learning and growth [6].

We argue that connecting students with the diverse experience levels and viewpoints of their global peer group peers improves learning outcomes. Online classes have massive scale and are widely accessible, potentially allowing for peer-interactions at any time of day. Furthermore, they attract students that are more diverse than in any offline setting [8]. For example, online classes routinely attract students from hundreds of countries in dozens of professions [15]. If this diversity is properly utilized, international relations classes could offer "mini-UN" discussions where students teaching each other global cultural perspectives and sharing experiences that cross professional cliques, design classes could offer global critiques of student work, and management classes could match students to mentors who suits them uniquely.

We argue that creating these applications will require us to simultaneously develop the pedagogical strategies that use the properties of the online space as an educational asset, as well as software designed for the global scale, asynchronous access, and diversity of online classes.

It is often not obvious how to design such systems. For example, a large number of students participate in an online class, but do so at different times. Therefore, systems (e.g. for video discussions) that assume that a number of students will be online at the same time are likely to fail. Instead, we found that systems are more successful when they induce students to be online together e.g. with scheduled discussions (see "Peer interactions for discussion"). Similarly, educators struggle to create in-person discussions with diverse viewpoints, in part because discussion groups have limited diversity [3]. Online, student diversity enables more geographically diverse groups, comprising students with meaningfully varied experiences. To leverage this diversity, new techniques are necessary so that diverse students are comfortable sharing and learning from each other's perspectives.

As these examples illustrate, pedagogical strategies that leverage class properties (such as diversity) create educational experiences unavailable elsewhere, and systems designed around class properties (such as large-scale but asynchronous access) enable large-scale adoption.

This dissertation introduces novel systems in massive online classes for two core educational processes: assessment and discussion. It discusses the design insights that enable these systems to leverage scale and diversity. Furthermore, it creates new pedagogical strategies that improve upon in-person peer assessment and discussion. Finally, it demonstrates how these pedagogical strategies can be re-encoded into software to enable them to be used by many educators.

PEER INTERACTIONS FOR DISCUSSION

Discussion and interaction among peers are central to learning in the classroom. Peers motivate each other, act as knowledge mediators, and contextualize knowledge. Unfortunately, peers in online classrooms don't often communicate. When they do, they use text-based forums where trust and common ground are hard to create.

We built Talkabout (https://talkabout.stanford.edu), a small-group real time video discussion system for MOOCs. Talkabout introduces an online learning environment and curricula that creates small, diverse groups in massive classes [4]. This environment connects students to their global peers via guided, synchronous video discussion to deepen their understanding of course concepts. In pilots, we found that the number of students who are spontaneously online at the same time is too small for reliable group discussions. Therefore, students choose their preferred time from a list (with times approx. every 6 hours), and the system forms groups of two to nine people with high national diversity for a video discussion. Discussion prompts encourage peers to relate course content to their local and personal experiences.

To date, more than 3,400 students from 134 countries have used Talkabout in seven online classes via Coursera. These classes include Social Psychology, Organizational Analysis, Behavioral Economics, Logic, and Design. The median discussion had six students from five countries.

The combination of availability and diversity creates discussions seldom seen in person. To encourage meaningful discussions in this new context, we co-created discussion guides with instructors. These guides embody a new pedagogical style based on three strategies. First, discussions are structured to encourage self-reference, i.e. connecting to the class material in a personal way such as recounting personal experiences [16]. Second, discussion guides use boundary objects to focus discussion. Everyday concepts such as the local government, workplace etc. have a coherent meaning but different forms around the world. This encourages students to reflect on previously unexamined assumptions about their own environments, deepening their learning [14]. Third, discussion guides often mention, but don't elaborate concepts from class. This encourages students who know the concepts to act as mediators and explain these to others.

Our experiments suggest that well-structured diverse discussions yield higher grades and engagement. A controlled experiment in two massive online classes varied the amount of geographic diversity present in the Talkabout discussions. Students in more geographically diverse groups performed significantly better on subsequent quizzes and exams; $t(129)=1.78$ and $t(110)=2.03$ respectively, $p<0.05$. Discussions also improved student engagement: students randomly assigned to a Talkabout group were significantly more likely to participate in class quizzes than those placed on a waitlist for future participation; $t(1123)=1.96$, $p<0.05$.

PEER INTERACTIONS FOR FEEDBACK AND CRITIQUE

My collaborators and I worked with Coursera to design their peer-assessment platform, which enabled classes to use open-ended assignments, such as essays and user interface designs. In addition to providing feedback and critique, peer assessment encourages reflection, and exposes students to inspiring work and new ideas. So far, more than 100,000 students have used it in more than a hundred classes, including Human-computer Interaction (our pilot class), Fantasy and Science Fiction, and Social

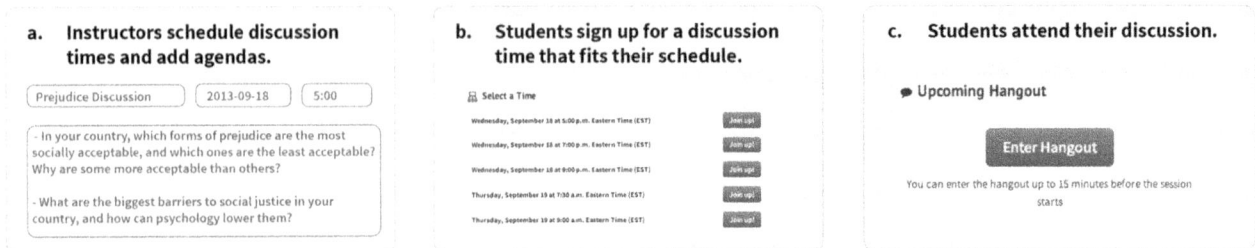

Figure 1: Talkabout discussion timeline: (a) Instructors enter a discussion agenda, and times for the discussion. (b) Students pick their preferred time. (c) When they log on to Talkabout at their selected time, Talkabout assigns them to a group, and creates a private hangout. (c) Students login at their selected time, and enter the discussion.

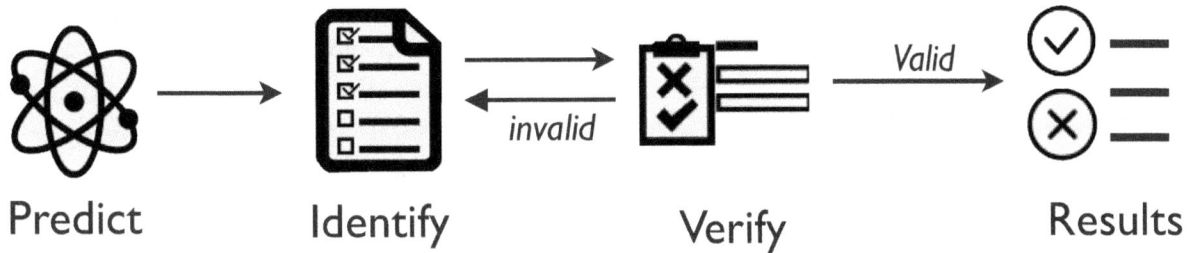

Figure 2: Augmenting peers with machine learning reduces busywork. In the identify-verify workflow an algorithm determines the number of peer raters. Raters then independently rate and verify each other's work.

Network Analysis.

This assessment system provides students feedback from their global classmates. We find that with well-defined grading criteria, the consensus opinion of anonymous reviewers is comparable to expert ratings. For instance, by aggregating grades from five peers, we estimate 80% of students in the HCI class got grades within 15% of the staff grade [11]. Furthermore, peer assessment leverages the diversity of opinion by collecting qualitative feedback from peers around the world (raters are randomly assigned). Finally, while peers may lack the expertise to articulate effective advice, they can recognize errors. To scaffold this, instructors identify and list common errors and advice; peers then recognize errors, and personalize advice. In our pilot class using this system (www.hci-class.org), 65% of students received personalized, qualitative feedback.

Machine learning reduces peers' busywork

In follow-up work, we investigated how to preserve the benefits of peer assessment, while reducing the grading burden on students.

Current automated grading algorithms alone aren't accurate enough to be used for assessment, and malicious students may game them [17]. However, we might combine human and machine assessment to improve grading quality and reduce work.

Through a pilot, we found that students and machines have complementary assessment strengths. While students are good at assessing ambiguous answers, they are easily swayed by eloquence over accuracy. Machine-learning based models, on the other hand, could grade unambiguous answers accurately, and reported low confidences for other answers. We also found students more accurately identified key features of answers, than they integrated these separate attributes into scores, consistent with prior work [5].

Therefore, we introduce the identify-verify assessment pattern, where a machine-grading algorithm estimates ambiguity in student answers and determines the number of peers who rate the work [12]. Peers identify key features of the answer using a staff-provided rubric, and verify each other's assessment. In an online HCI class (n=1370), this pattern produces richer feedback and yields roughly 80-90% of the baseline assessment quality that is achieved by taking the median of three student ratings, while saving up to 54% of the student time cost. Using machine learning with peer assessment allows students focus their attention where it has learning benefits, leaving machines to perform mundane but important classroom tasks.

Low-latency peer feedback to encourage iteration

Feedback timeliness is critical: when students receive feedback within a day, they apply the concepts they learn more successfully [10]. Feedback primarily succeeds when it makes the gap between current learning and desired learning salient [7] which is reduced by delaying feedback. Therefore, for creative tasks that involve more than simply recalling items, such as writing, design, or programming, fast feedback improves learning.

In addition, when students use feedback for iteration, they must receive it quickly enough to incorporate it in an iterative process. Except in the smallest classes, the significant effort to write feedback prevents traditional instructor-led classes from providing iterative feedback while it is most valuable.

In ongoing work, we propose to incentivize students to iteratively improve their work by requesting and integrating early peer feedback. To succeed, we must address two challenges. First, we need to design an online application that motivates peers to provide high quality formative feedback (the motivational challenge). Second, we need to create processes such that feedback is delivered quickly, ideally within an hour (the process challenge).

With *Peerstudio*, we propose to address the motivational challenge in part through community reciprocity, and the process challenge through the asynchronous massive nature of online classes. First, to receive feedback on their draft, each student must provide feedback on several other drafts. This reciprocity exposes students to other work and helps them understand the form of the feedback they will receive. Reciprocity designs can encourage contributions to social computing systems, especially when the user benefits by learning something about themselves or their work [1]. Second, thousands of students make it feasible to assume that another student will soon follow one who arrives wanting feedback. Finally, even when students are unavailable online, email allows us to draw out volunteers who review others' work. Together, this can enable quick, on-demand iteration-oriented feedback.

DISCUSSION AND PROPOSED CONTRIBUTIONS

This dissertation argues for the co-development of pedagogical strategy and supporting software systems that are designed for scale and diversity. With Talkabout, we demonstrate how a system can leverage diversity at scale. To do so, it also induces students to access the course in a more synchronous manner. In addition, Talkabout demonstrates how pedagogical strategies (e.g. encourage self-reference, use boundary objects etc.) can be co-developed iteratively with software systems. Iterative development can create new pedagogical strategies, but their widespread adoption depends on how well tools support them. Therefore, we are currently prototyping a version of the Talkabout interface that encourages instructors to use these strategies in their own structured discussions.

Our peer assessment platform similarly demonstrates how pedagogy and software can be co-developed (e.g. how can we structure feedback so students get personalized qualitative feedback?) In addition, in follow-up work, we demonstrate how assessment can be restructured to augment peer assessment with machine learning models, and how software can encode best practices (such as relying on feature identification, rather than scoring).

With Peerstudio, we intend to create a system that leverages the scale of online classes for fast formative feedback. By participating in this doctoral colloquium, we hope to refine our ideas for addressing motivational challenges and process structure. We also hope to discuss how co-development of software and pedagogy can create other novel educational experiences that not only leverage diversity and scale, but would be impossible without them.

ACKNOWLEDGMENTS

This work was supported by the Siebel Scholars Program, the Hasso Plattner Design Thinking Program, and NSF CAREER grant #1444865. I am grateful to Scott Klemmer and Michael Bernstein for their direction and guidance (as co-advisors), the many instructors who have used the software described here for their trust and feedback, and the many thousands of students who experienced both frustrations and delights with our prototypes.

REFERENCES

1. André, P. et al. Who gives a tweet? *Proceedings of the ACM 2012 conference on Computer Supported Cooperative Work - CSCW '12*, ACM Press (2012), 471.

2. Boud, D. *Peer Learning in Higher Education: Learning from and with Each Other*. Routledge, 2001.

3. Brookfield, S.D. and Preskill, S. *Discussion as a Way of Teaching: Tools and Techniques for Democratic Classrooms*. John Wiley & Sons, 2012.

4. Cambre, J. et al. Talkabout: Small-group Discussions in Massive Global Classes. *Learning@Scale*, (2014).

5. Dawes, R.M. The robust beauty of improper linear models in decision making. *American psychologist 34*, 7 (1979), 571.

6. Gurin, P. et al. Diversity and higher education: Theory and impact on educational outcomes. .

7. Hattie, J. and Timperley, H. The Power of Feedback. *Review of Educational Research 77*, 1 (2007), 81–112.

8. Ho, A.D. et al. HarvardX and MITx: The First Year of Open Online Courses, Fall 2012-Summer 2013. *SSRN Electronic Journal*, (2014).

9. Hollan, J. and Stornetta, S. Beyond being there. *Proceedings of the SIGCHI conference on Human factors in computing systems - CHI '92*, ACM Press (1992), 119–125.

10. Kulik, J.A. and Kulik, C.-L.C. Timing of Feedback and Verbal Learning. *Review of Educational Research 58*, 1 (1987), 79–97.

11. Kulkarni, C. et al. Peer and self assessment in massive online classes. *ACM Transactions on Computer-Human Interaction (TOCHI) 20*, 6 (2013), 33.

12. Kulkarni, C. et al. Scaling Short-answer Grading by Combining Peer Assessment with Algorithmic Scoring. *ACM Conf on Learning@Scale*, (2014).

13. Lawson, B. *How designers think: the design process demystified*. Architectual Press, 2006.

14. Lin, X. and Schwartz, D.L. Reflection at the Crossroads of Cultures. *Mind, Culture, and Activity 10*, 1 (2003).

15. Olds, K. Mapping Coursera's Global Footprint. *Inside Higher Ed*, 2013. http://www.insidehighered.com/blogs/globalhighered/mapping-courseras-global-footprint.

16. Symons, C.S. and Johnson, B.T. The self-reference effect in memory: A meta-analysis. *Psychological Bulletin 121*, 3 (1997), 371–394.

17. Winerip, M. Robo-Readers Used to Grade Test Essays - NYTimes.com. *New York Times*, 2012. http://www.nytimes.com/2012/04/23/education/robo-readers-used-to-grade-test-essays.html?pagewanted=all&_r=0.

Matter Matters: Offloading Machine Computation to Material Computation for Shape Changing Interfaces

Lining Yao
MIT Media Lab
Cambridge, MA
liningy@media.mit.edu

ABSTRACT

This paper introduces *material computation* to offload computing from machine to material, in the process of creating shape-changing output. It contains the explanation on the mechanism of transformation, the concept of material computation, the summary and analysis of literature research within and beyond the HCI field, the interaction loop integrating material computation, and my own practice in material computation technics and applications.

Author Keywords

Material computation; machine computation; hybrid material; shape change output; shape changing interface.

INTRODUCTION

With the unique capacity for dynamic affordances, symbolic and emotional representations, physicality of interaction, and physical embodiment of information, shape changing interfaces are gaining increasing interests in HCI community. The toolbox, containing sensing mechanisms, actuation mechanisms, material and fabrication techniques, is expanding rapidly. My thesis is situated in this context, while focuses on the mechanisms of actuation.

Through my own practice and the review of other relevant work, I argue that matter matters in the process of creating shape change output: the final output is a co-invention of machine computation and material structures.

MATERIAL COMPUTATION FOR SHAPE CHANGE
Energy Source for Shape Change

In order to achieve a certain deformation, we need actuators and energy sources. For actuators, except the most common electromagnetic motors, there are actuators responding to different types of energy stimulus (Here we only talk about physical stimuli, excluding chemical and biological stimuli). Energy source matters because material computation needs to be considered based on its stimuli type.

The ways we provide energy to actuators can be divided into two categories: the energy is directed either uniformly

UIST'14 Adjunct, October 5–8, 2014, Honolulu, HI, USA.
ACM 978-1-4503-3068-8/14/10.
http://dx.doi.org/10.1145/2658779.2661170

to all parts of a structure, or in a targeted fashion to some parts but not others. As an example, inForm table [1] using one linear motor for each pin. It has a higher controllability since each actuator is independently controllable. For some PneUI samples [9], on the other hand, one energy source, air flow, is directed to all parts of the material structure. Comparing different energy sources, the controllability with discrete energy sources is increasing, while the system simplicity and untetherness is decreasing.

Material Computation - Definition

Material computation refers to the concept that the design of material composition, geometry and structure has a programmable impact on the transformation. Material computation comes into play when we want to keep the simplicity of the control system, but achieve a shape change in a programmable and controllable manner. In addition, the material approach of achieving shape change can provide unique affordances and aesthetic representations.

Although the advantage of material computation can become more obvious if the energy source is directed uniformly to the entire material structure (e.g. PneUI[9]); it can be applied to the cases of discrete stimulus. Sometimes a combination of a dynamic discrete stimuli and material computation can create certain morphing motion in a bigger complexity (e.g. the photomobile robot from Table 1).

Material Computation- Literature Summary

To create dynamic material computation, the underlining principle is: we want to create hybrid material with components that respond to one or multiple stimulus (energy source) in an anisotropic manner. Table 1 is a summary of a literature research on existing ways of creating material computation for shape change output. Different cases have different stimuli types.

In Table 1, I pick one representative technique for each common type of energy source, and analyze the underlining design principle based on the logic of material computation. All the listed energy sources have been adapted in HCI before, and can be connected to digital information via a control loop.

Applied Stimuli	Material Computation Examples			
	Material Composition	**Computation Principles**	**Material Geometry and Structure**	**Shape Change Output**
Uniform distribution: Light	Top view / Side view 1. White thermal prestrained polymer sheets 2. Black ink	Heat Anisotropy in light absorption; the bending angle is related to the ink width and shrinking rate.		**Self folding polymer[4]**
Uniform distribution: Current	1 2 3 3 sections of Nitinol coil annealed at different temperature: 370°C, 480°C and 630°C.	Each segment expands and contracts at different current.		Micro muscle robot[3]
Uniform distribution: Humidity	Top view / Side view 1. Rigid plastic 2. Swelling polymer	Humidity Angle limiter set by rigid material defines the folding angle under water.		4D printing[8]
Uniform distribution: UV Light	Azobenzene Layer (photomobile polymer) PE film	Crosslinked LC elastomer extends under UV plastic film beneath does not.	Photomobile robot[2]	
Uniform distribution: Positive air pressure	Paper origami Elastomer	Pressured air flows towards the side with lower tensile strength.	Elastomeric Origami[5]	
Uniform distribution: positive air pressure; Discrete distribution: negative air pressure	Fluid 1. Unjammed cell 2. Jammed cell 3. Expanded actuator	Fluid Negative air pressure reconfigure stiffness distribution through jamming separate cells		Jamming Skin[7]

Table 1: Summary of approaches for material computation

Material Computation - My Own Practices

Through several research projects, I applied the principle of material computation and developed a series of techniques to fabricate shape changing samples.

PneUI Strip: Stiffness Anisotropy with Positive Air Pressure

In PneUI paper [9], one technique presented was pre-programmable bending curvature. The material computation lies in the stiffness distribution across the paper substrate, which constrains the elastomeric deformable in a pre-defined manner. 2D patterns in Figure 1 represent folding patterns on paper substrates.

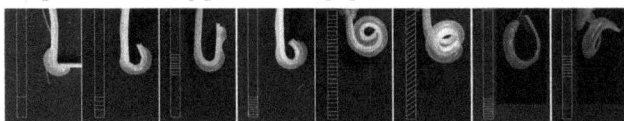

Figure 1: Material computation through stiffness anisotropy.

PneUI Ballon: Elasticity Anisotropy with Positive Air Pressure

PneUI [9] also presented another group of material samples that generate different surface textures when inflated. With uniform air supply, different cut patterns on the composite fabric layer create elasticity anisotropy and enable the generation of textures (Figure 2).

Figure 2: Fabric with cut patterns varies the surface elasticity distribution.

biologic: Anisotropic Hygroexpansivity with Relative Humidity

My current on-going work is to utilize an edible microorganism, the bacillus subtilis natto cell as a nanoactuator and deposit it on thin substrates to transform the substrates. The spore expands and contracts under the change of relative humidity. Digital printing technique is used to deposit the nanoactuators in orientation geometries, which defines the bending direction on a macro level (Figure 3).

Figure 3: Nanoactuator's geometrical alignment on latex substrate defines reversible bending angle.

jamSheets: Anisotropic Friction and Shear Strength with Negative Air Pressure

In JamSheets[6], we designed a stiffness reconfigurable mesh. The stiffness of each strip in the mesh is tunable. This material sample can hold shapes in different orientations, and it can be combined with other actuators (such as pneumatic actuators) and function as a stiffness reconfigurable substrate (Figure 4).

Figure 4: By pointing at each strip, the strip switches state from being soft to hard. In this case, the sheet is configured to have flexibility on only one side.

MATERIAL COMPUTATION IN AN INTERACTION LOOP

In the design of shape changing interfaces, without material computation, the physical material is merely a passive representation of form; with material computation, part of the computation can be offloaded from computers and microcontrollers to material. In the later case, material functions as both a representation of shape output and embodiment of computation.

Figure 5 summarizes three types of interaction loops. The later two include material computation. None of these three types is more advanced than the others. Depending on different applications, complexity requirements of the system configuration, and material affordability, different interaction loops can be adapted. In addition, although Type *c* material is not directly controlled by computer, it computes via material computation. In this case, it only "talks" to physical stimulus, but not digital information.

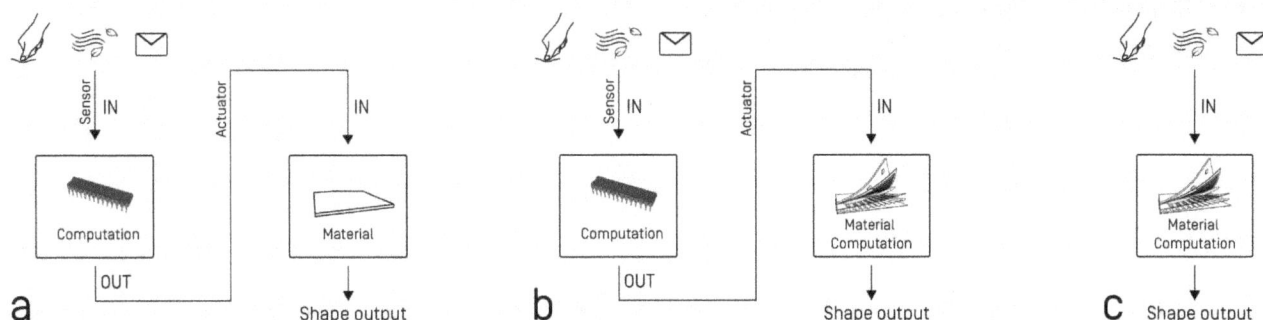

Figure 5: Interaction loops for Shape Changing Interfaces. (a) Without material computation. (b) Material computation partially offloads machine computation. (c) Material integrates all the computation: sensing, energy conversion and shape output.

Application Examples

To demonstrate the aforementioned interaction loops, I will describe several example applications through my research.

They share the design concept of material computation to offload computation from computer and enable the dynamic shape change in a controllable manner.

- PneUI Lamp[9]: This lamp has embedded liquid metal in elastomeric channels for sensing, and contains diagonal folding patterns on the paper substrate for transformation constraints (Figure 6). It follows the *b* type interaction loop in Figure 5.

Figure 6: PneUI lamp

- Living tea: The artificial tea leaves are made with green latex and bacteria nanoactuators introduced in the last section. The actuator deposition along the vein geometry generates the organic transformation that mimics nature. The tea leave responses to hot water vapor and gradually expands its body. This interaction follows the *c* type interaction loop in Figure 5.

Figure 7: Tea leaves that are wrapped at the beginning and unwrapped when tea is ready.

- jamChair [6]: jamChair is made of a stiffness reconfigurable sheet that senses the physical state of its shape and tunes its stiffness. When people try to wrap it, it is soft; and when it is formed into a chair shape, it becomes stiffer to hold shape and load (Figure 8).

Figure 8: Stiffness reconfigurable sheet

CONCLUSION

This paper is about the concept of *material computation* for shape change output by analyzing both literature research and my own work. I narrow down the research topic to material computation for shape change output due to the higher relevance of my own practice. However, I believe material computation is a powerful concept beyond shape change output, which can open a bigger space of better fabricating, programming and designing our physical world.

ACKNOWLSEG MENT

I appreciate the guidance, support and intellectual contribution from my advisor Hiroshi Ishii and my main collaborators, Jifei Ou, Ryuma Niiyama and Wen Wang.

REFERENCES

1. Follmer, S., Leithinger, D., Olwal, A., and Hogge, A. inFORM : Dynamic Physical Affordances and Constraints through Shape and Object Actuation. *Proc. of UIST 2013*, ACM Press (2013), 417–426.

2. Ikeda, T. and Ube, T. Photomobile polymer materials: from nano to macro. *Materials Today 14*, 10 (2011), 480–487.

3. Kim, S., Hawkes, E., Cho, K., Jolda, M., Foley, J., and Wood, R. Micro artificial muscle fiber using NiTi spring for soft robotics. *Proc. of IROS 2009*, IEEE/RSJ (2009), 2228 – 2234.

4. Liu, Y., Boyles, J.K., Genzer, J., and Dickey, M.D. Self-folding of polymer sheets using local light absorption. *Soft Matter 8*, 6 (2012), 1764.

5. Martinez, R. V., Fish, C.R., Chen, X., and Whitesides, G.M. Elastomeric Origami: Programmable Paper-Elastomer Composites as Pneumatic Actuators. *Advanced Functional Materials 22*, 7 (2012), 1376–1384.

6. Ou, J., Yao, L., Tauber, D., Steimle, J., Niiyama, R., and Ishii, H. jamSheets : Thin Interfaces with Tunable Stiffness Enabled by Layer Jamming. *Proc. of TEI 2014*, ACM Press (2014), 65–72.

7. Steltz, E., Mozeika, a., Rodenberg, N., Brown, E., and Jaeger, H.M. JSEL: Jamming Skin Enabled Locomotion. *2009 IEEE/RSJ International Conference on Intelligent Robots and Systems*, (2009), 5672–5677.

8. Tibbits, S. 4D Printing: Multi-Material Shape Change. *Archit Design 84*, 1 (2014), 116–121.

9. Yao, L., Niiyama, R., Ou, J., Follmer, S., Silva, C. Della, and Ishii, H. PneUI : Pneumatically Actuated Soft Composite Materials for Shape Changing Interfaces. *Proc. of UIST 2013*, ACM Press (2013), 13–22.

A Three-Step Interaction Pattern for Improving Discoverability in Finger Identification Techniques

Alix Goguey[1], **Géry Casiez**[2], **Daniel Vogel**[3], **Fanny Chevalier**[1], **Thomas Pietrzak**[2] **& Nicolas Roussel**[1]

[1]Inria Lille, [2]University of Lille, France, [3] University of Waterloo, Canada

{alix.goguey, fanny.chevalier, nicolas.roussel}@inria.fr, {gery.casiez, thomas.pietrzak}@lifl.fr, dvogel@uwaterloo.ca

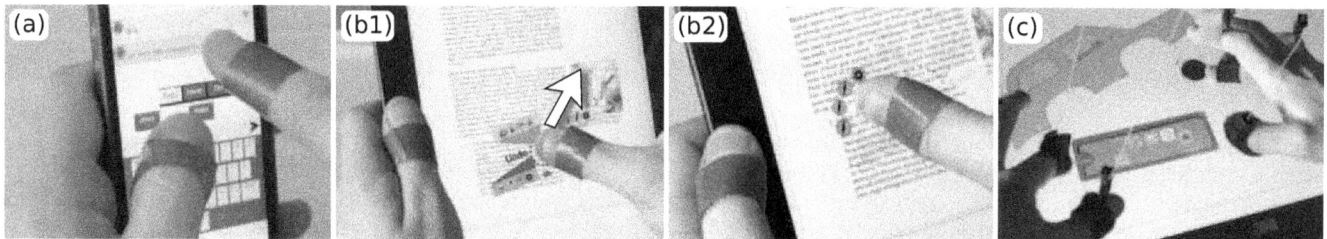

Figure 1: Our three-application demo: (a) SMS application: the thumb can be used to feed-forward the current mapping between individual fingers and commands; here, the index triggers the *copy* command. (b) PDF annotation application: (b1) thumb showing the different subsets of commands available for selection; after sliding the thumb in the corresponding direction, (b2) updated feed-forward corresponding to the top-right set. (c) Vectorial drawing application demo: non-dominant thumb and index select a command mapping enabling the dominant ring finger to draw an ellipse.

ABSTRACT

Identifying which fingers are in contact with a multi-touch surface provides a very large input space that can be leveraged for command selection. However, the numerous possibilities enabled by such vast space come at the cost of discoverability. To alleviate this problem, we introduce a three-step interaction pattern inspired by hotkeys that also supports feed-forward. We illustrate this interaction with three applications allowing us to explore and adapt it in different contexts.

Author Keywords

Multi-touch; finger identification; shortcuts; command selection; parameter control; direct manipulation

ACM Classification Keywords

H.5.2 Information interfaces and presentation: User interfaces

INTRODUCTION

Finger identification is a way to increase the multi-touch input space. Significant previous work has tackled the technical sensing problem with various approaches including inferring finger identity based on geometric relationships between touch contact points [6], using an overhead camera to track

UIST'14 Adjunct, October 5–8, 2014, Honolulu, HI, USA.
ACM 978-1-4503-3068-8/14/10.
http://dx.doi.org/10.1145/2658779.2659100

bare hands [4] or fingers with coloured rings [7], wearing gloves with fiducial markers [5], recognizing fingerprints [2], and forearm electromyography [1]. It seems inevitable that one day finger identification will be a standard feature of consumer multi-touch devices.

Robust finger identification sensing is on the horizon [1, 2], but its implications for interaction have only been considered in isolated point designs where chords were mapped to commands. Marquardt *et al.* built an exploratory toolkit for tabletops [5] and explored a number of interaction technique ideas to emphasize the toolkit's expressiveness. However, these explorations did not address the problem of discoverability brought by finger identification: discriminating fingers on a touch screen theoretically enables the access to up to 1023 finger combinations, a too large of a set to choose from for one who is not aware of the fingers-to-command mapping.

To address the discoverability problem associated with this large input space, we propose a three-step interaction pattern inspired by the combined use of keyboard shortcuts and a mouse in traditional graphical applications where 1) the non-dominant hand activates a mode with a key, 2) the dominant hand manipulates the mouse, and 3) the non-dominant hand optionally constrains the manipulation with a modifier key.

In our case, on *step 1*, a set of (*selector*) fingers determines a command mapping for another set of (*trigger*) fingers. On *step 2*, *trigger* fingers select a command and manipulate its parameters in a single stroke (Figure 1-c). On *step 3* (optional), *selector* fingers can constrain the manipulation. This three-step pattern only requires users to remember which fingers are in which one of the *selectors* set or the *triggers* set. More importantly, the separation between *selectors* and *trig-*

gers allows the introduction of on-demand feed-forward: the command mapping can be visualized on-screen as a crib sheet if the user pauses after the first step. This on-demand feed-forward makes it easy for novice users to browse the available commands, without hindering expert performance.

Depending on the context (*e.g.* smartphone, tablet, tabletop), the crib sheet can take different forms and be invoked in different ways by one or more *selectors* fingers. It may be triggered by a chord (Figures 1-a, 1-c) or a selection in a marking menu [3], for example (Figures 1-b1, 1-b2). We prototyped several applications to illustrate this three-step pattern in different contexts, that we describe in the following.

PROOF OF CONCEPT

We developed three applications: an SMS editor on a smartphone, a PDF annotation application on a tablet, and a vectorial drawing application on a tabletop system. For the smartphone and the tablet, considering the devices' form factors and the chosen applications, we assigned the *selectors* and *triggers* to a single hand and used only the thumb as a *selector*. For the tabletop application, we used the non-dominant hand's fingers as *selectors* and the dominant ones as *triggers*.

Hardware and low-level software configuration

Our focus is not on the technical problems of finger identification, but to experiment with our approach, we need to reliably identify which fingers are in contact with the display.

For this demonstration, we chose to attach rings tagged with two-dimensional barcodes to the user's fingers and to track their 2D position using a $640{\times}480$px RGB camera running at 20Hz and computer vision code. This technique can reliably track up to 6 fingers (Figure 2). The tracked positions are transformed into the display reference frame using an homography computed from a short calibration procedure. Our software makes it possible to generate custom touch events with hand and finger IDs in Qt applications running on Android or iOS devices.

Figure 2: Demonstration setup: the user wears tagged rings that are tracked by the computer using the webcam; the tablet sends the touch inputs to the computer via the router; the computer then merges both webcam and tablet information and identifies the touches which are sent back to the tablet via the router.

Applications

The SMS writing application (Figure 1-a) uses our three-steps pattern to support commands such as copy/cut/paste, spelling corrections and undo/redo, which are traditionally accessed on smartphones through contextual menus, dwell or gestures (*e.g.* shaking the device to undo). Considering the relatively low number of commands, we used one *selector* finger only for command selection – enabling two mappings of *trigger* fingers: with or without the *selector*.

For the PDF annotation application, we identified 19 common commands in our informal observations. Considering this number and inherent relationships between the commands, we decided to break down this set into three subsets that can be selected by moving the thumb in different directions: when the thumb crosses a threshold distance represented by the dotted circle in Figure 1-b1, the corresponding subset is selected (e.g., all different ink tools). Once a subset is selected, the feed-forward is updated to show the four tools associated to the remaining *trigger* fingers (Figure 1-b2). Some commands can also be constrained using the thumb (e.g., freeform vs. by-line highlighting).

For the vectorial drawing application, we identified 26 common commands. We grouped these commands into seven categories comprising at most five commands each. Chord combinations of three fingers of the non-dominant hand are used to select command mappings (i.e. categories), while the five fingers of the dominant hand are used to trigger the commands (Figure 1-c). Shape creation tools can be constrained in several ways (*e.g.* aspect ratio, snapping) and those constraints can be combined.

NOTE

The demonstration will be interactive. We will give people a take away set so they can try at the conference and at home.

REFERENCES

1. Benko, H., Saponas, T. S., Morris, D., and Tan, D. Enhancing input on and above the interactive surface with muscle sensing. In *Proc. ITS*, ACM (2009), 93–100.

2. Holz, C., and Baudisch, P. Fiberio: a touchscreen that senses fingerprints. In *Proc. UIST*, ACM (2013), 41–50.

3. Kurtenbach, G., and Buxton, W. User learning and performance with marking menus. In *Proc. CHI*, ACM (1994), 258–264.

4. Malik, S., Ranjan, A., and Balakrishnan, R. Interacting with large displays from a distance with vision-tracked multi-finger gestural input. In *Proc. UIST*, ACM (2005), 43–52.

5. Marquardt, N., Kiemer, J., Ledo, D., Boring, S., and Greenberg, S. Designing user-, hand-, and handpart-aware tabletop interactions with the TouchID toolkit. In *Proc. ITS*, ACM (2011), 21–30.

6. Wagner, J., Lecolinet, E., and Selker, T. Multi-finger chords for hand-held tablets: Recognizable and memorable. In *Proc. CHI*, ACM (2014), to be published.

7. Wang, J., and Canny, J. FingerSense: augmenting expressiveness to physical pushing button by fingertip identification. In *CHI EA*, ACM (2004), 1267–1270.

A Rapid Prototyping Toolkit for Touch Sensitive Objects using Active Acoustic Sensing

Makoto Ono, Buntarou Shizuki, and Jiro Tanaka
University of Tsukuba, Japan
Tennoudai 1-1-1, Tsukuba, Ibaraki, Japan 305-8571
{ono,shizuki,jiro}@iplab.cs.tsukuba.ac.jp

ABSTRACT

We present a prototyping toolkit for creating touch sensitive prototypes from everyday objects without needing special skills such as code writing or designing circuits. This toolkit consists of an acoustic based touch sensor module that captures the resonant properties of objects, software modules including one that recognizes how an object is touched by using machine learning, and plugins for visual programming environments such as Scratch and Max/MSP. As a result, our toolkit enables users to easily configure the response of touches using a wide variety of visual or audio responses. We believe that our toolkit expands the creativity of a non-specialist, such as children and media artists.

Author Keywords

Sensors; acoustic classification; tangibles; machine learning; prototyping; support vector machine; piezo-electric sensor; OpenSound Control; visual programming.

ACM Classification Keywords

H.5.2 [Information interfaces and presentation]: User Interfaces - Graphical user interfaces; Input devices & strategies.

INTRODUCTION

Touch input is commonly used in many consumer products such as mobile devices and tablets. However, making your own touch sensitive prototypes is still challenging for novices. This is because making touch sensitive prototypes usually requires special skills such as code writing and designing circuits.

Prototyping tools targeting touch sensitive prototypes have also been proposed. Most works construct touch sensitive prototypes by utilizing conductive elements such as thumbtacks [2], vinyl cut copper foil [6], and printed conductive patterns [3, 4, 1]. The sensing capabilities in these works depend on the number of electrical elements or patterns. Therefore, if the users want to use more touch gestures, its hardware configuration needs to be more complex. Moreover, the sensor replacement is cumbersome.

UIST'14 Adjunct, October 5–8, 2014, Honolulu, HI, USA.
ACM 978-1-4503-3068-8/14/10.
http://dx.doi.org/10.1145/2658779.2659101

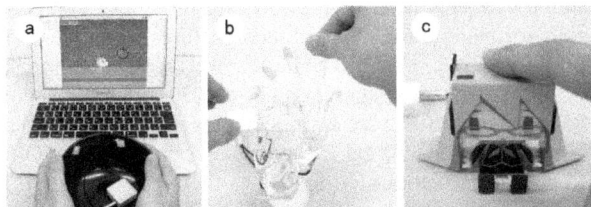

Figure 1. Examples of touch sensitive prototypes made by using our toolkit: a) game controller from ceramic bowl, b) musical instrument from hand-shaped acrylic object, and c) music player from character figure.

We present a rapid prototyping toolkit in this paper that is based on an acoustic touch sensing technique that uses the resonant properties of everyday objects [5]. This approach only requires attaching a pair of piezo elements to an object; the touch gestures for the object can be easily trained and/or modified by using machine learning. This enables users, even non-specialists, to rapidly and flexibly create touch sensitive prototypes like that shown in Figure 1.

IMPLEMENTATION

Our toolkit consists of a sensor module and software modules.

Sensor module

We implemented an original sensor module (Figure 2) that extracts the resonant feature from objects. A microcontroller (NXP LPC11u24) controls a programmable wave generator (Analog Devices AD5930) to emit sinusoidal sweep signals from 20–40 kHz in 5 msecs. This signal vibrates the piezo transducer and the vibration conducts the object. The vibration response is captured by a piezo microphone and its envelope is detected and amplified in the module. The microcontroller samples a 150-point acoustic feature vector from the envelope and sends it to a PC (Apple MacBook Air) via a Bluetooth Serial Port Profile.

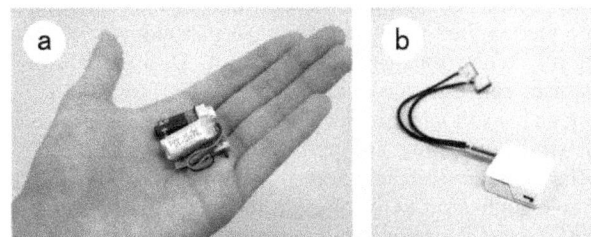

Figure 2. Our sensor module: a) 32 mm (W) x 32 mm (D) x 12 mm (H) core and b) module with case and cables.

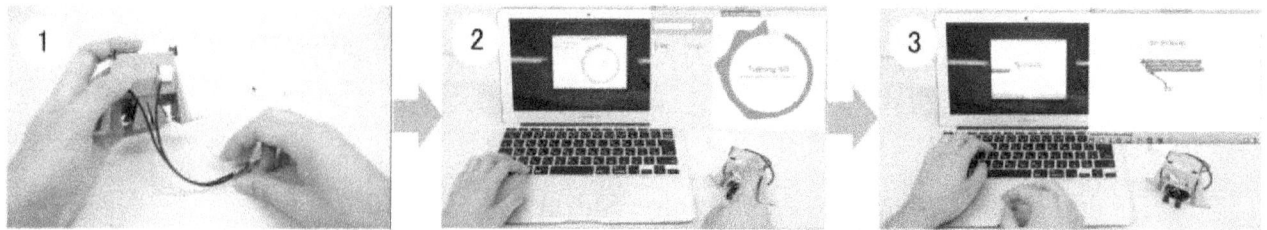

Figure 3. Workflow using our toolkit: 1) attaching sensor module, 2) training touch gestures, and 3) configuring response (using Max/MSP in this case).

Software modules

We implemented a recognition software and plugins for Scratch and Max/MSP as the software modules. The recognition software classifies the touch gestures using a Support Vector Machine. The 150-point feature vector from the sensor module is sent to the classifier at 30 frames per second. The recognition software communicates with the Scratch and Max/MSP plugins via HTTP and OpenSound Control (OSC), and sends the recognition results to them. For Scratch, the plugin behaves as a condition block that returns a true or false on the recognition result. For Max/MSP, the plugin behaves as a Max object that emits a bang corresponding to the recognition result. The user can set the label names as the arguments in the Max object; the Max object has outlets, each of which corresponds to each label. When the plugin receives a recognition result, the Max object sends a bang from the outlet corresponding to the recognition result.

WORKFLOW

Figure 3 shows the workflow using our toolkit. Our toolkit can be used in three steps: 1) attaching the sensor module, 2) training touch gestures, and 3) configuring the response. Note that none of these steps require any special skills such as code writing or designing circuits. Thus, our toolkit is readily accessible to everyone for prototyping touch sensitive objects.

1. Attaching sensor module

First, a user attaches a sensor module to an object that the user wants to make touch sensitive, making sure both piezo elements adhere to the object using double-sided tape. One limitation is that the objects that can be made touch sensitive using this toolkit are limited to hard and handheld sized ones just like [5] describes.

2. Training touch gestures

Second, the user trains the touch gestures using our recognition software. When the software starts, it automatically trains for a no touch gesture. After the no touch gesture is learned, the user can begin to define a new touch gesture by entering a label (i.e., the name of the gesture being defined) into the text box in the software. At that moment, the training of the new touch gesture will start. During the training, the user performs the touch gesture several times (e.g., five times); the software always compares the current feature vector with the feature vector of the no touch gesture. If the difference between them exceeds a certain threshold, the software recognizes it as the object is touched in a certain manner and trains the system with the current label. After the training is finished, the software starts the recognition of the touch gestures.

3. Configuring response

Finally, the user configures the response of the touch by using external software such as Scratch and Max/MSP. For example, by connecting the Max object's outlet to a shell object through a message object, which controls iTunes (e.g., *osascript -e 'tell application \"iTunes\" to play'*), the user can create a physical music player. For experts who have programming skills, the result from the recognition software can be sent as OSC messages to their program. Therefore, other environments such as Processing and Arduino also can be used to configure the response with more rich expressions.

FUTURE WORK

This toolkit is currently used by a few people who are interested in interactive arts for trial use; we are gathering their feedback about its usability. In our future work, we plan to conduct a workshop targeting children or media artists. In this workshop, we will evaluate the usability and explore how people's creativity can be expanded by using the toolkit.

REFERENCES

1. Gong, N.-W., Steimle, J., Olberding, S., Hodges, S., Gillian, N. E., Kawahara, Y., and Paradiso, J. A. PrintSense: A versatile sensing technique to support multimodal flexible surface interaction. In *Proceedings of the 32nd annual ACM conference on Human factors in computing systems*, ACM (2014), 1407–1410.

2. Hudson, S. E., and Mankoff, J. Rapid construction of functioning physical interfaces from cardboard, thumbtacks, tin foil and masking tape. In *Proceedings of the 19th annual ACM symposium on User interface software and technology*, ACM (2006), 289–298.

3. Kawahara, Y., Hodges, S., Cook, B. S., Zhang, C., and Abowd, G. D. Instant inkjet circuits: Lab-based inkjet printing to support rapid prototyping of UbiComp devices. In *Proceedings of the 2013 ACM international joint conference on Pervasive and ubiquitous computing*, ACM (2013), 363–372.

4. Olberding, S., Gong, N.-W., Tiab, J., Paradiso, J. A., and Steimle, J. A cuttable multi-touch sensor. In *Proceedings of the 26th annual ACM symposium on User interface software and technology*, ACM (2013), 245–254.

5. Ono, M., Shizuki, B., and Tanaka, J. Touch & Activate: Adding interactivity to existing objects using active acoustic sensing. In *Proceedings of the 26th annual ACM symposium on User interface software and technology*, ACM (2013), 31–40.

6. Savage, V., Zhang, X., and Hartmann, B. Midas: Fabricating custom capacitive touch sensors to prototype interactive objects. In *Proceedings of the 25th annual ACM symposium on User interface software and technology*, ACM (2012), 579–588.

Video Text Retouch: Retouching Text in Videos with Direct Manipulation

Laurent Denoue, Scott Carter, Matthew Cooper

FX Palo Alto Laboratory

3174 Porter Dr.

Palo Alto, CA, 94304 USA

{denoue, carter, cooper} @fxpal.com

ABSTRACT

Video Text Retouch is a technique for retouching textual content found in many online videos such as screencasts, recorded presentations and many online e-learning videos. Viewed through our special, HTML5-based player, users can edit in real-time the textual content of the video frames, such as correcting typos or inserting new words between existing characters. Edits are overlaid and tracked at the desired position for as long as the original video content remains similar. We describe the interaction techniques, image processing algorithms and give implementation details of the system.

Author Keywords

Video editing; video retouch; direct manipulation; text editing; web-based systems; HTML5 video processing

ACM Classification Keywords

H.5.2 Graphical user interfaces (GUI): Miscellaneous

INTRODUCTION

Millions of training videos or recorded meetings and lectures are available online. Unfortunately, when an author or another user needs to correct the content found in these videos, the process can be very time consuming. The whole sequence can be recaptured, or the user needs to edit the video using a standard video editor and retouch it frame by frame, e.g. to delete a word or add new content.

Instead, taking inspiration from past work on retouching static images [1], our system uses direct video manipulation as an interaction technique to more easily retouch the text (and ink) content displayed in these videos.

To edit a line of text, the user can click over that line in the video canvas. The tool automatically pauses the video, identifies the text line using visual content analysis, and allows the user to edit this text line, as shown in Figure 1.

The retouched content is automatically rendered over the original, giving viewers the illusion that the original video

UIST'14 Adjunct, October 5–8, 2014, Honolulu, HI, USA.
ACM 978-1-4503-3068-8/14/10.
http://dx.doi.org/10.1145/2658779.2659102

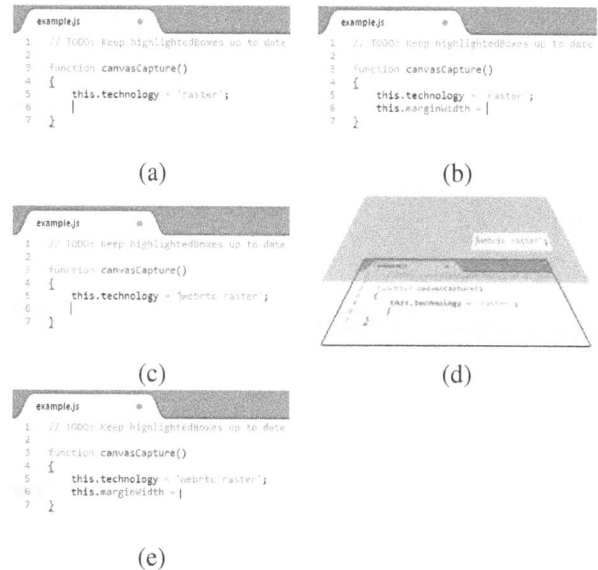

Figure 1. An example screencast video showing a code editor. In the original video the author types the first line of the function (a) and continues on to the second line (b). Using Video Text Retouch, the user can click directly on the first line to add "webrtc" before "raster" (c). Note in (c) that the cursor in the original video on the second line is black while the edit cursor on the first line is in red. As the user types, characters are automatically inserted, shifting the rest of the line to the right. Time-synchronized edits initially exist in a layer above the original video (d). Users can hide or show edits using our video player. When shown during playback the edits appear as if they are part of the video (e).

has been edited. The system automatically adjusts the edited content over new video frames and removes overlays when new frames appear but the original line is no longer found.

INTERACTION TECHNIQUE

To retouch a video, users simply drag and drop the video file onto the app's web page. The video plays inside an HTML5 video element. When the user clicks somewhere over the video canvas, the video is paused and a text insertion cursor is overlaid, prompting users to start editing the text line as if they were using a conventional text editor. New edits are appended to a time-synchronized layer above the video. Our video player collapses layers so that, to the user, it appears as if edits are part of the original video.

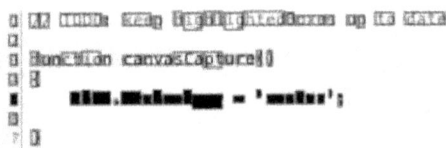

Figure 2. Each video frame is binarized and the bounding boxes of connected components are used to identify text lines (gray boxes); when a user clicks over the video, the text line is detected (black boxes) and its bitmap saved to build the overlay stripe.

The user can use backspace to delete, arrow keys to position, and type any character letter. The system visually adjusts the text line to reflect the changes.

When the user clicks again over the video, the system resumes playback and the newly created overlay is automatically shown over subsequent video frames for as long as the original content underneath the edited line is similar. When the original content becomes different, the overlays are also no longer displayed.

An option in our video player allows viewers to toggle edits on and off so they can compare the original video with the edits. Another option instructs the system to collapse the layers into a single, standard video file for sharing.

BROWSER-BASED IMPLEMENTATION IN HTML5

The system processes the video frames in real-time using lightweight and efficient image processing in JavaScript. The original video is hidden and incoming frames are instead drawn in real-time over a visible CANVAS element, from which we can extract and manipulate pixel data, as well as capture the user's mouse and keyboard events.

When the user clicks over the CANVAS, the video is paused and the current frame is binarized using automatic thresholding; the bounding boxes of connected components are extracted from this binary image, as illustrated in Figure 2 following [2]. Next, the system finds the closest bounding box located to the left of the click position, and identifies the line of text to be edited by looking to the left and right of this first bounding box. A bitmap corresponding to this text line is extracted from the current video frame as a horizontal band spanning the whole frame width, where its height and position are given by the text line's height and vertical position.

The line height is the mean of the bounding box heights, and the text color is determined by the average color of the pixels found in the underlying connected components. These values are used to choose the font size and color of the characters that will be drawn in the bitmap to render any added text.

Each bounding box is assumed to represent a character. When a keyboard event is received and corresponds to a character insertion, the system shifts the adjacent boxes to the right and draws the character glyph over the blank position. Similarly, if the key code is navigational, i.e. backspace/delete/left/right, the system moves the appropriate bounding boxes and updates the position of the cursor.

After each keyboard event, the edited version of the text line bitmap is then overlaid on the video canvas, giving users the perfect illusion that the edits are taking place.

PERSISTING EDITS IN REAL-TIME

When the user has finished editing and resumes playing the video, the system continues to analyze incoming frames, and applies the same technique of binarization and connected components extraction.

If boxes under the edited line are similar to any changes text lines, the system continues to show the corresponding overlay. However, two types of conflicts can occur: the original content may move somewhere else on the video canvas, or it has changed significantly.

When the underlying content changes, users may still wish for their edits to persist. Currently, we detect vertical shifts and reposition the overlays accordingly. For example, videos showing a text editor, web page, or word processor often scroll vertically. In those cases, the system automatically moves the overlay to correspond with the shift. However, when the content translates or new content appears, the system simply removes the overlay by default. Better tracking of content changes could be added to the system, e.g. tracking translations would allow the system to reposition the overlays when the video contains a desktop window moving on the screen. But our initial implementation is already very useful for many cases, including mostly static video recordings like lectures where the displayed slides do not change frequently, or even digital ink based tutorials such as Khan Academy videos where the content usually only scrolls vertically. Also, recreating edits later during the video playback is still much faster than using a regular video editing tool.

CONCLUSION AND FUTURE WORK

We presented a novel system that lets users quickly retouch text in videos such as lectures, and online screencasts. Users simply click over the video and start editing the text, reusing familiar metaphor for editing. The system monitors changes in subsequent frames and automatically adjusts the location of the overlays when the content scrolls vertically.

We are developing other tracking algorithms that will reposition the overlays when the content translates (e.g. a window is moved in the video); we are also applying the technique for ink-based content such as Khan Academy tutorials.

We believe that these editing systems will help people rapidly reuse and improve upon existing video content. Ultimately, our goal is to make it as easy to reuse and modify video content as it is to reuse and modify slide decks.

REFERENCES
1. Bagley, S. C. and Kopec, G. E. Editing images of text. *Communications of the ACM.* 37(12). 63-72. 1994.

2. Chang, F., Chen, C-J., and Lu, C-J. A linear-time component-labeling algorithm using contour tracing technique. *Computer Vision and Image Understanding.* 93(2). 206-220. 2004.

Inkantatory Paper: Dynamically Color-changing Prints with Multiple Functional Inks

Takahiro Tsujii
The University of Tokyo
tsujii@nae-lab.org

Koizumi Naoya
The University of Tokyo
koizumi@nae-lab.org

Takeshi Naemura
The University of Tokyo
naermura@nae-lab.org

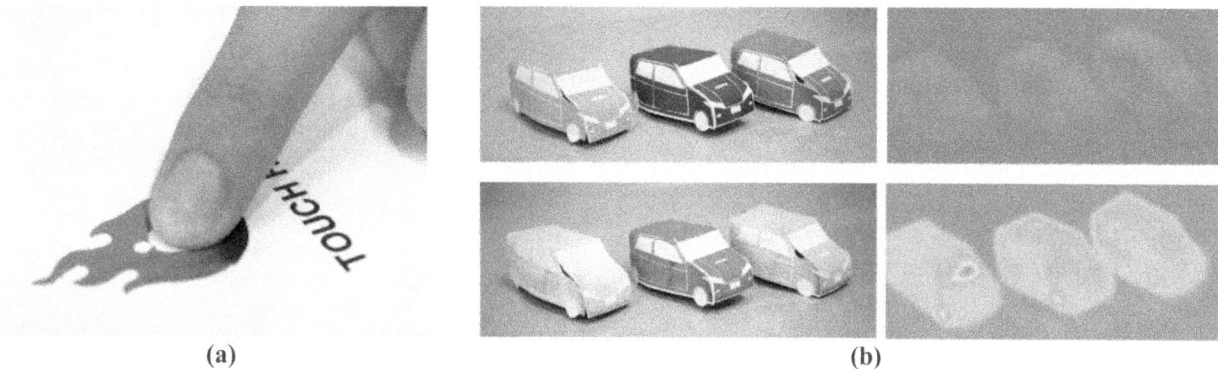

(a)   (b)

Figure 1. Inkantatory Paper. (a) Changing color by touch. (b) Changing color of paper crafts. It is caused by change of temperature, as shown in the thermal images at right.

ABSTRACT

We propose an effective combination of multiple functional inks, including conductive silver ink, thermo-chromic ink, and regular inkjet ink, for a novel paper-based interface called Inkantatory Paper that can dynamically change the color of its printed pattern. Constructed with off-the-shelf inkjet printing using silver conductive ink, our system enables users to fabricate thin, flat, flexible, and low-cost interactive paper. We evaluated the characteristics of the conductive silver ink as a heating system for the thermo-chromic ink and created applications demonstrating the usability of the system.

Author Keywords

Paper computing; conductive ink; prototyping; flexible printed electronics; inkjet printing; digital fabrication.

ACM Classification Keywords

H.5.m. Information interfaces and presentation (e.g., HCI): Miscellaneous.

UIST'14 Adjunct, October 5–8, 2014, Honolulu, HI, USA.
ACM 978-1-4503-3068-8/14/10.
http://dx.doi.org/10.1145/2658779.2659103

INTRODUCTION

Paper is used for a variety of purposes such as writing, reading, folding, packing, and so on, and recently there have been a number of studies on the augmentation of paper's function [1].

In 2012, Mitsubishi Paper Mill, Ltd. released commercial silver nano-particle inks [2] that are essentially conductive inks enabling inkjet printing of electrical circuits on paper or plastic film. Owing to this innovation, rapid prototyping of ubicomp devices is now attracting a lot of interest [3]. For example, Electronic Popables is an interactive pop-up book that sparkles, sings, and moves [4].

The focus of these studies has mainly been input techniques including touch, pressure, and bend sensing. In this work, however, we focus on output techniques, specifically, for a dynamic visual displaying method. For this purpose, we propose an effective combination of multiple functional inks including conductive silver ink, thermo-chromic ink, and regular inkjet ink. Our key concern in this paper is how to utilize the conductive silver ink as a heating system for the thermo-chromic ink. Constructed with off-the-shelf inkjet printing using silver conductive ink, our system enables users to fabricate thin, flat, flexible, and low-cost interactive paper that we call Inkantatory Paper. Our aim is to provide users with an easy way of integrating computing with paper.

We demonstrate two applications, as shown in Figure 1: (a) a printed fire image changing from black to red in response to a user's touch, and (b) the colors of paper crafts change according to the temperature as shown in the thermal image.

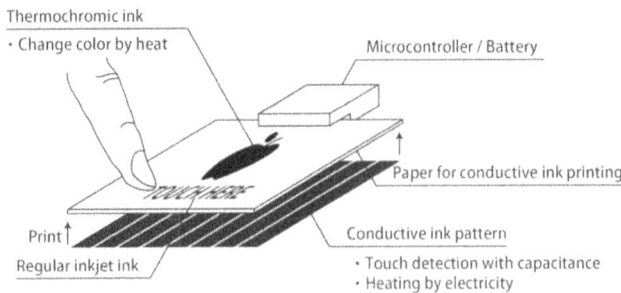

Figure 2: System overview.

SYSTEM OVERVIEW

The flow of this system includes three steps: 1) constructing the layout of the color-changing area and printing the pattern using an inkjet printer (PIXUS iP100) with conductive silver ink (MU01, Mitsubishi Paper Mill, Ltd.), 2) printing or painting with thermo-chromic ink (THERMO-CHROMIC Pigments 39°C, QCR Solutions Corp.), and 3) adding microcontroller and a power source. The system overview is detailed in Figure 2.

Layout and printing of conductive silver ink

To construct an adequate heating and touch detection system, we designed pre-composed patterns of conductive silver ink. Users can create their own heating patterns using a combination of these pre-composed patterns.

Painting thermo-chromic ink

Users can print the thermo-chromic ink on the backside of the printed heating pattern by using a screen printing kit or by hand-painting with brushes. We selected thermo-chromic ink with an activation temperature of 39°C in order to avoid the effect of body temperature and made sure that it did not go higher than 44°C to avoid harming users.

Hardware and power source design

We evaluated the relationship between the response speed of heat and the electricity consumption per unit area to design the hardware. Conductive silver ink patterns with 0.05–0.6 W/cm^2 were electrified and the time taken to reach the target temperature was measured. We utilized 200-μm non-layered paper and 270-μm-thick sticker-coated paper. The conductive silver pattern had a line width of 1 mm with 0.25-mm spacing between lines. The time taken to attain a temperature 10°C or 20°C higher than the original temperature is shown in Figure 3. As an example, 0.15 W/cm^2 of power is required to heat up 200-μm-thick paper by 10°C in three seconds. This means that one lithium polymer battery, which has 3 W of power, can heat up a 20-cm^2 area in this situation.

For the hardware in this research, we utilized the Arduino capacitive sensing library as input. This library requires an Arduino and 10 MΩ resistors, which we connected to paper with magnets.

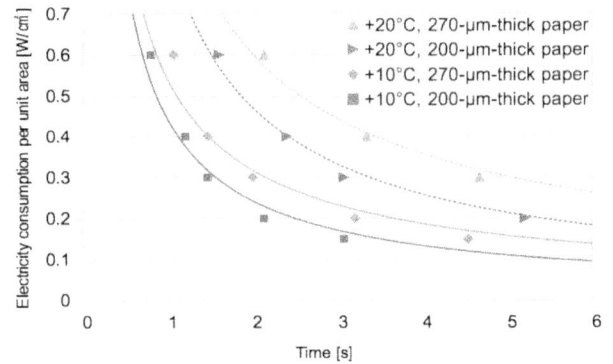

Figure 3: Characteristics of conductive silver ink as a heating system.

APPLICATION

In this section, we demonstrate 3 applications to showcase the capabilities of Inkantatory paper: a digital clock, a dynamic questionnaire, and a color-changing paper craft.

Digital clock: Inkantatory paper can be applied to ambient devices such as a clock because it displays reflected ambient light.

Dynamic questionnaire: Our system maintains the color of selected choices by providing continuous heat. Also, by adding a microcontroller and a battery to a magnet clip, it can function as a stand-alone system.

Paper craft: Since Inkantatory paper is composed of paper and inks, it is thin, flat, and flexible enough to make paper crafts.

CONCLUSION

This paper presented Inkantatory Paper, which adds a color-changing function to paper fabrications. We evaluated the relationship between the response speed of heat and the electricity consumption per unit area to design a given piece of hardware.

REFERENCES

1. Coelho, M., Hall, L., Berzowska, J., and Maes, P. Pulp-Based Computing: A Framework for Building Computers Out of Paper. In *the Extended Abstracts of Conference on Human Factors in Computing Systems CHI '09*, ACM Press (2009). 3527-3528.

2. http://www.k-mpm.com/agnanoen/agnano_ink.html.

3. Kawahara, Y., Hodges, S., Cook, B., Zhang, C., and Abowd, G. D. Instant Inkjet Circuits: Lab-based Inkjet Printing to Support Rapid Prototyping of Ubicomp Devices. In *Proc. of UbiComp '13*, ACM Press (2013), 363-372.

4. QI, J. and Buechley Li. Electronic Popables: Exploring paper-based computing through an interactive pop-up book. In *Proc. of the Fourth International Conference on Tangible, Embedded, and Embodied Interaction, TEI '10*, ACM Press (2010), 121-128.

StackBlock: Block-shaped Interface for Flexible Stacking

Masahiro Ando, Yuichi Itoh, *Toshiki Hosoi, *Kazuki Takashima, Kosuke Nakajima, *Yoshifumi Kitamura

Graduate School of Information Science and Technology, Osaka University
1-5 Yamadaoka, Suita, Osaka 565-0871, Japan
{ando.masahiro, itoh, nakajima.kosuke}
@ist.osaka-u.ac.jp

*Research Institute of Electrical Communication, Tohoku University
2-1-1 Katahira, Aoba-ku, Sendai, Miyagi 980-8577, Japan
{toshiki, takashima, kitamura}@riec.tohoku.ac.jp

ABSTRACT

We propose a novel building-block interface called *StackBlock* that allows users to precisely construct 3D shapes by stacking blocks at arbitrary positions and angles. Infrared LEDs and phototransistors are laid in a matrix on each surface of a block to detect the areas contacted by other blocks. Contact-area information is transmitted to the bottom block by the relay of infrared communication between the stacked blocks, and then the bottom block sends all information to the host computer for recognizing the 3D shape. We implemented a prototype of *StackBlock* with several blocks and evaluated the accuracy and latency of 3D shape recognition. As a result, *StackBlock* could sufficiently perform 3D shape recognition for users' flexible stacking.

Author Keywords
Tangible; building blocks; IR communication

ACM Classification Keywords
H.5.2 Information Interfaces and Presentation: User Interfaces.

INTRODUCTION

Many studies have recently focused on the block-shape user interface (Block UI), which allows users to interact with a computer using physical blocks. With intuitiveness for constructing 3D shapes, Block UIs are applied not only to industrial and architectural design but also to fields such as education and play therapy [1].

In existing Block UI systems, 3D shape recognition is basically achieved by image processing [2], optical markers [3], or electrical connections between blocks [4]. However, they have shortcomings of reduced flexibility for connecting and stacking several blocks because of the occlusion problem from the optical scheme, and the physical constraints of block connections such as hooks and

UIST'14 Adjunct, October 5–8, 2014, Honolulu, HI, USA.
ACM 978-1-4503-3068-8/14/10.
http://dx.doi.org/10.1145/2658779.2659104

magnets. Moreover, in most systems, users have to connect blocks at a predesigned angle and position. This limits potential applications with physical building blocks that need more delicate and natural building processes.

To tackle the problems of the existing block UIs, we propose a novel block UI called *StackBlock*. In this system, users can construct 3D shapes just by stacking blocks at arbitrary angles and positions like traditional wooden block toys, and the computer automatically recognizes the structure in real time as shown in Figure 1. An array of infrared LEDs (IR LEDs) and phototransistors (PTRs) is arranged on all six surfaces of a block to detect the areas contacted by other blocks. When a block (upper block) is stacked on a block that is already stacked (lower block), each block recognizes the contacted area by using infrared communication between IR LEDs and PTRs within the contacted area. IR LEDs and PTRs are also used to transmit the stacking information to the computer through relay of all stacking information by ordinary infrared data communication between the blocks.

Thus, since StackBlock utilizes infrared to recognize the constructed structure and communication between blocks, all block surfaces can be as smooth as traditional wooden block toys, and this allows users to flexibly and naturally construct 3D shapes. In addition, no occlusions occur when multiple users stack several blocks in tiers at the same time.

STACKBLOCK

Figure 1 shows an overview of the *StackBlock* system. As can be seen, the system detects the constructed structure. As described above, an array of IR LEDs and PTRs is arranged on all six surfaces of the block, and is utilized to detect areas in contact with other blocks and to transmit stacking information to the computer by infrared communication. Each block has a lithium ion battery (110 mAh, 3.7 V) and two R8C23 microcontrollers, and the substrates are covered and protected with a transparent acrylic box.

Figure 2 shows the workflow of the *StackBlock* system to recognize the constructed 3D structure according to the information about contact areas transmitted from stacked blocks. Normally, IR LEDs on each surface emit infrared light (IR light) at a constant interval. When a block is stacked on another block, both the lower and upper blocks

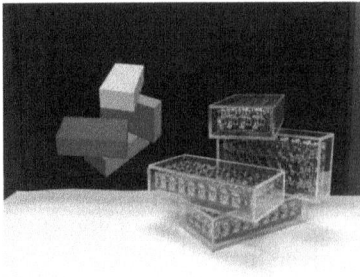

Figure 1 Implementation of *StackBlock*.

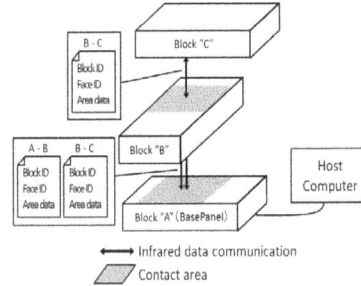

Figure 2 System Overview.

Figure 3 Recognition of the hand.

can estimate the contact area from the arrangement of the IR light received by PTRs. While a block is stacked on another block, the lower block regularly sends a request signal asking for the stacked block information (block ID, contacted surface ID, shape of contacted area) to the upper one via infrared communication (and the same information is relayed from blocks stacked higher up). After that, the upper block sends this information to the lower block. Then, the lower block pairs the received information with its own data. The block also sends this paired data as a response to the request from the underlying block. By repeating this communication, all stacking information of every pair of contacting blocks is finally gathered at the bottom block called a BasePanel, and is sent to the computer via a wired serial communication. The computer recognizes the whole 3D shape of the stacked blocks according to the gathered contact information that contains the identified block ID, surface ID and contacted area (also PTR IDs).

We designed and implemented several 50 x 100 x 25-mm blocks weighing approximately 100 g based on the design of commercial wooden blocks. On each surface, IR LEDs and PTRs are arranged at 10-mm intervals. We also developed software that visualizes the recognized 3D shape of stacked blocks in real time. With the implemented blocks, users can experience flexible, natural, and real-time 3D shape construction just by stacking the blocks.

For this shape recognition, we confirm recognition accuracy on changing positions of blocks, and latency. We found that the shape recognition was accurate (recognition accuracy was around 95 %), and latency was less than 1 sec. It will get better by examining the density and layout of the elements, and improving the software.

DISCUSSION

Recognition with IR-light
Since the design of blocks is very simple and primitive, and all users have to do is stack blocks, users can easily and intuitively construct a 3D shape in various ways. Also, since we use IR light to detect contact with other blocks, it is possible to recognize a user's touch interaction with the surfaces of blocks by detecting infrared light reflected by the user's hand. Figure 3 shows the actual result of recognizing the touched area. Thus, the system can examine the state transition: whether the block is grasped or not, and how a user grasps it.

Potential application
Unlike existing block UIs, the *StackBlock* system allows users to construct a 3D shape flexibly and naturally. We assume that this feature will enhance existing applications of physical blocks such as educational tools, cognitive testing, assessment of mental damage and play therapy [1], and so on.

In addition, *StackBlock* could be used in an application that recognizes not only the constructed structure but also users' interaction with blocks during the construction process, which is achieved by detecting users' touch interaction and transmitting the data via IR light communication as described above. For example, we can develop an application that assesses how efficiently a child grasps a block, and the data can be sent by emitting specific signals with IR LEDs.

CONCLUSION
We proposed the *StackBlock* system, which enables precise recognition of 3D shapes of blocks stacked at arbitrary angles and positions. In this paper, we described a method of achieving flexible stacking by using an array of IR LEDs and PTRs.

As future work, we are planning to examine the density and layout of the elements for more precise shape recognition, and to improve the software for faster shape recognition.

ACKNOWLEDGMENTS
This research was partially supported by the Grant-in-Aid for Young Scientists A (24680013) of the Japan Science and Technology Agency (JST), Japan.

REFERENCES
1. H. G. Kaduson et al., *101 more favorite play therapy techniques*, Aronson: Maryland, 2001.

2. M. Andrew et al., "Interactive 3D model acquisition and tracking of building block structures." *IEEE Trans. on Visualization and Computer Graphics*, Vol. 18, No. 4, pp. 651-659, 2012.

3. P. Baudisch et al., "Lumino: tangible blocks for tabletop computers based on glass fiber bundles," In *Proc. of CHI* '10, pp. 1165-1164, 2010.

4. R. Watanabe et al., "The soul of ActiveCube - implementing a flexible, multimodal, three dimensional spatial tangible," In *Proc. of ACE* '04, pp.178-180, 2004.

A Pen-based Device for Sketching with Multi-directional Traction Forces

Junichi Yamaoka
Keio University
5322, Endo, Fujisawa
yamajun@sfc.keio.ac.jp

Yasuaki Kakehi
Keio University
5322, Endo, Fujisawa
ykakehi@sfc.keio.ac.jp

ABSTRACT

This paper presents a pen-grip-shaped device that assists in sketching using multi-directional traction forces. By using an asymmetric acceleration of the vibration actuator that drive in a linear direction, the system can create a virtual traction force with the proper direction. We augment users' drawing skills with the device that arranged 4 vibration actuators that provides a traction force and a rotary sensation. Therefore the device is portable and does not have any limitation of needing to be in a particular location, this device can be used to guide the direction and assist the user who is sketching on a large piece of paper. Moreover, users can attach it to any writing utensil such as brushes, crayons. In this paper, we describe the details of the design of device, evaluation experiments, and applications.

Author Keywords

Creativity Supporting Tools; Pen-based UIs; Tactile and Haptic UIs; Pen and Tactile Input;

ACM Classification Keywords

H5.2 [Information Interfaces and Presentation]: User Interfaces.

INTRODUCTION

Until now, many researchers of Interactive Fabrication have attempted to expand the user's creativity by combining a hand working and a digital fabrication [1]. In these studies, digital technologies have augmented and supported user's drawing with pens and papers. For example, by using pens or styluses device, users can draw figures which are difficult by free-hand drawing and improve their skills by learning from the guidance. Specially, haptic guidance is effective because users can feel the sensation as if someone is leading the pen's movement during the drawing process.

The haptic representation technologies for supporting drawing can be classified into two classes. The first is the studies that can create traction force using nylon strings [2], actuators and arms [3], and magnets [4]. Although these studies can create a strong force by pulling the stylus

UIST'14 Adjunct, October 5–8, 2014, Honolulu, HI, USA.
ACM 978-1-4503-3068-8/14/10.
http://dx.doi.org/10.1145/2658779.2659105

physically, the required systems tend to be large. The second is the studies that include vibration actuators in pens and styluses and create tactile feedback [5]. These systems are portable because they include an actuator in each of the styluses. However, these systems specialize only in creating haptic feedback such as textures, and they cannot create a traction force. Traxion[6] is a tactile interaction device that generates the asymmetric actuation using a small tactile actuator. This system can create a virtual traction force; however, this device is used by holding them in the air, and application is such as a navigation system.

This time, we propose an augmented sketching system that provides a traction force and a repulsion force to help users. By attaching a pen-grip shaped device, on which multiple vibration actuators are arranged, to a writing utensil, the user's pen is controlled automatically. Therefore, users can use this system anywhere and attach it to any writing utensil such as pens, brushes, crayons, and styluses. This system allows users to draw pre-set figures, draw while being corrected by a computer.

SYSTEM DESIGN

The system consists of vibration actuators, a microcontroller (Arduino), amplifiers, and a computer. The pen-grip-shaped device uses four vibration actuators (Haptuator, Tactile Labs Inc.[7]) that drive in a linear direction. The signal is a 125-Hz square wave, and the duty cycle is 2 ms: 6 ms. Thus, the single vibration actuator can generate a unidirectional acceleration. Because the generated acceleration is transmitted to the tip and the paper, the tip moves as if it kicks the table surface and the pen itself generates the traction force. The strength of traction force is from about 0.5 N to 0.8 N. As shown in Figure 1, we placed two actuators oriented in the horizontal

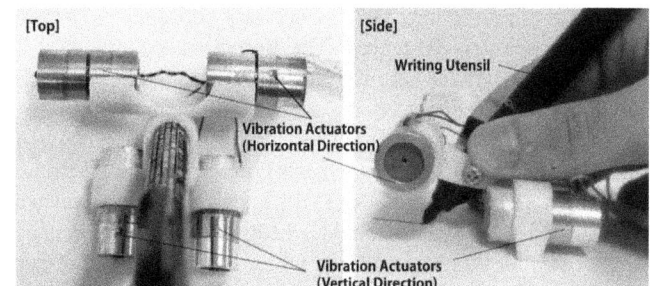

Figure 1: Design of device.

direction and two in the vertical direction. Specifically, as shown in Figure 2, toggling the direction of acceleration of the front actuators can create a force in the horizontal direction. The vertical direction corresponds to the rear actuators, and combining the traction forces produced by the four actuators creates a force in a diagonal direction, located at multiples of 45 degrees. Moreover, by reversing the traction direction of the rear actuators, the system can rotate the pen.

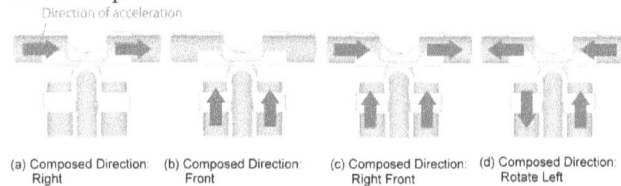

Figure 2. Control of multi-directional forces.

One Application of this system is drawing pre-set shapes semi-automatically. By attaching a writing utensil to the device and setting it on a piece of paper, the user can draw the pre-set shapes (Figure 3). In addition to pens and brushes, by using a digital pen or a stylus that can recognize the position of the pen, the system gives users access to interactive functionality. When the user is attempting to draw a straight line, this system corrects the position of the pen to the proper position when the line turns in the wrong direction.

Figure 3. Drawing shapes on a large place of paper.

EVALUATION

We conducted an experiment to determine whether users can feel the traction force in an arbitrary direction with this device. The subjects were 10 students. The subject held the felt-tipped marker with two fingers. The duration of stimulation was 3200 ms. The presented angle is arbitrary one of eight directions that divided at by 45 degrees, as the right direction is 0 degree. The participants completed a total of 40 trials, where 5 trials were completed for each direction. We compared the angles corresponding to the signals with the actual angles along which the subject's pen moved. The results are shown in Figure 4. As shown in the graph, there is one angle that is difficult to feel; however we confirmed that users could recognize the differences between the angles on the whole. The average error between the presented angle and the angle of the user's movement was 39.8 degrees.

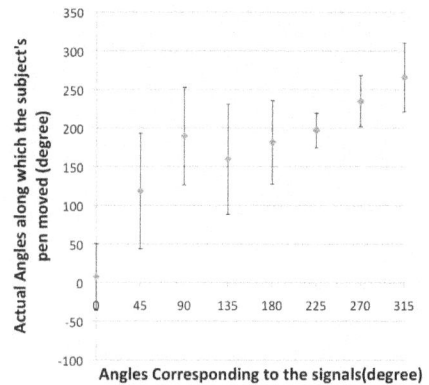

Figure 4. Results of the experiment.

Moreover, we examined the possibility of presenting rotary sensation by reversing the traction direction of the rear actuators. In this experiment, they reported whether the rotary sensation was to the right or the left. For each rotary direction sensation, there were 5 trials. The results showed that the subjects were able to correctly identify the direction of rotation 89 % of the time; hence, the participants were able to distinguish between rotary sensations to the right and to the left.

CONCLUSION AND FUTURE WORK

In this work, we proposed a pen-based device for sketching with multi-directional traction forces. The user could sense the difference in the two dimensional traction forces and the rotary sensation with few errors. However, it was difficult to differentiate the accurate directions. Therefore, rather than drawing accurately, we propose that this device can be used to guide the direction and assist the user who is sketching (Auto-correcting line-drawing function, etc.).

REFERENCES

1. Willis, K. D., et al. Interactive fabrication: new interfaces for digital fabrication. In Proceedings of TEI'11, 69–72, ACM, 2011.
2. Lin, L., et al. Spidar-pen: A 2t1r pen-based interface with co-located haptic-visual display. Transactions on Edutainment VIII, Volume 7220, 166-177, 2012.
3. Satoshi Saga, N. K., and Tachi, S. Haptic teaching using opposite force presentation, Mar.2005. In Conference Abstracts of World Haptics 2005 CD-ROM.
4. Yamaoka, J., and Kakehi, Y. dePENd: Augmented handwriting system using ferromagnetism of a ballpoint pen. In Proceedings of UIST '13, 203–210, ACM, 2013.
5. Poupyrev, I., et al. Haptic feedback for pen computing: Directions and strategies. In CHI EA '04, 1309–1312, ACM, 2014.
6. Rekimoto, J. Traxion: A tactile interaction device with virtual force sensation. In Proceedings of UIST '13, 427–432, ACM, 2013.
7. TactileLabs. Haptuator. http://www.tactilelabs.com/products/haptics/haptuator/.

Tangible and Modular Input Device for Character Articulation

Alec Jacobson
Columbia University
New York, USA
jacobson@cs.columbia.edu

Daniele Panozzo
ETH Zurich
Zurich, Switzerland

Oliver Glauser
ETH Zurich
Zurich, Switzerland

Cédric Pradalier
GeorgiaTech Lorraine
Atlanta, USA

Otmar Hilliges
ETH Zurich
Zurich, Switzerland

Olga Sorkine-Hornung
ETH Zurich
Zurich, Switzerland

ABSTRACT

We present a modular, novel mechanical device for animation authoring. The pose of the device is sensed at interactive rates, enabling quick posing of characters rigged with a skeleton of arbitrary topology. The mapping between the physical device and virtual skeleton is computed semi-automatically guided by sparse user correspondences. Our demonstration allows visitors to experiment with our device and software, choosing from a variety of characters to control.

Author Keywords

Novel input devices;character articulation

ACM Classification Keywords

H.5.2. Information Interfaces & Presentation: User Interfaces

Introduction

Interactively articulating virtual 3D characters lies at the heart of computer animation and geometric modeling. Expressive articulation requires control over many degrees of freedom: most often the joint angles of an internal skeleton. We introduce a physical input device assembled on the fly to control any character's skeleton directly. With traditional mouse and keyboard input, animators must rely on indirect methods such as inverse kinematics or decompose complex and integrated motions into smaller sequential manipulations—for example, iteratively positioning each bone of a skeleton hierarchy. While direct manipulation mouse and touch interfaces are successful in 2D [4], 3D interactions with 2D input are ill-posed and thus more challenging. Successful commercial products with 2D interfaces, e.g. Autodesk's MAYA, have notoriously steep learning curves and require interface-specific training.

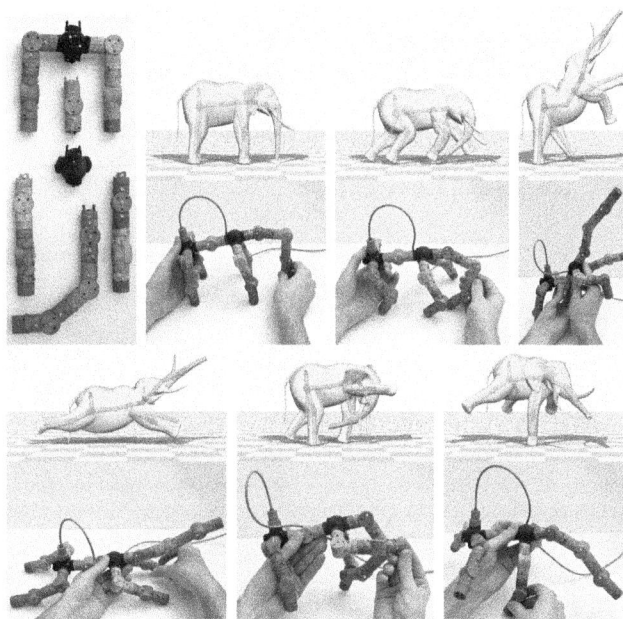

Figure 1. Assembled from modular, interchangeable, and hot-pluggable parts, our novel device forms a skeletal tree matching the *Elephant*. As the user manipulates each joint of the device, measured bone rotations animate a skeletal rig, and the *Elephant* comes to life.

Mouse and keyboard interfaces fall short because their control spaces do not match the perceptual space of the 3D interaction task [2]. Hence, we propose direct physical manipulation via a *tangible interface* [1] with degrees of freedom matching the 3D rotations at skeletal joints in the virtual character.

Our novel device is composed of modular, hot-pluggable mechanical parts. The user may quickly assemble measurement joints and branching splitters to create a custom device to control any virtual character with arbitrary topology skeleton (see Figure 1). Leveraging modern advances in 3D printing, our parts are compact and comfortably held with one or two hands.

UIST'14 Adjunct, October 5–8, 2014, Honolulu, HI, USA.
ACM 978-1-4503-3068-8/14/10.
http://dx.doi.org/10.1145/2658779.2659106

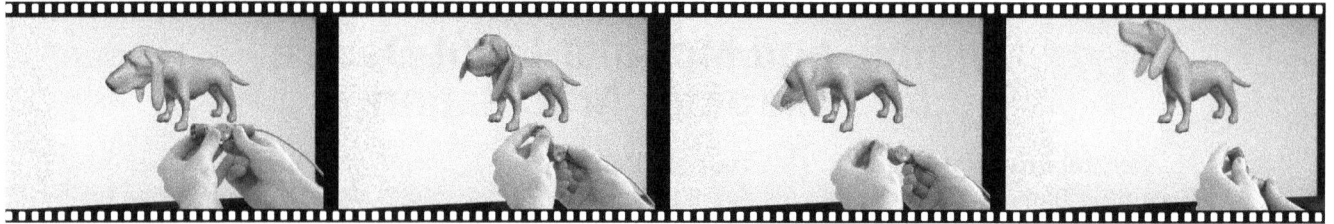

Figure 2. A user interacts with an elastic simulation of the *Basset Hound* in real time using a single joint to control the dog's neck.

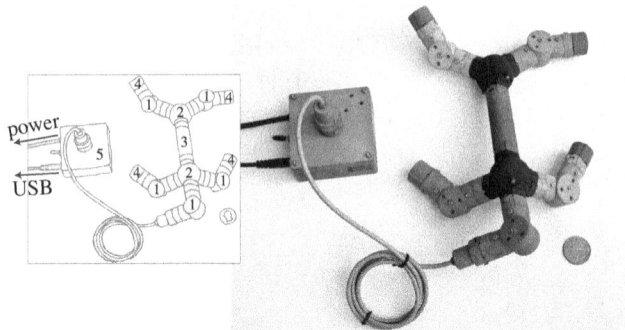

Figure 3.   A device instance may consist of joints, splitters, extension segments, endcaps, and a controller.

Technical Contributions

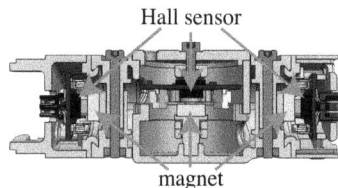

Exploiting human propri-oception and physical af-fordances, an assembled device allows interaction with a physical manifestation of the virtual character, without the need for a literal, fixed replication. Pairs of permanent magnets and Hall-effect sensors embedded in each joint measure rotations with accuracy of $\sim 1°$ at a frequency up to 250 Hz (more details in corresponding technical paper [3]). The device is well suited not only for rapid prototyping, but also precise control tasks such as meticulous keyframe posing and real-time animation capture. Complementary to the physical device, we introduce algorithms to facilitate the device's employment in the standard character rigging and animation pipelines. A novel semi-automatic registration algorithm accounts for the disparity between the device's physical proportions and the virtual character's. The user may quickly match the character's rest pose and immediately begin animating (see accompanying video).

Demo

Visitors may try our device in various 3D character articulation scenarios. Choosing from a catalog of virtual characters, visitors assemble a corresponding device from our kit of over 30 parts. Our system attaches the device to the character's virtual skeleton. Then the visitor manipulates the device while seeing the character animate on screen in real time. We also prepare more advanced demos where visitors use the device to control physically based simulations (see Figure 2) and explore variational geometric modeling techniques.

Our mechanical parts rely on internal electronic sensors rather than computer vision. Thus, the unpredictable light-

ing of the UIST Demonstrations exhibit space will emphasize that our device is suitable not only as a desktop tool at artist workstations, but also as a performance instrument in arbitrary environments.

Our input device intensifies immersion and tangibility in the context of posing, designing and animating deformable 3D shapes. As displays make leaping advances toward convincing autostereoscopy and 3D printing becomes commonplace, we see potentially large impact from tangible input devices for virtual 3D content. To this end, we release complete hardware blueprints (OpenHardware) and accompanying source code in the hopes of fostering future exploration in this direction. We will encourage visitors to download our blueprints and construct their own input devices at home.

REFERENCES

1. Ishii, H., and Ullmer, B. Tangible bits: Towards seamless interfaces between people, bits and atoms. In *Proc. CHI* (1997).

2. Jacob, R. J. K., Sibert, L. E., McFarlane, D. C., and Mullen, Jr., M. P. Integrality and separability of input devices. *ACM Trans. Comput.-Hum. Interact. 1*, 1 (Mar. 1994), 3–26.

3. Jacobson, A., Panozzo, D., Glauser, O., Predalier, C., Hilleges, O., and Sorkine-Horning, O. Tangible and modular input device for character articulation. *ACM Transactions on Graphics (proceedings of ACM SIGGRAPH) 33*, 4 (2014), to appear.

4. Shneiderman, B. Direct manipulation for comprehensible, predictable and controllable user interfaces. In *Proc. IUI* (1997), 33–39.

Digital Flavor Interface

Nimesha Ranasinghe
Department of Computer Science
New York University Abu Dhabi
Abu Dhabi, UAE
nimesha82@gmail.com

Gajan Suthokumar, Kuan Yi Lee,
Ellen Yi-Luen Do
Keio-NUS CUTE Center
National University of Singapore
gajan004@gmail.com, {idmleek, ellendo}@nus.edu.sg

ABSTRACT

This demo presents a unique technology to enable digital simulation of flavors. The Digital Flavor Interface, a digital control system, is developed to stimulate taste (using electrical and thermal stimulation methodologies on the human tongue) and smell (using a controlled scent emitting mechanism) senses simultaneously, thus simulating different virtual flavors. A preliminary user experiment was conducted to investigate the effectiveness of this approach with five distinct flavor stimuli. The experimental results suggested that the users' were effectively able to identify different flavors such as minty, spicy, and lemon flavor. In summary, our work demonstrates a novel controllable digital flavor instrument, which may be utilized in interactive computer systems for rendering virtual flavors.

Author Keywords

Flavor; Virtual flavor; Smell; Taste; Virtual reality

ACM Classification Keywords

H.5.1 Information Interfaces and Presentation (I.7): Multimedia Information Systems - Artificial, augmented, and virtual realities

INTRODUCTION

The sensation of flavor is mostly referred to the stimulus experienced in the mouth (or tongue) when consuming food or drinks. Thus, flavor is one of the most-apparent factors that contributes to successful food choice in humans. It is a multisensory experience mainly perceived as a combination of taste (gustation) and smell (olfaction) sensations [1]. Important contributions of taste and smell senses (including the interactions between the two senses) for flavor perception is highlighted in literature [4]. In addition to the senses of taste and smell, vision, audition, and taction (somatosensory - primarily the texture of food) are also involved in flavor perception.

However, at present, it has been difficult to share flavors digitally (or experience them virtually) other than verbal and pictorial descriptions of these sensations due to two main issues:

UIST'14, October 5–8, 2014, Honolulu, HI, USA.
ACM 978-1-4503-3068-8/14/10.
http://dx.doi.org/10.1145/2658779.2659107

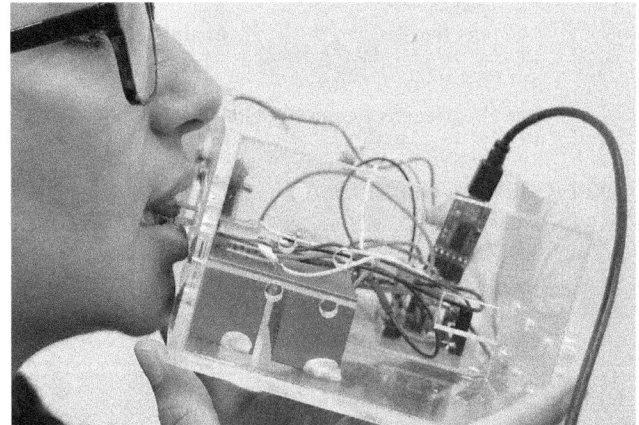

Figure 1. A participant is using the Digital Flavor Interface. Her tip of the tongue is contacting the two silver electrodes, while smell emitting module directs the corresponding scent using a small fan

1) there has not been a standard methodology to utilize flavors as a digitally controllable media, 2) lack of understanding of the sensation itself together with cross-sensory perceptions. Thus, this paper introduces the Digital Flavor Interface, a new form of digital technology to simulate flavors. As shown in Figure 1, when using the device virtual flavors are delivered as a combination of digital taste sensations and different scents. Distinct taste sensations are delivered using electrical and thermal stimulation on the tongue [2, 3], while smell sensations are delivered by heating an array of solid perfumes.

METHOD

The Digital Flavor Interface, consists of four different submodules for electrical stimulation, thermal stimulation, smell emitting, and a wearable tongue interface (which consists of a pair of silver electrodes). The electrical stimulation submodule sends weak and controlled electrical pulses (manipulating frequency 100Hz - 1000Hz and magnitude of current $20\mu A$ - $180\mu A$ of the electrical stimuli) to silver electrodes. Additionally, temperature changes are achieved on silver electrodes using a Peltier semiconductor element[1] that can heat and cool rapidly. A heat sink is used to provide an efficient temperature control. Currently, the smell emitting submodule has four small compartments to store four different scents in the form of solid perfumes. Each of these compartments has a resistor based heating mechanism to emit smells. In addition, a computer is connected to the device as a command center to manipulate various stimuli through a serial interface. The Digital Flavor Interface is displayed in Figure 2.

[1]http://www.peltier-info.com/

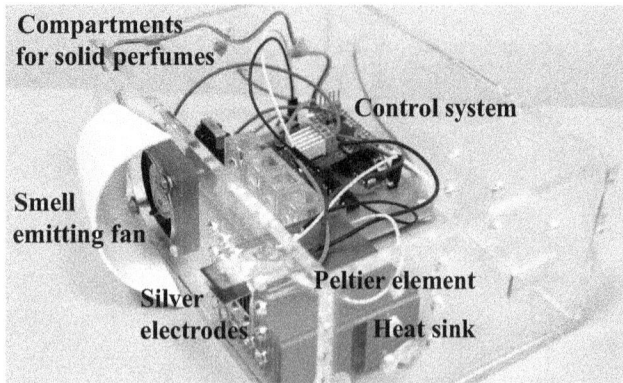

Figure 2. Main components of Digital Flavor Interface

EXPERIMENTAL RESULTS

A preliminary user experiment was conducted using several pre-defined flavor combinations. The participants were in good health conditions and did not report any tasting disorders. Output current was continuously monitored during the experiments for safety purposes. Furthermore, the silver electrodes were sterilized using alcohol swabs and deionized water to overcome possible hygiene problems.

The primary motivation of this experiment was to study the effects of flavors when different smells are overlaid on digitally simulated taste sensations. As studied in [3], sour (electrical stimulation), spicy (thermal stimulation), and minty (thermal stimulation) were reported as strong artificial taste sensations. Thus, we selected these three as basic sensations to experiment with different combinations of smells (solid perfumes[2]). A summary of formulated artificial flavor stimuli are described below:

1. Sour (magnitude of current: 180µA, Frequency: 800Hz) AND Tuscan orange

2. Sour (magnitude of current: 180µA, Frequency: 800Hz) AND Brazilian Mango Grapefruit

3. Sour (magnitude of current: 180µA, Frequency: 800Hz) AND Malibu lemon blossom

4. Spicy (magnitude of current: 20µA, Frequency: 400Hz, Temperature: 36°C) AND Madagascar Spice

5. Minty (magnitude of current: 20µA, Frequency: 400Hz, Temperature: 18°C) AND Malibu lemon blossom

The initial results clearly show that artificial taste sensations can be extended by overlaying different smells. For each stimulus, more than 60% agreed that the perceived sensations were richer than the taste sensations. Among all of the trials, minty has shown the highest improvement by integrating with the smell of lemon. Many participants explained that they sensed 'minty + lemon' flavor similar to a refreshing menthol sensation. In addition, participants identified the spicy flavor as a hot and spicy burning sensation on their tongue. Several users also mentioned that the scent stimuli make the flavor sensations clearer and easier to distinguish between them.

[2]http://www.pacificaperfume.com/beauty/perfume/solid-perfumes

Moreover, in stimulus 1 (sour + orange), 2 (sour + mango), and 3 (sour + lemon) participants were able to recognize different flavors although the same taste sensation was incorporated. However, in several occasions (between trials 1 and 3) elicited flavors were found to be subjective. We believe this occurs due to the similarity of citrus scents used in these trials (orange and lemon scents) and individual differences in perceiving them.

DEMO EXPERIENCE

During the demonstration, users can experience aforementioned digital flavor stimuli through the Digital Flavor Interface. In addition, they may also select different combinations of taste and smell sensations apart from the predefined sensations by changing the output parameters (current: 20µA - 180µA, frequency: 100Hz - 1000Hz, and temperature: 18°C - 36°C).

CONCLUSION

In conclusion, this paper introduced a method to synthesize virtual flavors digitally. The technology is based on actuating various combinations of taste and smell sensations using electrical stimulation, thermal stimulation, and solid perfumes. Five different stimuli with distinct taste - flavor combinations were examined during the initial experiment. Importantly, it has highlighted that the range of taste perceptions can be enhanced by incorporating other modalities into the digital taste experiences. We believe this technology can be developed further in several directions. Besides using sensation of flavor as a digital media, findings of this approach may also provide insights into novel applications such as Digital food ingredients. For instance, in the future, this technology might facilitate adding virtual chicken or beef flavors while eating a cup of plain noodles or converting a glass of water into a virtual soft drink digitally.

ACKNOWLEDGEMENT

This research is supported by the Singapore National Research Foundation under its International Research Center Keio-NUS CUTE Center @ Singapore Funding Initiative and administered by the IDM Program Office.

REFERENCES

1. Auvray, M., and Spence, C. The multisensory perception of flavor. *Consciousness and cognition 17*, 3 (2008), 1016–1031.

2. Cruz, A., and Green, B. Thermal stimulation of taste. *Nature 403*, 6772 (2000), 889–892.

3. Ranasinghe, N., Nakatsu, R., Nii, H., and Gopalakrishnakone, P. Tongue mounted interface for digitally actuating the sense of taste. In *16th International Symposium on Wearable Computers (ISWC)*, IEEE (2012), 80–87.

4. Stevenson, R. J., and Boakes, R. A. Sweet and sour smells: learned synesthesia between the senses of taste and smell. *The handbook of multisensory processes* (2004), 69–83.

Interactive Exploration and Selection in Volumetric Datasets with Color Tunneling

Christophe Hurter
University of Toulouse
ENAC, France
Christophe.hurter@enac.fr

A.R. Taylor
University of
Calgary, Canada
russ@ras.ucalgary.ca

Sheelagh Carpendale
University of Calgary
Canada
sheelagh@cpsc.ucalgary.ca

Alexandru Telea
University of Groningen
Netherlands
a.c.telea@rug.nl

ABSTRACT

Interactive data exploration and manipulation are often hindered by dataset sizes. For 3D data, occlusion, important adjacencies, and entangled patterns make visual interaction via common filtering techniques hard. This demonstration presents Color Tunneling, a toolset for interactive exploration and selection in large datasets. Our toolset uses a set of real-time multi-dimensional exploration techniques (animation between view configurations, semantic filtering and view deformation) to help users to easily select, analyze, and eliminate spatial-and-data patterns. Any data subset can be selected at any step along the animation. Data can be filtered and deformed to reduce occlusion and ease complex data selections. Our techniques are simple to learn and implement, flexible, and real-time interactive with datasets of tens of millions of data points. We demonstrate our toolset on three domain areas: 2D image segmentation and manipulation, 3D medical volume exploration, and astrophysical exploration.

Author Keywords

Data cube visualization, data exploration, GPU techniques

ACM Classification Keywords

I.3.6 [Methodology and Techniques]: Interaction techniques

INTRODUCTION

Interactive data exploration and manipulation are often hindered by dataset sizes. For 3D data, occlusion, important adjacencies, and entangled patterns make visual interaction via common filtering techniques hard. To this end, we developed Color Tunneling [1], a set of techniques to interactively unveil occluded structures of interest in dense 3D multivariate datasets which exhibit significant overlap between groups of voxels or pixels. Color Tunneling extends Focus + Context interactive exploration of 2D and 3D datasets in several directions. It proposes a set of linked *views* that display subsets of data attributes: 3D volume rendering plots, 2D scatterplots, and 2D and 3D histograms.

UIST'14 Adjunct, October 5–8, 2014, Honolulu, HI, USA.
ACM 978-1-4503-3068-8/14/10.
http://dx.doi.org/10.1145/2658779.2659108

Views are linked by brushing and free-form selection. Using the optimal view(s), one can find structures of interest, e.g. spatially compact zones in images/volumes or peaks in histograms, and highlight or erase such structures in all views at once. We enhance classical *histogram* views with shading, sorting, and depth, to allow spotting complex patterns with greater ease. We propose a smooth *animation* between multiple views, to locate (and select) data patterns which are hard to isolate in single views. We integrate a focus + context *deformation* that adds the ability to uncover locally-occluded spatial patterns in any view. For this, we propose five interactive techniques (Figure 1) as follows:

- **View linking:** Three configurable views (2 exploration views and one lock view) are linked for data exploration.
- **Warp:** Animates any view between two configurations.
- **Lock:** Locks items not to be affected by brush or dig.
- **Brush:** With the lock view, brushing allows adding or removing data in any view.
- **Dig:** With the lock view, digging pushes data points away from the lens center to unveil occluded structures.

EXPLORATION EXAMPLES

Color Tunneling can handle large datasets (up to tens million records with a modern graphics card). We next demonstrate Color Tuneling on three use-cases involving different datasets in three application domains.

Medical imaging: Consider the 3D CT scans in Figure 1 and in the video. We want to "peek" inside the head and expose the *top part* of the brain structure in our head scan. Simply filtering out the bone voxels does not display the brain since the skin will not be filtered and will occlude it. Conversely, filtering out the skin will also remove the brain which has a similar density value. To solve our task, we use Color Tunneling and its associated tools. This effectively produces a combination of density-based, gradient-based, and geometry-based filtering that lets us remove the upper skin and skull cap, and unveil the brain in its spatial context, by means of just a few mouse clicks (video; 37 seconds).

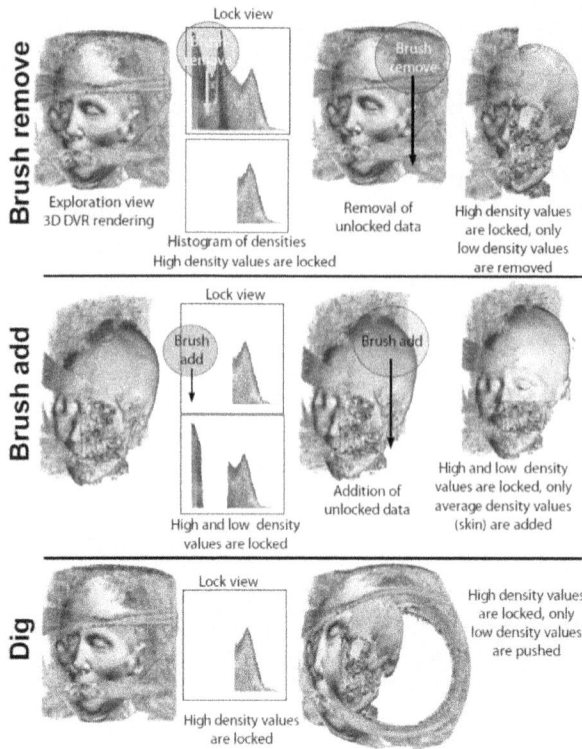

Figure 1: Brush, dig, and lock tools with Color Tunneling.

Astrophysical data: We consider a cube of astro-physical measurements of the large-scale structure of hydrogen gas intensities in our Milky Way Galaxy in 3D polar-coordinate-wavelength space. Thanks to the animation between the 3D cube and the density histogram, we can easily brush and extract constant-intensity outliers which are deep buried in the data cube (Fig. 3; video, 51 seconds). Astronomers require isolating such outliers for reasoning about various early-Universe formation patterns [6].

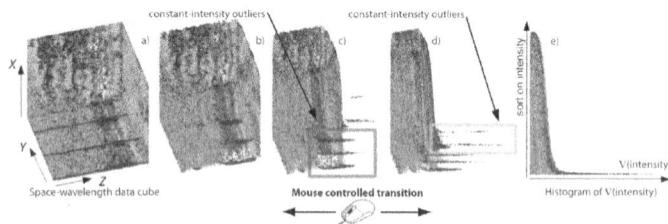

Figure 2: Locating constant-intensity line outliers in a 3D astronomical data cube.

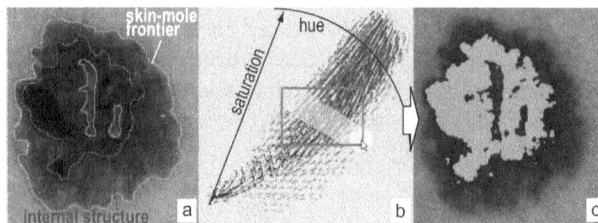

Figure 3: Skin tumor segmentation.

Image segmentation: Figure 3 shows a skin scan of a naevus, or mole. Dermatologists need to segment such scans into normal skin, the mole, and the internal mole structure prior to applying various metrics to predict the mole's potential malignity, such as shown in Fig. 2a. Producing such segmentations in the RGB image space is a delicate manual process. Using Color Tunneling, a dermatologist could produce comparable segmentations in a fraction of the time, by using brushing in a hue-saturation plot and animation towards the classical RGB image plot (Fig. 2c; video 3 minutes 20 seconds).

CONCLUSION

We have presented Color Tunneling, a set of interactive techniques for exploration and selection of structures from multidimensional datasets. In contrast to earlier animation techniques [2] [3], users can control and stop the animation at any stage. This yields an *infinite* set of in-between views where one can brush, dig, select, and explore the data. We thus use animation as a first-class exploration tool rather than only to preserve the mental-map between two views. We also present a new interaction tool: the lock view. Locked items are not affected by our dig, warp and brush tools. Locking leverages brushing by allowing complex selections of brushable items, in contrast to brushing compact ranges [4] [5]. Concluding, Color Tunneling's contributions are as follows:

- using **animation** as a controlled data exploration-and-selection technique,
- improved **brushing** with a flexible selection of brushable items,
- improved lens deformation (**dig tool**) with a flexible selection of pushable items,
- a simple implementation able to handle over 10M displayed data points at over 20 images/second on a modern GPU (e.g. NVidia 750m) on a recent PC computer (e.g. core I7 processor).

REFERENCES

[1] C. Hurter, R. Taylor, S. Carpendale, and A. Telea, "Color tunneling: Interactive exploration and selection in volumetric datasets", *Proc. IEEE PacificVis*, 2014, pp. 225–232.

[2] C. Hurter, A. Telea, and O. Ersoy, "MoleView: An attribute and structure-based semantic lens for large element-based plots" *IEEE TVCG* 17(12), 2011, pp. 2600–2609.

[3] F. Chevalier, P. Dragicevic, and C. Hurter, "Histomages: fully synchronized views for image editing", Proc. *ACM UIST*, 2012, pp. 281–286.

[4] C. Hurter, B. Tissoires, and S. Conversy, "FromDaDy: Spreading aircraft trajectories across views to support iterative queries," *IEEE TVCG* 15(6), 2009, pp. 1017–1024.

[5] M. Ward, "XmdvTool: integrating multiple methods for visualizing multivariate data", *Proc. IEEE Visualization*, 1994, pp. 326–333.

[6] A. Taylor, S. Gibson, M. Peracaula, P. Martin, T. Landecker, C. Brunt, P. Dewdney, S. Dougherty, A. Gray, L. Higgs, C. Kerton, L. Knee, R. Kothes, C. Purton, B. Uyaniker, B. Wallace, A. Willis, and D. Durand. The Canadian galactic plane survey. Astron J, 125(6):3145–3164, 2003.

FeelCraft: Crafting Tactile Experiences for Media using a Feel Effect Library

Siyan Zhao, Oliver Schneider
Disney Research Pittsburgh
4720 Forbes Avenue, Pittsburgh
{siyan.zhao, oliver.schneider}
@disneyresearch.com

Roberta Klatzky
Carnegie Mellon University
5000 Forbes Avenue, Pittsburgh
klatzky@cmu.edu

Jill Lehman, Ali Israr
Disney Research Pittsburgh
4720 Forbes Avenue, Pittsburgh
{jill.lehman, israr}
@disneyresearch.com

ABSTRACT

FeelCraft is a media plugin that monitors events and states in the media and associates them with expressive tactile content using a library of *feel effects* (FEs). A *feel effect* (FE) is a user-defined haptic pattern that, by virtue of its connection to a meaningful event, generates dynamic and expressive effects on the user's body. We compiled a library of more than fifty FEs associated with common events in games, movies, storybooks, etc., and used them in a sandbox-type gaming platform. The FeelCraft plugin allows a game designer to quickly generate haptic effects, associate them to events in the game, play them back for testing, save them and/or broadcast them to other users to feel the same haptic experience. Our demonstration shows an interactive procedure for authoring haptic media content using the FE library, playing it back during interactions in the game, and broadcasting it to a group of guests.

Author Keywords

Feel effect; haptic vocabulary; haptic gaming experience; haptic authoring tool.

ACM Classification Keywords

H.5.2. Information interfaces and presentation: User Interfaces—Haptic I/O

INTRODUCTION

In recent years, haptic feedback has been frequently utilized to enhance user experience in movies, shows, games, rides, virtual simulations, and social and educational media [1-4, 6]. Despite a long history of use in communication, haptic feedback is a relatively new addition to the toolbox of special effects. Unlike sound or visual effects, haptic designers cannot simply access libraries of effects that map cleanly to media content, and they lack even guiding principles for creating such effects. Recently, Israr and colleagues [5] compiled a library of FEs that extended the

richness of an interaction by engaging the haptic senses in the same way that libraries of sound and visual effects are used to engage the auditory and visual senses.

FEEL EFFECT LIBRARY

A key feature of an FE is that it correlates the semantic interpretation of an event (as judged by human users) with the parametric composition of the sensation in terms of physical variables, such as intensity, duration, temporal onsets, etc. In carefully designed perceptual studies, Israr et al. [5] showed that:

- semantically similar FEs lie in close proximity in haptic parameter space,
- semantic reasoning for relating events can be applied to the haptic space to derive new FEs.

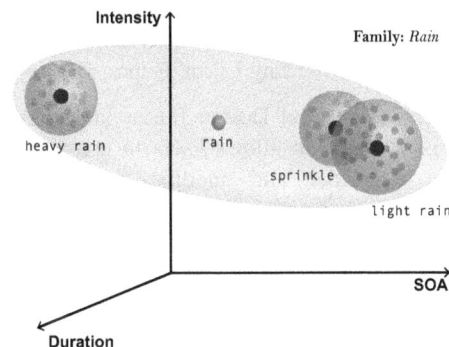

Figure 1. Feel Effects spanning a parametric sub-space

For example, FEs associated with **heavy rain** and **light rain** are located at the extreme ends of the "*Rain*" family in the haptic parametric space (see Figure 1). We compiled a library of FEs associated with the six families of events shown in Figure 2. Each family has a predefined parametric structure and the FEs in a family vary with respect to one, two or three parameters [6].

FEELCRAFT ARCHITECTURE

The FeelCraft plugin channels media events to dynamic tactile sensations on a haptic device. Figure 3 shows the architecture of authoring and playback haptic media. In a typical **playmode**, *media* (1) triggers action monitored in *media plugin* (2). The *Event2Haptic* (3) associates events to a specific FE stored in the *FE library* (4). The associated

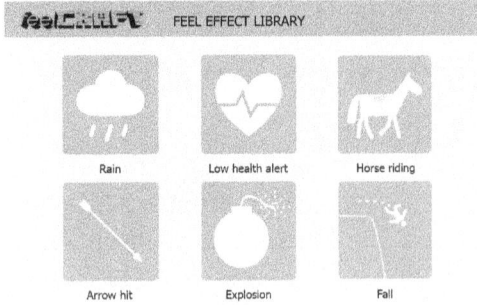

Figure 2. Families in the current Feel Effect library

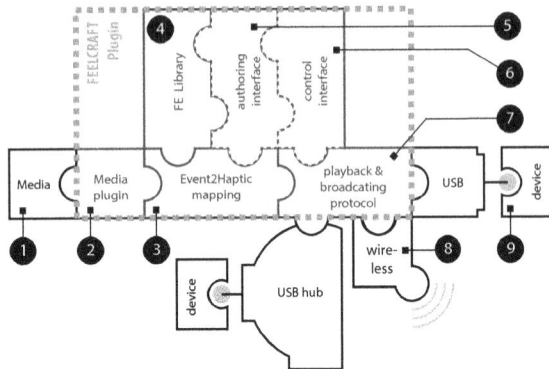

Figure 3. Haptic authoring and playback architecture

FE is *played back* (7) using custom protocols that either send the FE to a specific *haptic device* (9) or *broadcast* (8) it. In **craftmode**, users create and save new FEs and tune, edit and playback existing FEs on the *authoring and playback interface* (5,6). Users can also assign FEs to media events by overwriting Event2Haptic mappings.

Figure 4 shows the Feel Design Editor (an authoring and playback interface) that allows users to create new haptic sensations or select and modify previously created sensations from the existing FE library and associate them to actions from the media.

DEMONSTRATION

The demo is interactive and engages up to six guests at one time. Figure 5 shows the demonstration layout. Guests sit on chairs with commercially available Marvel Avengers haptic pads (Vybe Haptic Gaming Pad, Comfort Research, USA). Guest A interacts with the authoring tool interface and generates new FEs or uses existing FEs from the library. Guest 1 sits by and interacts with guest A during media production process. Guest U plays the game with a hand controller and the multisensory experience is broadcasted to guests 2-4 sitting on gaming pads waiting for their turns. Host H explains the demonstration and interacts with guests.

Figure 5 also highlights interactions spaces for the demonstration. Two gaming pads are attached to a computer running the game, plugin and Feel Design Editor (space I), while the remaining gaming pads are connected to a wireless hub (space III), which receives the broadcasted haptic media. One monitor screen shows the authoring tool

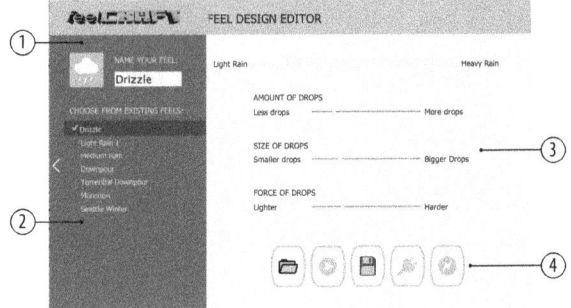

Figure 4. FeelCraft Design Editor. (1) FE Library, (2) presets, (3) authoring interface and (4) control interface

and the other screen shows the game. The game is also projected on a wall for stand-by, passing-by and engaged guests G (space II).

Our plugin runs on a PC and monitors actions, states and events from a popular sandbox indie game "Minecraft" (*https://minecraft.net/*). It extracts six recurring events from the game and associates them with six FEs from the families in the FE library. Guests can play FEs, tune them, make new FEs, save them and broadcast them for other guests for this entertaining and exciting sensory experience.

Figure 5. Installation at UIST

REFERENCES

1. D-BOX Technologies Inc., http://www.d-box.com/

2. Farley, H. & Steel, C. A quest for the Holy Grail: Tactile precision, natural movement and haptic feedback in 3D virtual spaces. In *Same places, different spaces. Proc. ASCILITE Aukland (*2009), 285-295.

3. Immersion Corporation. http://www.immersion.com/

4. Israr, A. *et al.* Surround Haptics: Sending Shivers Down Your Spine. *E-tech ACM SIGGRAPH* (2011).

5. Israr, A., Zhao, S., Schwalje, K., Klatzky, R., and Lehman, J. 2014. Feel Effects: Enriching Storytelling with Haptic Feedback. ACM Trans. Appl. Percept. 17 pages (in press).

6. Waltl, M., Rainer, B., Timmerer, C., and Hellwagner, H. A toolset for the authoring, simulation, and rendering of sensory experiences. In *Proc. International Conference on Multimedia.* AMC Press (2012), 1469-1472.

SikuliBot: Automating Physical Interface Using Images

Jeeeun Kim   **Michael Kasper**   **Tom Yeh**   **Nikolaus Correll**

Computer Science, University of Colorado, Boulder

430 UCB, Boulder, CO 80309, USA

{Jeeeun.Kim, Michael.Kasper, Tom.Yeh, Nikolaus.Correll}@colorado.edu

ABSTRACT

We present SikuliBot, an image-based approach to automating user interface. SikuliBot extends the visual programming concept of Sikuli Script[2] from the graphical UIs to the real world of physical UIs, such as mobile devices' touch-screens and hardware buttons. The key to our approach is using a physical robot to see an interface, identify a target, and perform an action on the target using the robot's actuators. We demonstrate working examples on MakerBot 3D printer that could move a stylus to perform multi-touch gestures on touchscreen to automate tasks such as swipe-to-unlock, playing a virtual piano, and playing the Angry Bird game. A wide range of automation possibilities are made viable using a simple scripting language based on images of UI components. The benefits of our approach are: generalizability, instrumentation-free, and high-level programming abstraction.

Author Keywords: Automation; Robotics; Visual Programming; Tangible User Interfaces

ACM Classification Keywords

H.5.m. Information interfaces and presentation

INTRODUCTION

Physical user interface is the most traditional type of user interface, such as pressing buttons to enter a number to a calculator, moving a slider to control volume. Modern personal computing devices tend to be a mix of physical and graphical interfaces. iPhone, for instance, has a touchscreen (physical), a home button (physical), and can run a wide variety of app each of which has a unique interface (graphical). UI automation is a paradigm for automating machines or devices at the interface level rather than at the underlying hardware level. For GUI, a variety of UI level automation tools have been developed, such as Chickenfoot [1] for web automation and Sikuli [2] for general-purpose pixel-based automation. These tools allow users to express their automation intent based on how they would do it manually themselves through an interface The UI automation paradigm is difficult to apply to devices or machines whose user interface is physical. We propose SikuliBot, a new approach to automating physical UI using images of real-world widgets. To apply the same concept of Sikuli,

UIST'14 Adjunct, October 5–8, 2014, Honolulu, HI, USA.
ACM 978-1-4503-3068-8/14/10.
http://dx.doi.org/10.1145/2658779.2659110

automating GUI to a physical UI, we need to replace the software robot with a physical one, which can see a physical UI and simulate physical actions.

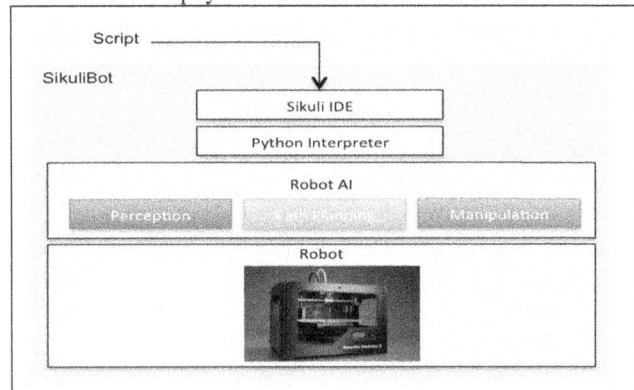

Figure 1. SikuliBot is automating physical UI by allowing users to write simple scripts using images of UI components.

APPROACH: SIKULI BOT

The basic operation unit of UI automation is a pair of target and action. The target refers to a user interface widget and the action refers to an input operation to be performed automatically on the widget. User can express the automating intention on a physical UI by writing a unary function that carries the name of the action and supplying the function with an image of that as an argument, such as click(🗑). It takes trash bin icon as target, invokes a findall() operations, do task to the entire array result.

SYSTEM ARCHITECTURE

SikuliBot has four major layers (see Figure 1). At the topmost level, a user composes a visual script over IDE, which is adaption of Sikuli Script, by capturing images and import them into a script. SikuliBot's functions are interpreted as Python modules, implementing the underlying robot AI routines to carry out the high-level automation. These AI routines roughly fall into three categories: (1) *perception,* seeing the interface and finding target, (2) *path planning,* finding a way for the robot to reach the target, and (3) *manipulation,* executing physical actions on the target, such as press, touch, and drag. AI routines are loaded to a robot, running them and carry desired automations to interact with a target physical user interface. We present MakerBot as the first manipulation of SikuliBot.

IDE

IDE captures an image representation of a target and use it in a script to refer to an UI element, by capturing image pixels from target region. Makerbot takes a digital photo of the target and import the photo in the IDE. This photo of the target is imported to IDE, working as target.

ROBOT: MAKERBOT

Image processing is performed on a separate computer, since the MakerBot does not have processing power other than what is necessary to control 3D printing. We attached the camera to conveyor bar, which is stationary, in order to see and detect visual interface placed on the print base. Stylus is used to implement touch gestures on the screen, attached to print head. (see Figure 2.)

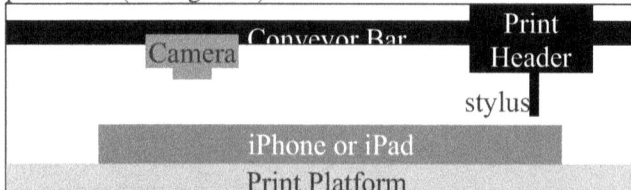

Figure 2. MakerBot's setting to see and detect interface, and execute automating task on the physical interface.

Programmatic control of the MakerBot is achieved through G-code, a widely used CNC programming language that can be understood by the MakerBot. G-code commands that could perform the desired movement is generated dynamically and transmitted to the MakerBot to execute. A camera is attached right next to the print head facing downward to the print platform to observe.

GESTURES AND AUTOMATION APPLICATIONS

We applied our approach to a wide variety of physical UI with same gestures to assess our approach's generalizability across many types of interface while staying instrumentation free.

Press, Drag & Drop: Physical home button and Slider

```
Press (   )
dragDrop(   ,   )
```
http://youtu.be/sbQQfM0qTdA

In this example, the automation intent is to press the home button, a physical UI. Given an button image, SikuliBot finds the area looks like the home button, through a camera. Once the target is found, it executes a "press" action by bringing the print head to a 2D position where attached stylus is above. Then, it raises the printing base. Finally, the platform is lowered until the stylus is no longer in contact with the home button, thereby completing the press action, and Drag & Drop the slider icon to play swipe to unlock.

Press, Drag & Drop: Play a Piano

```
for x in [ A4 , B4 , F4 ]
  press(x)
press( F4 .front(10).right(5))
press( F5 )
dragDrop( G5 , E4 )
```
http://youtu.be/-YLrG8VvMuM

In this example, the challenge is to play piano keys that are visually ambiguous but have setting to display a "symbol" on each key (e.g., A4, B4), which is distinctive to match, through physical contact. SikuliBot first iterates through an array of three notes and press each note. Then SikuliBot script intends to play the note F4#, a black key. There is no symbol on the black key, so SikuliBot locates the symbol F4 nearby and uses spatial operators front and right, to locate to the desired black key. Finally, SikuliBot completes playing with *Glissando* from E4 to G5, using a dragDrop.

Drag & Drop: Play Angry Bird

```
dragDrop(   ,   )
dragDrop(   ,   )
dragDrop(   ,   )
```
http://youtu.be/WXrnyc9Gubk

Sikuli Script has been used to play a wide range of games. For instance, one user has managed beat Map 1 to 4 of Angry Bird (http://youtu.be/GzKII3nssP8). SikuliBot can also play Angry Bird physically. In this example, three birds are available, so we hard coded a dragDrop action for each bird with enough time of waiting before launching the next bird. Without any complex logic, and just by luck, the map can be beat about one out of ten times.

Press, Drag & Drop: Type a Keyboard

```
for x in [ E , G , G , ?123 ]:
  press(x)
longpress( w )
dragTo( S )
```
http://vimeo.com/91805153

iPad provides an extended keyboard layout on a long press. Each key requires an image, so we built a library of key images of all possible characters and access them through a Hash table, where a key is a character and a value is the character's image. This library can then be imported and reused by other scripts that interact with physical keyboard.

CONCLUSION

We presented Sikulibot, a new automating physical UI by image-based scripts such as buttons that can be used as arguments for acting pres. We demonstrated a series of examples to demonstrate our approach's applicability to Makerbot, over a wide range of physical UI.

REFERENCES

[1] Bolin, Michael, Matthew Webber, Philip Rha, Tom Wilson, and Robert C. Miller. 2005. Automation and customization of rendered web pages. In Proceedings of the 18th annual ACM symposium on User interface software and technology (UIST '05). ACM, New York, NY, USA, 163-172.

[2] Yeh, T., Tsung-Hsiang Chang, and Robert C. Miller. Sikuli: using GUI screenshots for search and automation. In Proceedings of the 22nd annual ACM symposium on User interface software and technology (UIST '09)

THAW: Tangible Interaction with See-Through Augmentation for Smartphones on Computer Screens

Sang-won Leigh   **Philipp Schoessler**   **Felix Heibeck**   **Pattie Maes**   **Hiroshi Ishii**

{sangwon, phil_s, heibeck, pattie, ishii }@media.mit.edu

MIT Media Lab, 75 Amherst Street, Cambridge, MA, United States

Figure 1: A smartphone screen can be used as a user interface intervening into the display space of a computer screen.

ABSTRACT

In this paper, we present a novel interaction system that allows a collocated large display and small handheld devices to seamlessly work together. The smartphone acts both as a physical interface and as an additional graphics layer for near-surface interaction on a computer screen. Our system enables accurate position tracking of a smartphone placed on or over any screen by displaying a 2D color pattern that is captured using the smartphone's back-facing camera. The proposed technique can be implemented on existing devices without the need for additional hardware.

Author Keywords

Multi-device Interaction; Tangible Magic Lens;

ACM Classification Keywords

H.5.2 User Interfaces: Input devices and strategies (e.g., mouse, touchscreen)

INTRODUCTION

A growing number of people own a smartphone in addition to their computer. The collocated interaction with those devices poses the question of how to seamlessly connect the different display spaces and their afforded interactions.

The physical body of the smartphone affords tangible manipulation, while the screens on both devices can display virtual graphics that augment or interact with each other. If the interaction between the devices happens in close proximity, the graphics on each device and the phone's physicality in combination with our strong visual-motor skills bridges the gap between spatial reality and the digital.

UIST'14 Adjunct, October 5–8, 2014, Honolulu, HI, USA.
ACM 978-1-4503-3068-8/14/10.
http://dx.doi.org/10.1145/2658779.2659111

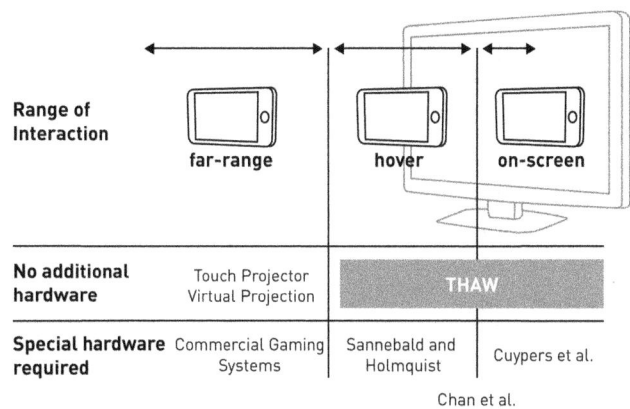

Figure 2. Systems based on tracking of handheld devices

Prior Augmented Reality (AR) styled interaction systems explored interactions between a phone and a computer screen over a distance, however, none thoroughly explored near surface (on-screen) interactions. This is mainly because the proposed tracking techniques require a certain distance between the devices to work properly [1, 2] or special tracking hardware / setups as seen in [3, 4, 5]. (Figure 2)

In this paper we present THAW (Tangible, Handheld, and Augmented Window), a system that enables near-surface interaction with ordinary computer displays and smartphones without any necessary hardware modifications. We also present a framework that explains and classifies possible interactions.

IMPLEMENTATION

The very close distance from the smartphone to the screen (< 2cm) makes conventional feature-based tracking impossible due to the camera's lack of near-focusing capability and limited field of view (FOV). In our system, a computer screen displays a distinct color pattern. The phone's back-facing camera detects the pixels' color shown on the screen behind the phone. Sampled points are used to infer the phone's position from the RGB values through linear transformation. Calibration needs to be performed only once per device (Figure 3). Additionally, by comparing two frames' color delta we can measure the smartphone to screen distance reliably up to 15 cm.

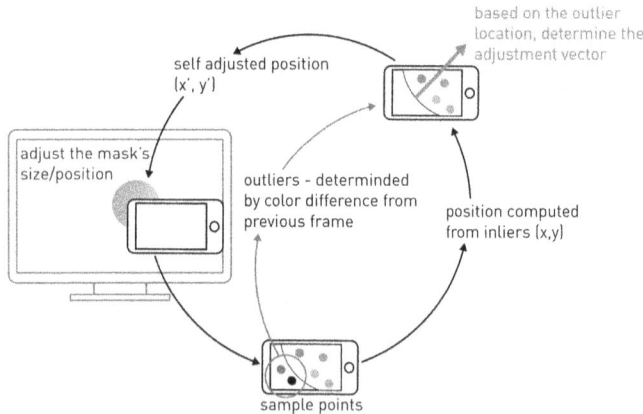

Figure 3. Sequence diagram of the tracking algorithm

Non-invasive Tracking

One advantage of using a dynamically displayed tracking pattern is its adjustability. It is sufficient for the pattern to only be visible in the camera's FOV to achieve continuous tracking. Therefore, we can hide the pattern in the area occluded by the phone, which allows tracking without sacrificing valuable information space.

INTERACTION

Here we present a framework for classifying possible interactions with our system (Figure 4). The phone can be used as a physical token to directly interact with digital entities based on their relative positions (Figure 4(a-b)). It can act as a lens for controlling or augmenting objects on a computer screen (Figure 4(c)) and also offers an additional space to be used for extended control or as a physical clipboard. (Figure 4(d)). The presented interactions can be used in combination or interchangeably, thus enabling variable combinations of tangible interaction and see-through augmentation.

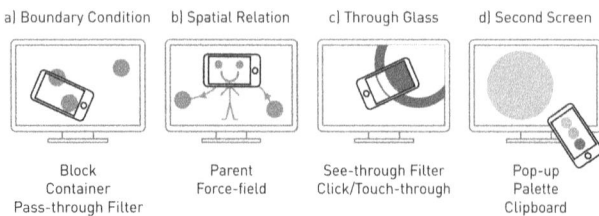

Figure 4. Categories of interaction

DEMO APPLICATIONS

See-through Mouse

We use the phone as an advanced see-through mouse tool. The phone serves both as a tangible clipboard and a see-through touch tool, enabling intuitive drag/drop or copy/paste of digital content (Figure 5). This largely extends the modality of a conventional mouse, enabling more sophisticated functionality such as opening a web link on the mouse or performing kinetic gestures.

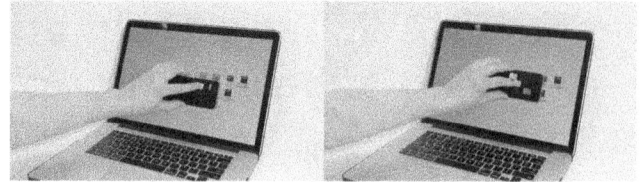

Figure 5. Seeing and touching through the smartphone

Game

We developed a simple game in which the goal is to help the character reach the flag. The smartphone acts as an active controller that can be used to physically intervene in the gameplay (Figure 1). Players have to choose different strategies to clear each stage, which is designed to showcase a specific interaction or a mix of interactions of our framework. It is notable that, in each stage, the phone is perceived to have versatile physicality through showing different uses of visual augmentation and interactions. This potentially promises countless more novel gaming scenarios than the ones presented here.

CONCLUSION

In this paper, we proposed an easy to deploy technology as well as interaction scenarios to better utilize the near-range interaction space on and above computer screens with smartphones. The combination of AR and Tangible User Interfaces (TUI) enables versatile user interfaces for context-aware seamless interactions. As a growing number of people own these two complementary devices, we believe that our system can unlock the potential of those collocated technologies in the immediate future and contributes an easy to deploy near surface interaction technology.

REFERENCES

1. Baur, D., Boring, S. and Feiner, S. Virtual Projection: exploring optical projection as a metaphor for multi-device interaction. In Proceedings of CHI'12. ACM.

2. Boring, S. et al. 2010. Touch projector: mobile interaction through video. Proceedings of the SIGCHI Conference on Human Factors in Computing Systems (New York, NY, USA, 2010), 2287–2296.

3. Chan, L.-W., Wu, H.-T., Kao, H.-S., Ko, J.-C., Lin, H.-R., Chen, M. Y., Hsu, J., and Hung, Y.-P. Enabling beyond-surface interactions for interactive surface with an invisible projection. In Proc. ACM UIST '10 (2010), 263–272.

4. T. Cuypers, Y. Francken, C. Vanaken, F. V. Reeth, and P. Bekaert. Smartphone localization on interactive surfaces using the built-in camera. In Proc. Procams, pages 61–68, 2009.

5. Sanneblad, J. and Holmquist, L.E. Ubiquitous Graphics: Combining Hand-held and Wall-size Displays to Interact with Large Images. ACM AVI Conference on Advanced Visual Interfaces 2006.

Projectron Mapping:The Exercise and Extension of Augmented Workspaces for Learning Electronic Modeling through Projection Mapping

Yoh Akiyama
Meiji University
Nakano, Tokyo, Japan
akyoh9933@gmail.com

Homei Miyashita
Meiji University and JST CREST
Nakano, Tokyo, Japan
homei@homei.com

ABSTRACT

There has been research using software simulations to support the learning of electronic modeling by beginners. There have also been systems to extend workspaces and support electronic modeling on tabletop interfaces. However, in the case of software-based circuit operation, as it is not possible to operate the actual elements, the feeling of actually moving the elements is lacking. For this reason, we are proposing a system that extends the sense of reality in software simulators through the use of projection mapping. This will make it possible to actually give the impression of moving the elements by using a software simulator, and to achieve both high speed and a sense of reality through trial and error.

Author Keywords

Projection Mapping; Electronics; Pseudo Lighting Understanding Electricity; Tangible user interface;

ACM Classification Keywords

H.5.m. Information Interfaces and Presentation (e.g. HCI): Miscellaneous

INTRODUCTION

The complexity of trial and error is an obstacle to beginners looking to learn electronic modeling. With trial and error, it is necessary to perform the same kind of hard-wired work, and that hard wiring itself may take a significant amount of time. A software simulator is one means of improving the speed of the trial and error process. However, with the illumination of elements in software, the sense of reality pales in comparison to the illumination of actual elements.

Therefore, we are proposing an augmented workspace that can extend the sense of reality in a software simulator. Using projection mapping, the real elements can be extended as if they are in operation. By using a touch panel display and projector in the system, it is possible to achieve both learning support and a sense of reality with the software. By using projection mapping to make the elements appear as though

UIST'14 Adjunct, October 5–8, 2014, Honolulu, HI, USA.
ACM 978-1-4503-3068-8/14/10.
http://dx.doi.org/10.1145/2658779.2659113

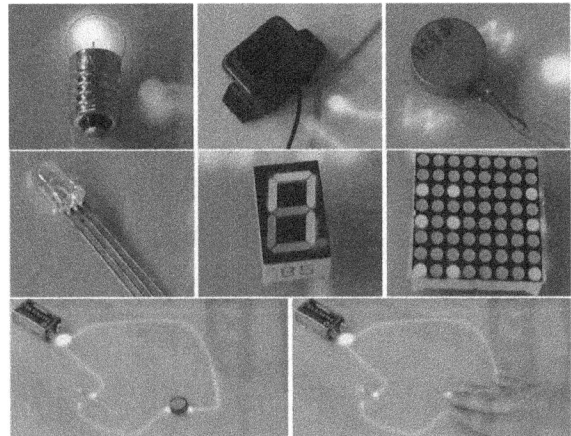

Figure 1. Electronic kits using projection mapping

they are actually shining, as shown in Figure 1, an intense experience is provided to the user. Furthermore, a tangible interface is used so that trial and error can be carried out at high speeds as in the software simulator. The user can create circuits using a drag operation.

RELATED WORKS

Fritzing[3] and CCK[4] have adopted the approach of using software simulators to study electronic modeling. Fritzing carried out simulations by creating circuits using a software bread board. CCK, rather than a breadboard, is a tool that can freely create circuits to perform trial and error. In this way, trial and error can be attempted at high speeds using a software simulator. Furthermore, Conradi et al. extended the electronic modeling workspace in software, and proposed a Flow of Electrons in which electronic modeling takes place on a tabletop interface [2]. Conradi et al. stated that a tool kit was essential for supporting beginners and that an augmented workspace should be prepared, as well. However, software simulators, including Flow of Electrons, have been unable to provide an intense experience in which there is the "enjoyment of actual elements moving." Therefore, we propose an augmented workspace that extends the feeling of reality in software simulators using projection mapping.

APPLICATIONS

The user can perform hard-wiring by pulling a virtual jumper wire through a drag operation, without using an actual lead. The virtual jumper wire can be disconnected with a touch

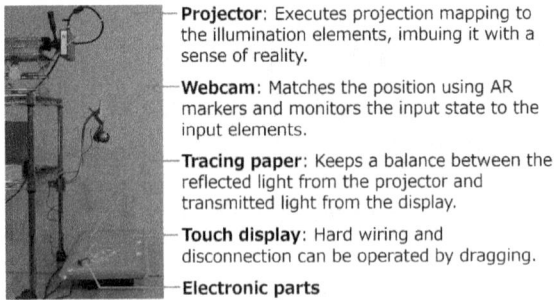

- **Projector**: Executes projection mapping to the illumination elements, imbuing it with a sense of reality.
- **Webcam**: Matches the position using AR markers and monitors the input state to the input elements.
- **Tracing paper**: Keeps a balance between the reflected light from the projector and transmitted light from the display.
- **Touch display**: Hard wiring and disconnection can be operated by dragging.
- **Electronic parts**

Figure 2. System

gesture as if you were snapping the wire. The currently supported elements are shown in Figure 1.

A touch panel display is installed horizontally and a projector is placed in the top section (Figure 2). The projector is fixed in a position so that the display range of the projector is exactly the same as the display. The web camera is installed in a position so that the entire display can be seen. The projector is mirrored on the display so that the position of the touch panel and the display location of the projector are matched.

Input system

Input into this system is operated by the two operations of both the fingers via the touch panel display and, using the camera, an exaggerated operation in which the touch panel is not touched with the fingers but uses image recognition. The former is used for installation of virtual elements and hard wiring and disconnection of circuits. The latter is used for grasping the state of input elements, such as switches and variable resistance, etc. As the pixels in which elements exist can be obtained from the camera image, AR markers can be used to match the positions of the display area for the display and the camera image. Skin recognition is carried out using the hsv surface colors, and it is then determined whether there is input to the device. The switch state is reflected in the circuit state using image recognition (Figure 1).

Projection mapping from the top

By carrying out projection mapping on output elements and light elements in particular, it is possible to make it look as though they are actually moving even if they are not actually electrically connected. It is not necessary to carry out projection mapping for all illuminated areas of the elements, and if projected in a way so that the illuminated areas overlap to a certain extent, it can appear as if they are illuminated. If the elements are specularly reflected, the area that you wish to illuminate may be artificially lit even if they are transparent. In the case of miniature lamps, as particles are displayed around the area that is being artificially lit, through projection of the illumination area using a single color, illumination with a sense of reality has been successfully achieved. Figure 1 shows the implementation results when projection mapping on to the illuminated elements using the respective proposed systems.

By projection mapping from above, the lower touch panel display is increased. Therefore, it is necessary to maintain a bal-

ance between the reflective light from the projector and the transmitted light from the display. For this reason, by laying tracing paper over the top of the display, a balance is maintained between the reflected and transmitted light. In this way, even if the projection is covered with a hand, it is possible to display the wiring state via the transmitted light from the display. This has almost no effect on touch input even via the tracing paper.

Other output systems

The system rings an operating noise from the PC to express ringing of the buzzer or vibrator. In addition, the system displays an animation around the vibrator that makes it appear that it is shaking. Projection mapping is not carried out on batteries; however, it becomes the starting point for an electrical conductivity check within the program. The circuit simulator is linked to the Circuit Simulator Applet[1]. As there is a bug in the external simulator, a simple circuit judgment program can be integrated into the system to handle switchovers at necessary times.

DISCUSSION

We believe that the proposed system combines both a sense of reality in which the elements are actually moving and a high speed software simulator. It is felt that illumination of the actual elements provides beginners with the impression and experience of elements actually moving, by illuminating the elements of the simulator within the display. Furthermore, as hard wiring and disconnecting is performed by dragging, as with a simulator, trial and error can be carried out simply.

We plan to further extend the electronic modelling environment using projection mapping. Currently, projection uses a single color. However, the actual elements are not illuminated equally. By performing gradation that matches the shape of the elements for projection mapping, we believe that projection mapping with an increased sense of reality can take place. Furthermore, we feel that by projecting the reflected light around the element with the projector, photo-real projection mapping can take place. Additionally, as there are few varieties of elements that are supported, we think that it will be necessary to increase the number of supported elements moving forward.

REFERENCES

1. Circuit Simulator Applet
   `http://www.falstad.com/circuit/`

2. Conradi, B., Lerch, V., Hommer, M., Kowalski, R., Vletsou, I., and Hussmann , H. Flow of Electrons: An Augmented Workspace for Learning Physical Computing Experientially. Proceedings of the ACM International Conference on Interactive Tabletops and Surfaces, pp.182-191, 2011.

3. Knrig, A., Wettach, R., and Cohen, J. Fritzing: a tool for advancing electronic prototyping for designers. Proceedings of the 3rd International Conference on Tangible and Embedded Interaction, pp.351-358 ,2009.

4. Wieman, C.E. and Perkins, K. K. A powerful tool for teaching science. Nature Physics 2, 5, pp.290-292, 2006.

Extension Sticker: A Method for Transferring External Touch Input Using a Striped Pattern Sticker

Kunihiro Kato
Meiji University
Nakano, Tokyo, Japan
kunihiro162@gmail.com

Homei Miyashita
Meiji University
Nakano, Tokyo, Japan
homei@homei.com

ABSTRACT

A method for transferring external touch input is proposed by partially attaching a sticker to a touch-panel display. The touch input area can be extended by printing striped patterns using a conductive ink and attaching them to overlap with a portion of a touch-panel display. Even if the user does not touch the touch panel directly, a touch event can be generated by touching the stripes at an arbitrary point corresponding to the touched area. Thus, continuous touch input can be generated, such as a scrolling operation without interruption. This method can be applied to a variety of devices including PCs, smartphones, and wearable devices. In this paper, we present several different examples of applications, including a method for extending control areas outside of the touch panel, such as the side or back of a smartphone (Figure. 1).

Author Keywords

Striped pattern sticker; continuous touch input; conductive ink; capacitive touch panel.

ACM Classification Keywords

H.5.2 Information Interfaces and Presentation: User Interfaces Input Devices and Strategies.

INTRODUCTION

Mobile devices with touch-panel displays such as tablets and smartphones are widespread; users can instinctively operate these devices by touching the display with their finger. Many tangible interfaces on touch-panel displays have been explored. The interface on a capacitive touch panel was introduced by Rekimoto [1]. In addition, interfaces may operate on the touch-panels in CapStones and Clip-on gadgets, and other studies have been carried out on the interfaces of these devices to extend the operation of the touch panel [2] [3]. However, although studies have been proposed, the environment that allows a user to create an interface requiring the user himself has not yet been realized.

UIST'14 Adjunct, Oct 05-08 2014, Honolulu, HI, USA.
ACM 978-1-4503-3068-8/14/10.
http://dx.doi.org/10.1145/2658779.2668032

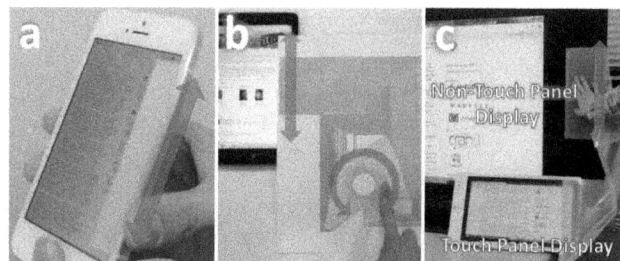

Figure 1. a) Smartphone side-input controls, b) rotation-scrolling control conversion, and c) touch controls for non-touch-panel displays

Recently, conductive ink used in prototyping has been attracting attention. In the Instant inkjet circuits proposed by Kawahara, a conductive ink was used for prototyping the circuits and sensors [4]. In addition, PrintSense has been used to create touch sensors [5].

In this study, we focused on the conductive ink and proposed a method for transferring external touch input by partially attaching a sticker to a touch-panel display. By attaching a sticker printed with a striped pattern using a conductive ink, devices may be operated without directly touching the display. By extending the striped pattern outside the display, the user can use any surface including the back or sides of a smartphone, the surface of a desk, or even the walls of a room as a touch-capable interface. Furthermore, this method is not only ON-OFF control of touch input but allows for continuous touch input such as scrolling within the scope of the attached sticker (Figure. 1).

PROPOSED METHOD

General touch-panel displays are controlled with input using human fingers. Therefore, one point can be recognized by touching an area the size of a human finger, but a touch input will not be generated if the touch area is a small point or a line less than 1 mm in width. In this paper, we propose a method for generating touch input by placing multiple lines that are too thin to be recognized by the touch-panel at intervals of a few millimeters. The user attaches the stickers with striped patterns printed using a conductive ink onto the edge of the display (Figure. 2). By touching one side of the sticker, the user can transfer the touch input to the display attached to the other side of the sticker. In addition, touch input can be generated by touching a number of closely spaced lines less than 1 mm in width. Therefore, the finger in contact with the lines of the striped pattern will be activated in order when the

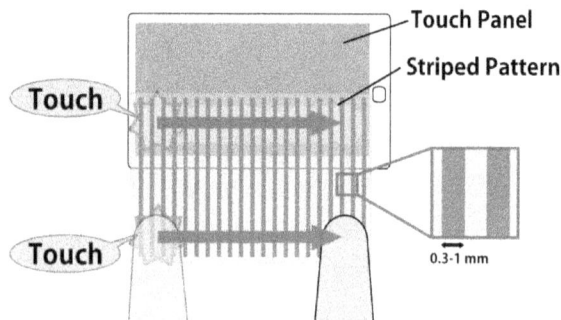

Figure 2. Striped Pattern Using a Conductive Ink

user slides his finger on the sticker. Thus, continuous touch input such as scrolling is generated without interruption.

APPLICATION EXAMPLES
In this section, we discuss examples of applications using the proposed method. Changing the form of the touch input area allows a user to create a variety of touch interfaces.

Smartphone Side-Input Controls
Stickers with striped patterns printed using a conductive ink are attached to the sides of the display and side surface of the smartphone. In this way, the user can touch the side of the smartphone to scroll and view a browser or other applications without obscuring the screen with a finger (Figure. 1a). By extending the striped pattern to the back of the smartphone, back-panel touch input can be realized for use in applications. Alternatively, the stickers could be applied to the sides of a smartwatch display equipped with a touch panel and to the watch band, thereby allowing the device to be controlled by touching the band.

Rotation-Scrolling Control Conversion
Rotation controls can be converted to scrolling controls by attaching a striped pattern printed with lines arranged in a circle, as shown in Figure. 1b. This makes it possible to create a wheel mechanism that allows for scrolling by simply attaching a sticker to a smartphone or tablet. This could be used to realize a jog dial that recreates the classic iPod controls on an iPhone.

Touch Controls for Non-Touch Panel Displays
It is possible to adjust the touch input speed difference by changing the spacing of the stripes on the input and output sides. Thus, a touch input operation using the user's hand can be converted to a touch input of fingertip size. For example, a smartphone or tablet is attached to a large non-touch-panel display and displays a reproduction of the image. By attaching the sticker onto these two displays, it is possible to scroll the side of the large non-touch-panel display by hand. Figure 1c shows the transference of touch input from the sticker attached to the large non-touch-panel display to the tablet device.

Applications for Other Devices and Equipment
This method can be applied to a variety of other devices equipped with capacitive touch panels. For example, the method could be used for a digital camera with touch-panel zoom controls. When users touch a digital camera, they tend to press the body of the camera strongly, which can shift the camera's position. By using this method to extend the touch panel to the camera's tripod, we could realize more stable controls. Air-conditioner controllers have also used touch panels in recent years, and these controllers are often located on a wall where they cannot be moved. Using this method, the user interface could be brought from the panel to the sofa or another location following the wall or floor. Because thin materials such as paper are used, they could be attached to the back of the carpeting or wallpaper. The method also allows for free design interaction with daily-use objects.

CONCLUSION
In this paper, we reported a method for transferring external touch input by using a conductive ink.

Although the portion of the display covered by the pattern is difficult to see, the touch area could be extended without reducing the display visibility by using transparent materials such as a transparent conductive ink. In addition, the printed surface is degraded while using the interface because we have used a conductive ink to create the stickers; thus, it is necessary to consider more appropriate materials.

Presently, the touch input can only be controlled in a single axial direction, but we hope to create a mechanism for controlling touch input at an arbitrary point in an x-y plane via future improvements. The examples in this paper are only a portion of the total number of applications. Because this method can be used with a variety of devices equipped with capacitive touch panels, we expect that it can be used in a wide variety of applications.

REFERENCES
1. Jun Rekimoto: SmartSkin: An Infrastructure for Freehand Manipulation on Interactive Surfaces, In *Proc. CHI'02*, pp.113-120, 2002.

2. Neng-Hao Yu, Sung-Sheng Tsai, I-Chun Hsiao, Dian-Je Tsai, Meng-Han Lee, Mike Y. Chen, Yi-Ping Hung: Clip-on Gadgets: Expanding Multi-touch Interaction Area with Unpowered Tactile Controls, In *Proc. UIST'11*, pp.367-372, 2011.

3. Liwei Chun, Stefanie Muller, Anne Roudaut, Patrick Baudisch: CapStones and ZebraWidgets: Sensing Stacks of Building Blocks, Dials and Sliders on Capacitive Touch Screens, In *Proc. CHI'12*, pp.2189-2192, 2012.

4. Yoshihiro Kawahara, Steve Hodges, Benjamin S. Cook, Cheng Zhang, and Gregory D. Abowd: Instant Inkjet Circuits: Lab-based Inkjet Printing to Support Rapid Prototyping of UbiComp Devices, In *Proc. UbiComp'13*, pp.363-372, 2013.

5. Nan-Wei Gong, Jürgen Steimle, Simon Olberding, Steve Hodges, Nicholas Gillian, Yoshihiro Kawahara, Joseph A.Paradiso: PrintSense: A Versatile Sensing Technique to Support Multimodal Flexible Surface Interaction, In *Proc. CHI'14*, pp.1407-1410, 2014.

LiveSphere: Immersive Experience Sharing with 360 degrees Head-mounted Cameras

Shunichi Kasahara
Sony CSL
Shinagawa, Tokyo, Japan
kasahara@csl.sony.co.jp

Shohei Nagai
The University of Tokyo
Shinagawa, Tokyo, Japan
shohei.nagai14@gmail.com

Jun Rekimoto
The University of Tokyo, Sony CSL
Shinagawa, Tokyo, Japan
rekimoto@acm.org

ABSTRACT

Sharing full immersive experience in real-time has been the one of ultimate goals of telecommunication. Possible application can include various applications such as entertainment, sports viewing, education, social network and professional assistance.

Recent head-worn wearable camera enables to shoot the first person video, however, view of angle is limited with the head direction of the person who is wearing, and also captured video is shaky that makes us dizzy.

We propose LiveSphere, immersive experience sharing system with wearable camera headgear that provide 360 degrees spherical images of the user's surrounding environment. LiveSphere system performs spherical video stabilization and transmits it to other users, so that they are enable to view shared video comfortably and also look around at the scene from a different view angle independently from the first person. In this note, we explain the overview of the LiveSphere system implementation, stabilization and viewing experience.

Author Keywords

First person view streaming; 360 degrees spherical image; wearable computer;

ACM Classification Keywords

H.5.1. Information Interfaces and Presentation (e.g. HCI): Multimedia Information Systems

INTRODUCTION

Completely sharing or recording one's experience is one of the ultimate goals of telecommunication. As envisioned by the SF movie Brainstorm [1], immersive experience sharing can have very broad applications including an entertainment and content distribution (i.e., the audience can share the view from professional sports player), and communication and teaching (i.e., an expert can share the surrounding scene of the person who is doing a task, and gives proper and context-aware guidance).

UIST'14 Adjunct, October 5–8, 2014, Honolulu, HI, USA.
ACM 978-1-4503-3068-8/14/10.
http://dx.doi.org/10.1145/2658779.2659114

Figure 1. LiveSphere headgear captures 360 degrees images of the user's surrounding scene.

Recently a small wide-angle camera (GoPro or action cameras) has been popular, and people can attach it to his/her body to record a movie from his/her viewpoint. However, when it is used for experience sharing, the view angle of these cameras is still limited and it is difficult to watch the scene from a different direction. Also when such a camera is mounted on the user's head, his/her head-motion would also cause image shaking that it would be cumbersome to the viewer. One possible solution to these problems is merging images from the head-worn camera to create a pseudo wider view [2], but it is not robust.

Then we introduce LiveSphere, an experience sharing system with head-worn cameras that provides 360 degrees images of the user's surrounding environment. We embed multiple cameras within a form-factor of a head band for comfortable wearability. Head-motion effect of 360 degrees images is compensated by analyzing image rotation, and is recorded or transmitted to another user. This second user can look around the shared scene of the first user with different view angle from the first user.

LIVESPHERE SYSTEM

LiveSphere consists of two parts (Figure 2). The first one is a head-worn device, called the headgear, for a person who is acting in a real-world environment (we refer this person the Body). The other part is a viewing device for another user who watches the Body's surrounding scene and might give guidance to the Body (we refer this user the Ghost). These two components are connected by a wireless network.

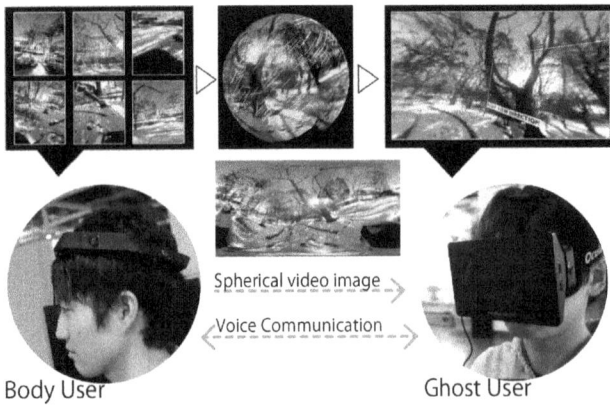

Figure 2. LiveSphere system configuration. A Body user wears the headgear and transmits surrounding scene images that are obtained from head-worn cameras. A Ghost user is allowed to look around stabilized 360 degree spherical streaming.

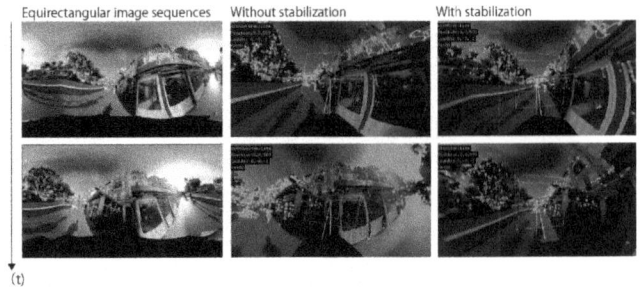

Figure 3. Rotate Motion Stabilization. In each frame, image feature points are extracted and tracked. The tracking motion are mapped into spherical coordinate, then quotation for the each video frame is estimated

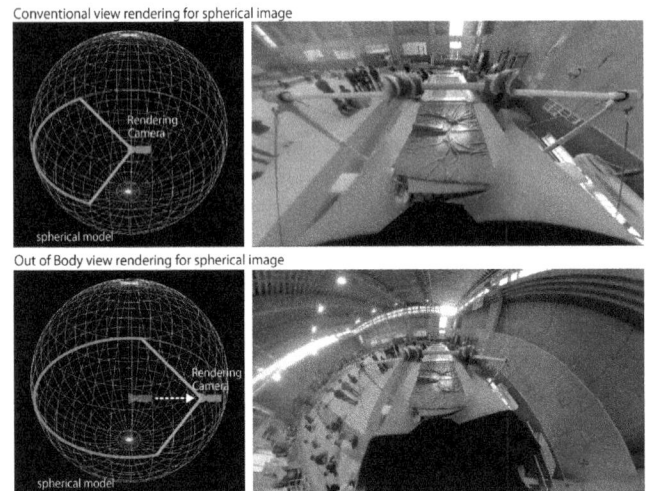

Figure 4. Out Of Body viewing experience .

The headgear has six wide-angle cameras. Each has 120 degrees horizontal and 90 degrees vertical fields of view and is connected to a laptop. Video images from these cameras are stitched together into a spherical video and image stabilization is performed. This image is streamed to the viewer device of the Ghost side. As viewing device, we both use a normal display and a head mounted display (Oculus rift). In the latter case, the Ghost can see the Body's 1st person view, with the freedom of looking around from the view direction of the Body. Adding to image sharing, voice communication between the Body and the Ghost is available

And also we developed a non realtime version of headgear which consists of six GoPro cameras and helmet to examine the stabilization for high resolution and high frame rate video. Six recorded videos are stitched together into a spherical video and analyzed afterward. Then LiveSphere system also can playback the spherical video with stabilization on the viewing device.

IMAGE STABILIZATION

Unlike a handheld camera, the first person video from the wearable camera contains intense movement due to user's physical motion such as nodding in the conversation, turning head in the walking, and sports activity, and these are unconscious and inevitable. Then if the Ghost just watches the image from the Body, he/she would suffer from image shaking and might feel motion sickness. Conventional video stabilization is to counteract distracting vibrations, however to solve this problem, stabilization should be also considered to cancel the intense motion caused by the first person.

In LiveSphere system, rotational motion in spherical video is estimated at each frame by tracking image feature points (Figure 3). By performing inverted rotation for spherical image rendering, rotational motion can be canceled and the video image can be seen spatially registered in spherical environment. With this image stabilization, the ghost would be able to see the Body's surrounding scene, but with Ghost's own view direction and look around the scene independently.

We examined this stabilization with various activities from walking in the town and beach, riding a motorcycle, gymnastics and bungee jumping. Then we confirmed that our stabilization algorithm works well even for intense sport motion as well as walking motion.

OUT-OF-BODY VIEWING

Adding to spatial registration of the spherical image, LiveSphere generates Out-of-Body view that the viewer can virtually look around as exocentric view, by sifting rendering camera for spherical video. This view gives the pseudo wider view from upper of first person body and shows embodiment motion of the body's head motion on top of the spherical view (Figure 4). In LiveSphere application, the Ghost user can manually switch Out-of-Body viewing and conventional first person view with smoothed rotational transition.

REFERENCES

1. Douglas Trumbull (director), "Brainstorm," Advanced Robotics, Metro-Goldwyn- Mayer, 1983.

2. L. Cheng and J.Robinson, Dealing with Speed and Robustness Issues for Video-Based Registration on a Wearable Computing Platform. In Proc. ISWC98, pp.84-91, 1998.

Nishanchi: CAD for hand-fabrication

Pragun Goyal
MIT Media Lab
Responsive Environments
75 Amherst St
E14-548
pragun@media.mit.edu

Pattie Maes
MIT Media Lab
Fluid Interfaces
75 Amherst St
E14-548G
pattie@media.mit.edu

Joseph A. Paradiso
MIT Media Lab
Responsive Environments
75 Amherst St
E14-548P
joep@media.mit.edu

ABSTRACT

We present Nishanchi, a position and orientation aware hand-held inkjet printer which can be used to transfer the reference marks from CAD to the workpiece for use in manual fabrication workflows. Nishanchi also has a digitizing tip that can be used to input features about the workpiece to a computer model. By allowing for this two-way exchange of information from CAD to a nonconcormal workpiece, we believe that Nishanchi might help make inclusion of CAD in manual fabrication workflows more seamless.

Author Keywords

Computer-Aided Design (CAD); Digital Fabrication; Printing

ACM Classification Keywords

H.5.m. Information Interfaces and Presentation (e.g. HCI): Miscellaneous

INTRODUCTION

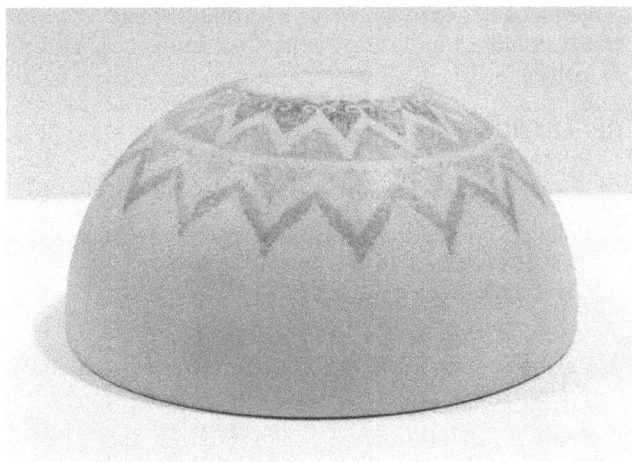

Figure 1. Final output: A CAD-Defined pattern printed by hand.

UIST'14 Adjunct, October 5–8, 2014, Honolulu, HI, USA.
ACM 978-1-4503-3068-8/14/10.
http://dx.doi.org/10.1145/2658779.2659116

Before the advent of NC (numeric machine) control, the designs for objects were described on paper in the form of blueprints and sketches. Elements from these designs would then often be copied on the workpiece for reference using pencils and/or stencils. CAD (Computer Aided Design) now allows for creating detailed designs in the form of computer models. However, CAD does not work seamlessly in manual fabrication workflows. One of the problems is the sudden change of medium from the workpiece to the computer and vice versa while taking features from the workpiece in the software and bringing design parameters back on the workpiece. Our work, Nishanchi [2], is a position and orientation aware handheld inkjet printer which can be used to transfer the reference marks from CAD to the workpiece. Nishanchi also has a digitizing tip that can be used to input features about the workpiece in a computer model. By allowing for this two-way exchange of information between CAD and the workpiece, we believe that Nishanchi might help make inclusion of CAD in manual fabrication workflows more seamless.

Our work is similar in spirit to [4] where the CAD design for a model is changed based on annotations made on the workpiece. Although Nishanchi can do this too, we also support the opposite mode, where mechanical operations are initiated in the computer and translated onto the workpiece. Our approach was inspired the approach used by [5] and [3], where the hand tool actuates automatically based on its position and orientation with respect to the workpiece. Our approach differs from other handheld inkjet printers, for example [1], in that Nisanchi is aware of its 3D position and orientation as well as the 3D form of the workpiece.

SYSTEM DESIGN

The Nishanchi system consists of a several components (Figure 3). A handset, (Figure 2, handheld device) that lets the user operate on the workpiece and the software; the software itself, which is in the form of a plugin for Rhinoceros 5.0 software and a Polhemus FASTRAK Magnetic Motion Tracking system (an AC 6D magnetic tracking system) to estimate the 3D position and 3D orientation of the handset.

Handset

The handset is made out of 3D printed plastic. The handset has an HP C6062 inkjet printhead to print on the workpiece. To allow the user to use the same device as a means to import features of the object into the computer, the handset is equipped with a pointed tip, which can be used like a 3D digitizing pen to input pointclouds into the CAD software. Further, the handset is mounted with two buttons that allow for the selection of operation mode: digitzing versus printing.

Tracking system

The tracking system has two parts: transmitter and reciever, and it gives the position and orientation of the receiver with respect to the transmitter. The transmitter is mounted to the workbench. The receiver is mounted on the handset. The digitizing tip and the inkjet nozzles on the handset are computed using the orientation and position given by the tracking system using simple 3D translations in the frame of reference of the handset.

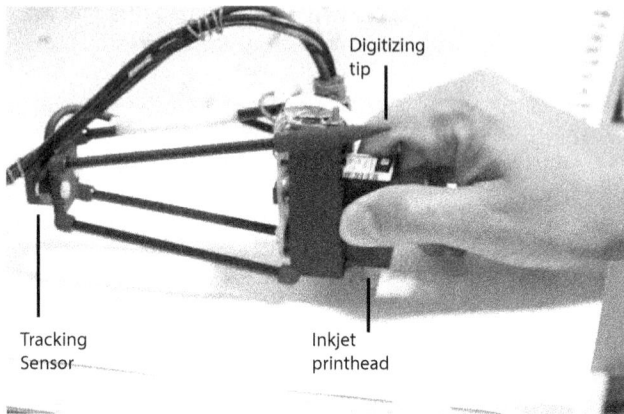

Figure 2. A photograph of a user using the Nishanchi handset to make a print.

Software

The software consists of a plugin written for Rhino (Rhinocerous 5.0 3D modeling software). Rhino was chosen for its support of standard CAD operations, and popular use in architecture and furniture design. The plugin has accesss to all the elements in the active document, and can introduce new elements in the document.

Print mode

The print mode allows the user to print a selected shape in Rhino on the object. The user moves the handset back and forth on the workpiece much like a paint roller to raster the desired area with the selected shape.

In this mode, the software plugin computes the nozzle trajectories for each tracking frame, and whether a nozzle trajectory intersects with the desired shape to be printed on the object. The nozzles that are within 20mm from the point of intersection are issued commands to fire. The trajectory of an ink droplet is modeled as a straight line originating from the nozzle. As this computation is to be done in realtime, the shapes are represented as wire-mesh, which allows for much faster computation of nozzle trajectories and surfaces; as compared to Rhino's native representation: NURBS.

Digitizing mode

The digitizing mode lets the user create a pointcloud scan of the workpiece. In digitizing mode, the plugin introduces a

new 3D point corresponding to the position of the digitizing tip in the active document for each tracking frame.

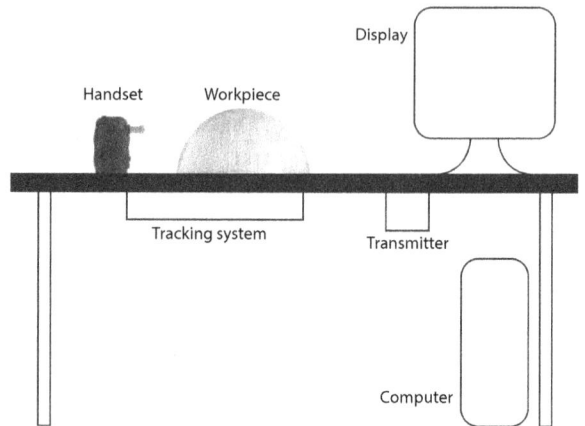

Figure 3. System

WORKFLOW AND CONCLUSIONS

The Nishanchi handheld printer was designed for the following workflow. 1. The user uses the digitizing tip to create a point cloud for the features of interest of the workpiece. 2. The user performs operations on the point cloud. 3. The user transfers the operations back to the workpiece.

This allows one to move design problems that are best solved in CAD to the computer, and then take the results back onto the workpiece, thus allowing one to include CAD in the fabrication workflow more seamlessly. We built a prototype device and used it in the described workflow on a test object: an IKEA wooden bowl to render a graphic on the bowl. This model also incorporates two microswitches for programmable user input (e.g., overriding computer control of the printhead, inserting markers not in the original CAD model, etc.).

REFERENCES

1. Printbrush 4x6 handheld printer. http://www.printdreams.com. Accessed: 2014-07-01.

2. Pragun, G. CAD Enabling Smart Handtools. Master's thesis, Massachusetts Institute of Technology, Cambridge, September 2014.

3. Rivers, A., Moyer, I. E., and Durand, F. Position-correcting tools for 2d digital fabrication. *ACM Trans. Graph. 31*, 4 (July 2012), 88:1–88:7.

4. Song, H., Guimbretière, F., and Lipson, H. The modelcraft framework: Capturing freehand annotations and edits to facilitate the 3d model design process using a digital pen. *ACM Trans. Comput.-Hum. Interact. 16*, 3 (Sept. 2009), 14:1–14:33.

5. Zoran, A., and Paradiso, J. A. Freed: a freehand digital sculpting tool. In *Proceedings of the SIGCHI Conference on Human Factors in Computing Systems*, ACM (2013), 2613–2616.

Enhancing Virtual Immersion through Tactile Feedback

Mounia Ziat
Northern Michigan University
Marquette, MI, 49855
mziat@nmu.edu

Taylor Rolison
Northern Michigan University
Marquette, MI, 49855
trolison@nmu.edu

Andrew Shirtz
Northern Michigan University
Marquette, MI, 49855
anshirtz@nmu.edu

Daniel Wilbern
Northern Michigan University
Marquette, MI, 49855
dwilbern@nmu.edu

Carrie Anne Balcer
Northern Michigan University
Marquette, MI, 49855
cabalcer@nmu.edu

ABSTRACT
The lack of tangibility while interacting with virtual objects can be compensated by adding haptic and/or tactile devices or actuators to enhance the user experience. In this demonstration, we present two scenarios that consist of perceiving moving objects on the human body (insects) and feeling physical sensations of virtual thermal objects.

Author Keywords
Tactile feedback; Oculus Rift; Temperature perception

ACM Classification Keywords
H.5.1. Multimedia Information Systems: Artificial, augmented, and virtual realities; H.5.2. User Interfaces: Haptic I/O

INTRODUCTION
Head-mounted displays are not only used in gaming and simulation, but also science, military defense, and perception research. More paticularly, the Oculus Rift offers a field of view (FOV) superior to 90 degrees that creates a great sense of immersion [5]. Despite this characteristic, the lack of tactile and proprioceptive feedback could affect and limit the virtual interaction. "Haptic Turk", a motion platform based on people, represents an innovative approach that reduces drastically motion sickness in VR [2]. Our focus in this demonstration is related to passive or marginally-active situations, where we present low-cost tactile feedback related to events or objects in the virtual world that could enhance the interaction with virtual objects while watching a movie or playing a game. Two perceptual phenomena have been explored:

Haptic Hallucinations
Also known as formication are the sensations of crawling insects on or beneath the skin. They are experienced by several psychotic disorder patients, drug addicts, or alcohol withdrawal patients. More interestingly, crawling insects have been the facination of the public, gamers and moviemakers. Probably the most famous scenes comes from the Mummy [6] where scarabs crawl under the skin and Indiana Jones and the Temple of Doom [7] where the two lead actors are trapped in a catacomb literally crawling with every type of insect. Our proposed setup combines a virtual perception of an insect with a sensation of crawling on/beneath the skin to offer an immersive situation that could be added to a game or a video/movie to complete the experience.

Temperature Perception
Temperature is felt in every moment of the day: the sun shining through a window or the cool of ice water as it touches your lips. Although all of our senses contribute to the perception of temperature, the true sensation of temperature can only be provided by a direct contact with the object and hence through the tactile sense. In a virtual environment, more specifically for game and movie makers, several visual and auditory cues are used to judge the temperature of an object. For instance, we can hear ice cubes clink in the glass of our lemonade, hear the sizzle of frying bacon, or hear the shrill whistle of a teapot that inform us that the boiling point of the water has been reached. However, the experience remains limited to the information provided by our auditory or visual senses, restricting therefore the true sense of temperature. Our second setup associates visual and tactile cues of temperature to offer a tangible experience of virtual thermal objects.

IMPLEMENTATION
Haptic Hallucinations
A sleeve that produces two types of sensations was built: 1) sensation of insects crawling on the skin, and 2) sensation of insects crawling beneath the skin. In order to give the sensation of a crawling bug on the surface of the skin, a motor dragged tinny fibers connected at the end of a cable. The fiber, unseen by the participant but in contact with the skin, moves at a specific speed that gives the sensation of crawling ants. Creating sensations beneath the skin was obtained by using a vibrating actuator also pulled by a cable controlled by a motor. The vibrations and their displacement along the

UIST'14 Adjunct, October 5–8, 2014, Honolulu, HI, USA.
ACM 978-1-4503-3068-8/14/10.
http://dx.doi.org/10.1145/2658779.2659116

forearm generate sensations of something moving under the skin. A servos motor controlled by an arduino board was used to dragged the cable at a specific speed. The haptic hallucination sleeve was selected among the finalists (top 3) and nominated for best demo award at Worldhaptics 2013 [3].

Temperature Perception
The setup consists of a steel cup that is either warm or cold while displaying a virtual hand touching an virtual cup that is either red or blue. The virtual environment was created using the UNITY game engine that was connected to the Oculus Rift. Mounted to the Oculus Rift, a CREATIVE interactive gesture camera was used to track participants hand movements, using the iisu middleware, a platform for tracking gestures. Hand movements were synchronized with the movements of the virtual hand in the UNITY environment. The interactive camera was attached to the Oculus using a holder printed on a 3D printer (MakerBot Replicator 2X).

Two stainless steel cups are utilized to present thermal stimuli to the participants hand. The thermal properties of stainless steel allow for a larger heat flux out of skin contact than other materials [4]. Thermal stimuli are maintained at a mean of 17C, SD = .24C for the cold cup and a mean 36.9C, SD = .8C for the warm cup (below pain temperature thresholds). The cold temperature is controlled by a 12V Peltier thermo-electric cooler mounted to a heatsink and 12V fan. The warm temperature is controlled by an electric heating pad 10cm x 5cm, powered by a 5VDC.

DEMO SCENARIOS
The audience will have the opportunity to try different tactile feedback in two virtual scenarios while wearing the Oculus Rift.

Haptic Hallucinations
The visitors will be asked to wear a sleeve-like device (Figure 1) that is worn on the forearm [3], which simulates sensations that are similar to insects crawling on or beneath the skin. The visitors will have the opportunity to experience two different sensations: 1) small fibers will brush over the surface of the forearm to create the sensation of insects on top of the skin while a virtual ant is crawling on the forearm, and 2) a small vibration motor is dragged across a track to simulate the movement of something under the skin while a virtual worm is crawling beneath the skin.

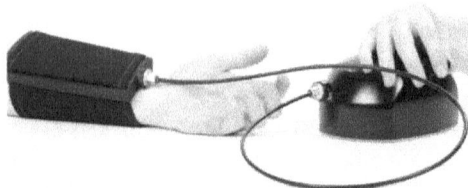

Figure 1. Haptic hallucination sleeve

Temperature Perception
The audience will have to experience whether a virtual cup's is either warm or cold. While wearing the Oculus rift, the

visitors will be asked to grasp a virtual cup that is either red or blue. Their virtual hand matches the real hand movements tracked by a creative camera. Simultaneously, they will be touching a steel cup that could be either cold or warm and is spatially synchronized with the virtual cup. There will be four sets of stimuli, comprising of visual (V) and tactile (T) modalities (V:red-T:warm, V:blue-T:cold, V:red-T:cold, and V:blue-T:warm). These four configurations provide both an objective (real temperature) and a subjective (virtual temperature) experience of temperature. Indeed, any warm temperature in a "red" condition is rated higher than the same temperature in the "blue" condition (Figure 2). Conversely, a cold temperature is rated lower when a red cup is presented comparing to a blue cup [1]. This aspect is important during gaming as sensations of warm and cold fluctuate and are affected by external factors such as color of the objects or the room.

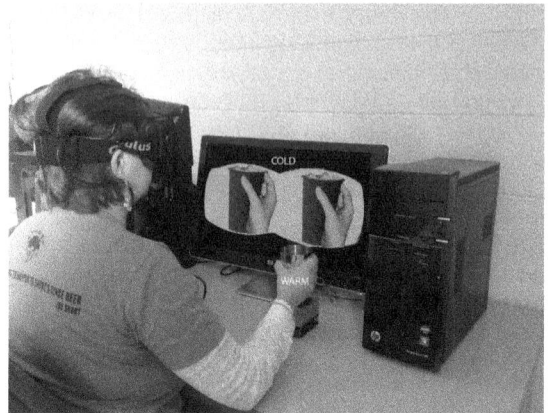

Figure 2. Is seeing cold, feeling warm?

CONCLUSION
The suggested scenarios provide tactile feedback for an enhance virtual interaction through low cost actuators. As future work, we are planning to use additional scenarios where other tactile cues such as texture and different tactile vibrations provide the user with a richer multisensory experience.

REFERENCES

1. Balcer, C., Shirtz, A., Rolison, T., and Ziat, M. Visual cues effects on temperature perception. In *Psychonomic Society Meeting*, PS (2014).

2. Cheng, L., Lhne, P., Lopes, P., Sterz, C., and Baudisch, P. Haptic turk: a motion platform based on people. In *ACM CHI 2014*, ACM (2014).

3. Fancher, J., Smith, E., and Ziat, M. Haptic hallucination sleeve. Nominated for best demo award.

4. Galie, J., and Jones, L. Thermal cues and the perception of force. *Experimental Brain Research 200*, 1 (2000), 81–90.

5. Oculus. Oculus rift. http://www.oculusvr.com/.

6. Sommers, S. The mummy, 1999. Universal Pictures.

7. Spielberg, S. Indiana jones and the temple of doom, 1984. Paramount Pictures.

Ubisonus: Spatial Freeform Interactive Speakers

Yoshio Ishiguro, Eric Brockmeyer, Alex Rothera, Ali Israr
Disney Research Pittsburgh
4720 Forbes Avenue, Pittsburgh
{yoshio.ishiguro, eric.brockmeyer, alex.rothera, israr}
@disneyresearch.com

ABSTRACT

We present freeform interactive speakers for creating spatial sound experiences from a variety of surfaces. Traditional surround sound systems are widely used and consist of multiple electromagnetic speakers that create point sound sources within a space. Our proposed system creates directional sound and can be easily embedded into architecture, furniture and many everyday objects. We use electrostatic loudspeaker technology made from thin, flexible, lightweight and low cost materials and can be of different size and shape. In this demonstration we will show various configurations such as single speaker, speaker array and tangible speakers for playful and exciting interactions with spatial sounds. This is an example of new possibilities for the design of various interactive surfaces.

Author Keywords

Interactive architecture; furniture design; interactions; electrostatic loudspeakers; freeform speakers

ACM Classification Keywords

H.5.2. Information interfaces and presentation (e.g., HCI): User Interfaces - Auditory feedback.

INTRODUCTION

Sound and visuals are important ingredients for creating interactive systems that produce an engaging and believable user experience. Display technology has progressed into more flexible, scalable and freeform configurations by use of OLED screens, projectors and other emerging display technologies. Sound technology has lagged behind relying on traditional surround sound systems limited by audible area, calibration, and bulky components [4].

We introduce *Ubisonus: Spatial Freeform Interactive Speakers*, that can reproduce sound directly from *architecture*, *furniture* and many other *everyday objects* as shown in Figure 1. *Ubisonus* utilizes electrostatic loudspeakers (ESL) that are lightweight, flexible, scalable, and can be made into almost any shape and size. They are

highly durable and ideal for use in spatially restrictive and dynamic spaces and structures.

Ubisonus demonstrates a novel method for realizing *Programmable Matter* [1], *Programmable Physical Architectures* [6], and *Organic User Interfaces* [3].

DESIGN OF FREEFORM SPEAKER

Principal of Electrostatic Loudspeaker Technology

The basic principles of electrostatic sound reproduction are simple and were explored in depth in the 1930s [2]. An audio signal is amplified to ~1000 V and applied to an electrode, charging it relative to the ground potential that is connected to a diaphragm. As the electrode is charged, an electrostatic attraction force is developed between the electrode and the diaphragm. The whole diaphragm produces sound and can continue to produce sounds as objects are placed on it. Additionally, this structure can be used as a microphone by measuring the changing potential between the electrode and the diaphragm.

Configurations of Our Electrostatic Loudspeaker

Single-Side Configuration

The conventional form of ESL (Figure 2a) has both electrode and diaphragm charged. However, this can be dangerous to the human body that normally has the same potential as ground. In our previous work on *3D printed speakers* [5], we connected the diaphragm to ground and the electrode to a HV signal (Figure 2b). Furthermore, we limited the current (~1.25mA) protecting the user from electrical shocks. This simple *single-side* configuration can be used as the surface of tabletops, walls, toys, floating objects, and more.

UIST'14 Adjunct, October 5–8, 2014, Honolulu, HI, USA.
ACM 978-1-4503-3068-8/14/10.
http://dx.doi.org/10.1145/2658779.2659117

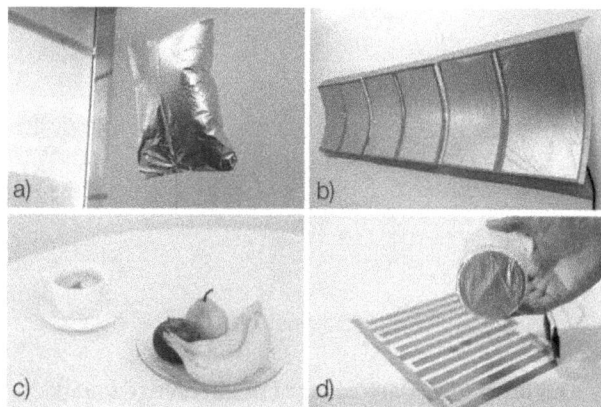

Figure 1. Examples of *Ubisonus*. (a) *Balloon*. (b) *Large curved wall*. (c) *Speaker table*. (d) *Tangible objects*.

Array Configuration

An extension of the *single-side* is an *array* configuration as shown in Figure 2c. The array allows ESL to be placed sequentially, where each speaker is independently controlled. Multiple sound patterns can be channeled through individual speakers creating a moving and dynamic sound system (Figure 3).

All speakers in the array can share a common ground plane. Therefore, a single diaphragm surface could be used with multiple speaker electrodes as shown Figure 3 *left*.

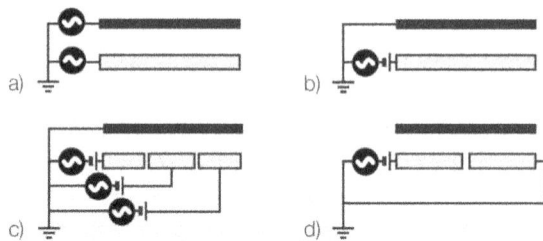

Figure 2. Configurations of electrostatic speakers.

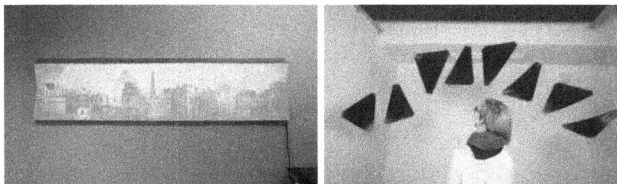

Figure 3. Freeform electrostatic speakers are arranged to form a curved surface and morphing structures.

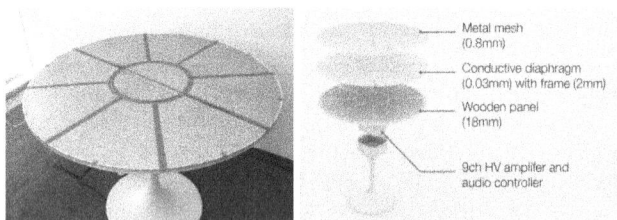

Figure 4. The surface of a large round table is embedded with an array of freeform speakers.

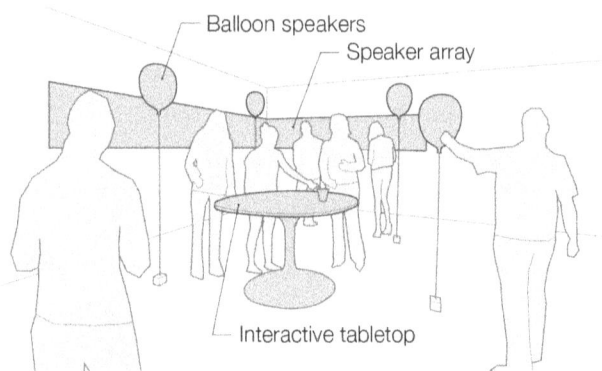

Figure 5. Users are engaged in interactive sound environments that show *Ubisonus* in architecture, furniture and floating objects.

Passive Speaker Configuration

Figure 2d shows the *passive speaker configuration*. In this configuration, HV and ground electrodes are arranged on the same surface, and an object with a passive diaphragm is placed on the surface. The surface itself cannot produce sound, however, the conductive surface of the object creates a difference in potential between the diaphragm and the HV electrode as well as between the diaphragm and ground.

DEMONSTRATION AT UIST 2014

We will demonstrate our freeform speaker technology in an interactive sound environment made with *architecture*, *furniture*, and *everyday objects* (Figure 5).

Architecture: *Wall Scale Speaker Array*

Freeform speakers are a good candidate for embedding in large and complex shaped walls due to their flexibility and scalability. We will integrate the ESL into a wall setting as shown in Figure 1b and will build a small wall for our demonstration.

Furniture: *Interactive Tabletops*

In this installment, we will integrate an array of nine freeform ESL into the surface of a wooden table to enhance tabletop interactions as shown in Figure 4. Due to the minimal effect of loading on ESL, the weight from plates and cups placed on the table do not affect sound quality. In addition to the use of the panels as speakers, they will also be used as microphones.

A projector will allow us to collocate responsive animated content with sound on the table and wall to create an immersive and engaging experience for the user.

Everyday Objects: *Tangibles and Floating Speakers*

In some situations, interactions are desired with passive tangible objects. In our demonstration we will include a variety of objects equipped with *passive speakers* as described previously. Figure 1d shows a table with a grid pattern made from conductive tape and a cup with a thin aluminized film diaphragm.

Finally, due to the lightweight nature of ESL, floating objects, such as balloons (Figure 1a) will provide ambient sounds to the user.

REFERENCES

1. Goldstein, S. C. *et al.*, Programmable matter. *Computer*, *38*(6), pp. 99-101. (2005)

2. Hanna, C.R., Theory of the electrostatic loud speaker. The Journal of the Acoustical Society of America 2, 2, pp. 143–149. (1930)

3. Holman, D. *et al.*, Organic user interfaces: designing computers in any way, shape, or form. *Communications of the ACM*, *51*(6), pp. 48-55. (2008)

4. IOSONO GmbH, www.iosono-sound.com

5. Ishiguro, Y. *and* Poupyrev, I., 3D printed interactive speakers. *Proc. of CHI*, pp. 1733-1742, ACM. (2014)

6. Rekimoto, J., Squama: modular visibility control of walls and windows for programmable physical architectures. *Proc. of AVI*, pp. 168-171, ACM. (2012)

Eyes-Free Text Entry Interface Based on Contact Area for People with Visual Impairment

Taedong Goh[1] and Sang Woo Kim[2]
[1]Creative IT Engineering, POSTECH
[2]Electrical Engineering, POSTECH
Pohang 790-784, Republic of Korea
{ehd1116, swkim}@postech.ac.kr

ABSTRACT

We developed an eyes-free text entry interface using contact area to determine pressed state for mobile device with touchscreen. The interface gives audio feedback for a touched character similar to VoiceOver of iPhone, but audio feedbacks of two simultaneous touches are considered. A desired character is entered by pressing once. Independent entry of two fingers can reduce movement distance for searching a character. Whole interaction occurs in touched states, additional tactile feedback can be augmented.

Author Keywords

Pseudo-pressure detection; touchscreen interface; text-to-speech

ACM Classification Keywords

H.5.2. Information interfaces and presentation (e.g., HCI): User Interfaces.-Input devices and strategies.

INTRODUCTION

Touchscreen of smartphone is generally used to supply recognition of various gestures and relatively wide screen by removing physical buttons. However, people with visual impairment cannot recognize visual information. Voiceover of iPhone, a commercialized assistive technology, reads text information indicated by focus, and has specialized gesture entry [1]. In the text entry of Voiceover, a finger should be frequently moved for long distance between keys because QWERTY keypad was originally designed for two-handed users. Therefore, the distance causes significantly slow and uncomfortable text entry. Our research goal is to develop fast text-entry interface of smartphone for people with visual impairment which two thumbs can be used to enter texts independently. For independent confirming interaction, pressure detection was considered.

Several interfaces detecting pressure in touchscreen have been proposed. SimPress was suggested to detect clicking gesture based on contact area for tabletop [2]. Researchers made an interface which detect pressure values, and strongly pressed state was corresponded to enter capital character in resistive touchscreen [3]. Touched time was used to determine pressed state [4], and additional hardware for

UIST'14 Adjunct, October 5–8, 2014, Honolulu, HI, USA.
ACM 978-1-4503-3068-8/14/10.
http://dx.doi.org/10.1145/2658779.2658780

detecting pressure was used to detecting pressure between two smartphone [5]. In addition, one handhold interface was developed to control size of map of smartphone in the interface, contact area was used to detect pressure state [6]. In this study, we suggested an interface which determines pressed state by detecting acute variation of contact area for entering small character key, and enables simultaneous interaction of two touched fingers to enter characters.

PROPOSED INTERFACE

The proposed eyes-free text entry interface is text-to-speech interface similar to VoiceOver. The interface should be handled without sight, so audio feedback is supplied when each character is touched. The interface was implemented on iPhone 5S (Apple), and has two remarkable differences from the VoiceOver, which are pseudo-pressure detection and independent touch interaction. On the QWERTY keyboard of the interface, two thumbs can be touched to search desired characters and pressed to confirm the desired character separately (Figure 1). In this prototype, English capital characters of QWERTY keyboard were only implemented.

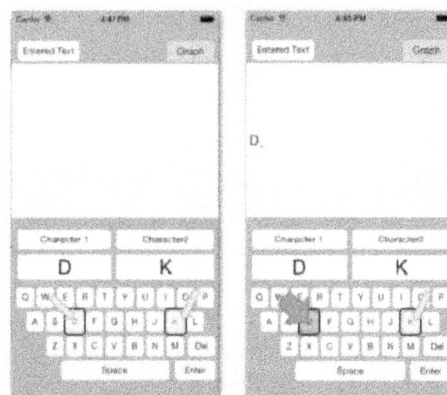

Figure 1. Searching (left) and confirming (right) in the prototype interface. Information of touched characters ("D", "K") are supplied by audio feedback, and the pressed character ("D") is entered to string.

API of iPhone supports a function acquiring major radius of the contact area. It was assumed that the acquired major radius is proportional to the size of contact area. As the finger is more strongly pressed to a point on the touchscreen, the size is larger. However, the size can be changed without additional pressure by location or angle of finger. For example, slightly touched fingertip of thumb including entire fingerprint has much larger size than thumb pressed vertically on the touchscreen. The pressure-independent variation of the size is major obstacle to confirm a key when the finger is moved on the screen to acquire feedback. To prevent the unintended pressure detection, moved length of touched point was used.

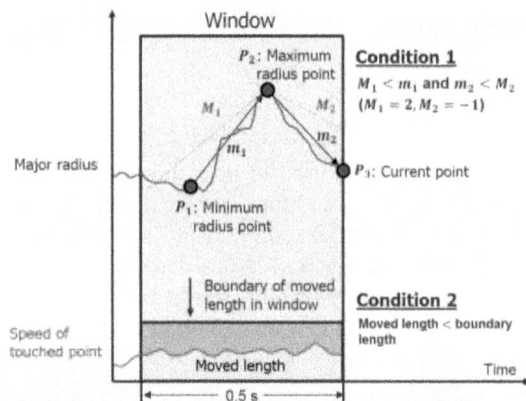

Figure 2. Pressed state detection conditions.

We took two conditions to determine pressed state (Figure 2). First condition is that slope (m_1) between minimum radius point and maximum radius point is high enough (M_1), and slope (m_2) between maximum radius point and current point is low enough (M_2). The algorithm actually finds the sharp climb in the radius graph, which means acute variation of contact area. The second condition is that length of moved finger for the period is less than the boundary length. The condition prevents pressed state detection from false detection by moving like sweeping gesture.

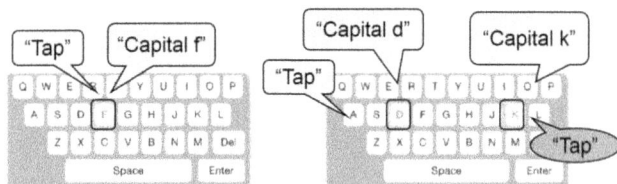

Figure 3. Audio feedbacks when a finger is touched (left), and two finger is touched (right).

Audio feedback is similar to VoiceOver. When a character key is touched, sound effect ("Tap") is played once immediately. Then, character utterance is also played once after 0.1 sec from touching (Figure 3, left). In two fingers are simultaneously touched, the sound effects and the character utterances are played consecutively. However, to distinguish each touched fingers, different sound effects are played, but the utterances have same tone.

We found some limitations in the proposed interface during several usability tests. If we pressed so frequently within the window period, then each pressed state is often not detected because only a minimum radius point and a maximum radius point are found within the period in spite of actual pressing number. In addition, characters at edge of touchscreen are

not easily determined to pressed state because finger cannot be fully touched in the area.

The proposed interface supplies the intuitive text entry distinguishing touched and pressed state and enables people to use each finger independently for entering text. The interface is based on QWERTY keypad, so people familiar with keyboard or QWERTY keypad of smartphone can use easily. With this approach, people will handle QWERTY keypad fast without sight, and comfortably communicate with other people in mobile messenger.

CONCLUSION AND FUTURE WORK

In this poster, we proposed an eyes-free text entry interface for people with visual impairment. To use each finger independently for entering text, we made pseudo-pressure detection algorithm based on contact area. In addition, audio feedbacks distinguishing each touched fingers were applied to acquire information of simultaneous touches without sight. With this interface, moving distance of fingers for search could be reduced.

For future plan, we will evaluate this interface with other eyes-free text entries for people with visual impairment. In addition, tactile feedback will be augmented to the proposed interface to enhance fast discrimination between adjacent character keys.

ACKNOWLEDGMENTS

This research was supported by the MSIP(Ministry of Science, ICT and Future Planning), Korea, under the "IT Consilience Creative Program" (NIPA-2014-H0201-14-1001) supervised by the NIPA(National IT Industry Promotion Agency)

REFERENCES

1. Voiceover, http://www.apple.com/accessibility/osx/voiceover/.

2. H. Benko, A. D. Wilson, and P. Baudisch., Precise Selection Techniques for Multi-Touch Screens, *Proc. CHI'06*, ACM Press (2006), 1263-1272.

3. Brewster, S. A., and Hughes, M., Pressure-Based Text Entry for Mobile Devices, *Proc. MobileHCI'09*, ACM Press (2009), 73-76.

4. Arif , A. S., and Stuerzlinger, W., Pseudo-Pressure Detection and Its Use in Predictive Text Entry on Touchscreens, *Proc. OzCHI'13*, ACM Press (2013), 383-392.

5. Stewart, C., Rohs, M., Kratz, S., Essl, G., Characteristics of Pressure-Based Input for Mobile Devices, *Proc. CHI 2010*, ACM Press (2010), 801-810.

6. Boring, S., Ledo, D., Chen, X., Marquardt, N., Tang, A., Greenberg, S., The Fat Thumb: Using the Thumb's Contact Size for Single-handed Mobile Interaction, *Proc. MobileHCI'12*, ACM Press (2012), 39-48.

Third Surface:
An Augmented World Wide Web for the Physical World

Valentin Heun, Kenneth Friedman, Andrew Mendez, Benjamin Reynolds, Kevin Wong, Pattie Maes

Fluid Interfaces Group

MIT Media Lab

20 Ames Street, Cambridge, MA 02139 U.S.A.

{heun, ksf, mendeza, benolds, kevinw} @ mit.edu, pattie@media.mit.edu

ABSTRACT

The ubiquitous use of Augmented Reality (AR) applications is dependent on an easy way of authoring and using content. Present systems depend on specific authoring tools or content delivery systems that provide a limited amount of freedom and content ownership to the author compared to the possibilities of the World Wide Web (WWW). Third Surface is a system that allows the user to publish and use WWW content saved on personal HTTP servers for augmented reality applications in the physical environment. The contribution of this work is a system that allows a web developer to post location-based augmented reality content and AR marker on one's own HTTP server. A Global Location Service (GLS) provides a browsing application with location-based URLs that link the browsing application to content, AR markers, and data for the right positioning of content in the augmented reality interface. The Third Surface has three advantages compared to other concepts. It is globally scalable able to millions of users. The interactive possibilities for developers and users are the same as for the WWW. The developers are in charge of their own content distribution.

Author Keywords
Augmented Reality; Web; User Interface

ACM Classification Keywords
H.5.2 User Interfaces; H.5.1 Multimedia Information Systems

INTRODUCTION AND RELATED WORK

We live in two separate worlds: the physical world in which graphic designers design and place content onto physical surfaces such as book covers, magazines and billboards, and a digital world in which web designer and engineers generate content for the WWW. Second Surface [1] explored the usability of collaborative content placed in physical spaces and envisioned a world where digital

content overlays the physical environments we inhabit. However, the authors have not found a solution for how to place content ubiquitously and simply into the physical world. Solutions like Layar [2] provide an easy interface to generate AR content, but the interface has limitations compared to digital content generated for the WWW. With a system like Layar, it is difficult to generate content that can compete with content that can be found on the WWW. Kharma [3] in contrast allows the generation of web similar content based on a combination of Google Earth KML and HTML that can be used for delivering AR content that has web functionality. Kharma aims at providing the content in its markup language. Due to the Kharma content delivery concept, a user is not able to just walk around and experience content based on his location without further interaction requirements. Furthermore a developer is not able to just host marker data, simple html content, and services on their own Internet HTTP server.

THIRD SURFACE

Third Surface does offer these possibilities and brings a new concept of publishing augmented reality content into the physical space. Based on a user's location the Third Surface application loads content and AR marker information from the developer's own HTTP servers in order to give complete freedom to the designer or developer of the AR content. For browsing AR content, the system works in the background and the user only needs to open the browsing application to engage with surrounding content. Since GLS servers provide location-based URLs to the browsing application and the content is stored on developer-owned HTTP servers, the system is scalable to a global multi-user scenario. The GLS server can also be run on any computer reachable by the browsing application via either TCP/IP (so that complete private content systems are possible) or a distribution service structure similar to Domain Name Systems (DNS) (used to match Internet IPs with domain names).

PUBLISHING

Inspired by the World Wide Web and the structure of the Internet, Third Surface consists of a mobile application, developer owned content HTTP servers and a central register (GLS) that stores locations and URLs for the surfaces a developer wants to place content on (See Figure 1).

UIST'14 Adjunct, October 5–8, 2014, Honolulu, HI, USA.
ACM 978-1-4503-3068-8/14/10.
http://dx.doi.org/10.1145/2658779.2658781

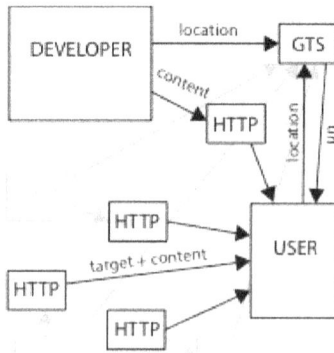

Figure 1. This Networking Diagram for Third Surface shows a developer publishes to the Web and the GLS and user sends his position to the GLS and loads the content from the web according to the information received from the GLS.

To publish content, a developer needs to perform four steps. First a developer creates the content as HTML-conform content and stores it on an HTTP server of their choice. The developer then uses the Qualcomm Vuforia [4] online service to generate an AR marker for the surface where the content should be placed. Then, the developer stores the generated AR marker in the same folder as the HTML content on their HTTP server.

Third, the developer pushes an "add" button within the Third Surface application to get a popup window that asks for a URL to enter. The Developer adds the URL that points to his HTTP server. The application then starts loading the AR marker as well the content from the HTTP server. Once loaded, the application starts to augment the content on to the marker. The application uses CSS 3D transformations provided by the iOS WebKit to map the content onto the AR marker. For providing the right mapping of the web content in to the AR video stream, the application translates the OpenGL transformation matrix provided by Vuforia in to right scaled WebKit transformation matrix. This is necessary as the OpenGL and the Webkit CSS 3D rendering pipelines work differently.

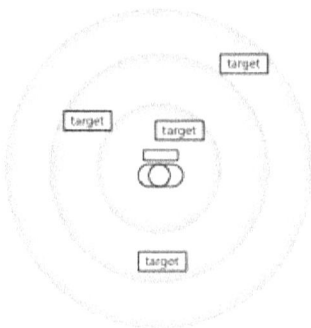

Figure 3. Diagram of the search performed around the user.

Now that the content and AR markers are loaded, the Developer performs a final step by positioning the content on the marker. The application allows the developer to rotate, scale and translate the content to a desired position. The Developer can now push a button to publish the content to a GLS. The application sends the URL and transformation data together with the location of the iOS device to a GLS that registers the data based on its location.

BROWSING

Once a user opens the application, the application sends its location to the GLS. The GLS searches entries in its database in an expanding radius around the user (see Figure 2). A list of these entries is sent to the application. The application then downloads the AR marker data and HTML content from the developer's HTTP server. Once the application detects an AR marker, it presents related HTML content. The User can now interact with the content. Since the Webkit used for rendering the content might have to display HTML content from more then one developer, it uses HTML iFrames to encapsulate each source. The application loads and unloads these iFrame snippets via Javascript, so that the visualization is performed uninterrupted.

Using ThirdSurface, a web designer and engineer have a simple tool to generate augmented reality content and keep maximum control over the content, as every technology developed for the WWW is also enabled using the Third Surface. Since the system builds on Vuforia, it also has the benefits and limitations of Vuforia.

ACKNOWLEDGMENTS

We would like to thank Shunichi Kasahara, Austin Lee and Hiroshi Ishii for valuable discussions while writing the Second Surface, which eventually lead to the motivation for this work.

REFERENCES

1. Kasahara, S., Heun, V., Lee, A., Ishii, H., Second Surface: Multi-user Spatial Collaboration System based on Augmented Reality, SIGGRAPH Asia 2012

2. Layar. Layar. http://www.layar.com.

3. Hill, A., MacIntyre, B., Gandy, M., Davidson, B., Hafez, R., KHARMA: An Open KML/HTML Architecture for Mobile Augmented Reality Applications, IEEE International Symposium on Mixed and Augmented Reality 2010.

4. Qualcomm Vuforia, http://www.qualcomm.com/Vuforia.

Tactile Cue Presentation for Vocabulary Learning with Keyboard

Daichi Ogawa[1], Sakiko Ikeno[1], Ryuta Okazaki[1, 2], Taku Hachisu[1, 2], Hiroyuki Kajimoto[1, 3]

[1]The University of Electro-Communications   [2]JSPS Research Fellow   [3]Japan Science and Technology Agency

1-5-1 Chofugaoka, Chofu, Tokyo 182-8585, Japan

{ogawa, ikeno, okazaki, hachisu, kajimoto}@kaji-lab.jp

ABSTRACT

This paper presents the results of a pilot experiment observing the effect of tactile cues on vocabulary learning. Considering that we generally memorize words by associating them with various cues, we designed a tactile cue presentation device that aids vocabulary learning by applying vibrations to the finger that is associated with the next key to press when typing on a keyboard. Experiments comparing tactile and visual cues indicated that tactile cues can significantly improve long-term retention of vocabulary after one week.

Author Keywords

Haptic; tactile cue; vocabulary learning; wearable device

ACM Classification Keywords

H5.2 [Information interfaces and presentation]: User Interfaces - Training, help, and documentation.

INTRODUCTION

Vocabulary learning is one of the most time-consuming aspects of language learning and known to be assisted by the association with various cues. Oxford et al. evaluated language learning for a second or foreign language assisted by visual, aural, tactile, and kinesthetic associations [1].

We focused on tactile association to support vocabulary learning when using a keyboard, because adults typically use typing more than writing and typing naturally involves an accompanying tactile sensation to each finger. Bojinov et al. designed a game using the keyboard to unconsciously memorize a password [2]. Huang et al. designed Mobile Music Touch as a means for learning piano key sequences [3].

In this study, we focused on adult first language speakers of Japanese who were learning English words. To present tactile cues to the keyboard, we designed a glove-type tactile device with eight vibrators situated at the root of each finger, excluding the thumbs (Figure 1).

In contrast to previous work that has used one-to-one mapping between fingers and keys [3, 4], our system used a one-to-many mapping feature, i.e., each finger can press a range of keys so that vibration to the finger does not uniquely determine the key to press. For example, if a tactile cue is given to the little finger of the left hand, the next key to press could be either A, Q, or Z. We speculated that this uncertainty does not hinder, but would rather facilitate learning.

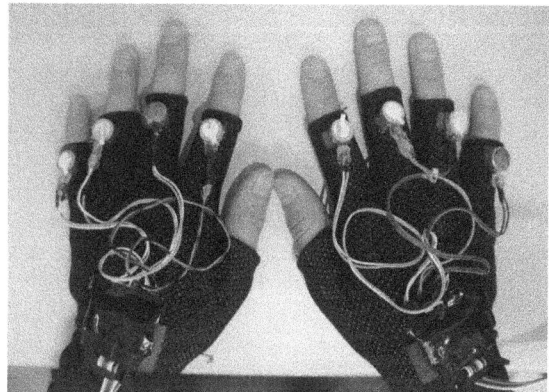

Figure 1. Glove-type tactile device

SYSTEM

The system is composed of a glove-type tactile device, a PC and a keyboard. The device has eight small vibration motors (FM34FTokyo Parts Ind. Inc.), transistors to drive the motors, and a microcontroller (mbed NXP LPC1768 NXP Inc.) to control the motors and communicate with the PC. Users see the LCD monitor of the PC, which displays a Japanese word (the question) and its English translation (the answer).

EXPERIMENT

To determine if our system is effective for learning words, we performed an experiment comparing tactile with ordinary visual cueing. One hundred words required to yield 729 points or more in TOEIC (Test of English for International Communication) were selected and 40 words were randomly chosen from these for each participant. The set of 40 words was divided into two: 20 words for tactile cues and 20 words for visual cues.

Procedure

We recruited seven participants consisting of four males and three females, 21–23 years of age. Each participant learned 20 words in tactile condition and 20 words in visual condition.

In the first phase, a Japanese word (the question) was displayed in a white font, and an English word (the answer) in gray font was displayed on the LCD against a black background. When the participants pressed the corresponding key, each gray letter was changed, one by one, to white. The participants were asked to input the 20 words once in this phase.

In the next phase (Training Phase), only the Japanese word was displayed, and the English answer was displayed in a letter-by-letter fashion when the participant typed the correct letter. After this phase, all words were tested (Test Phase) without tactile or visual cue. The Training and Test Phases were repeated five times. In the Training Phase, only the words that were missed in the previous Test Phase were used so that the experiment time was reduced. After one week, the Test Phase was performed to see the long-term effect.

In the Training Phase, the participants were either presented tactile or visual cue. The tactile cue was a vibration presented to the finger that should be used for the next letter (assuming general finger-keys mapping with a QWERTY keyboard). The visual cue was a gray color display of the next letter. In both cases, the cues were presented only when the participants could not press the next key for 0.5 s. The participants were randomly divided into two groups, A and B. Group A participated in the experiment with tactile cues given first, and group B in the experiment with visual cues given first.

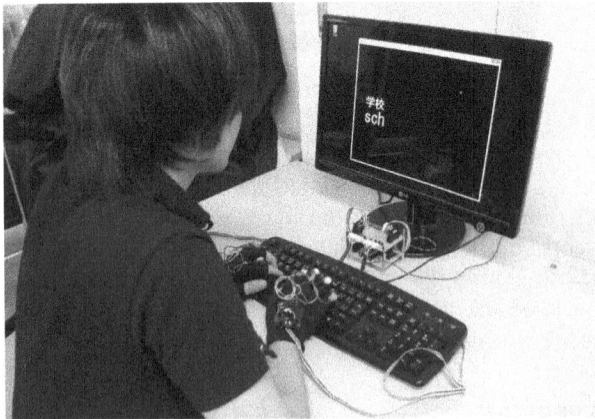

Figure 2. Overview of experiment

Result and Discussion

Figure 3 shows the results of the Test Phase for the two conditions. The horizontal axis shows the number of the Test Phase. We found a significant difference between the two conditions after one week (Wilcoxon matched-pairs signed-rank test, p<.05) with tactile cues outperforming ordinary visual cues. No difference was observed between group A and B.

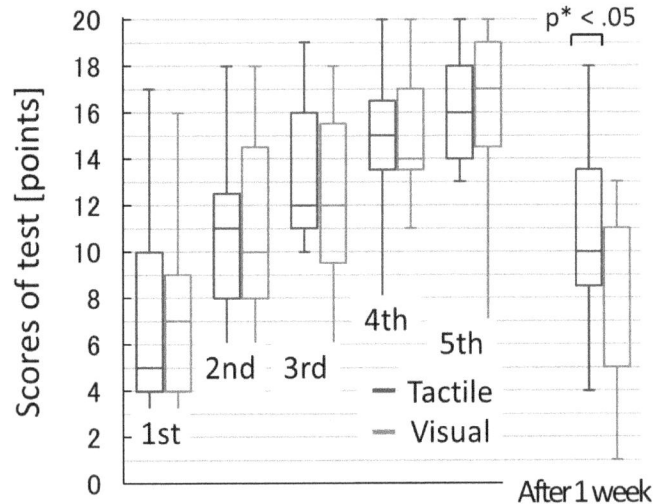

Figure 3. Result for the Test Phase using two different conditions

Results indicate that the tactile cues were effective for ensuring that information was retained for a long term. This may be owing to the fact that our tactile cue has ambiguity (i.e. the cue was presented to the finger and the user must still actively determine which key to press), while the visual cue gave a more complete cue (i.e. user can passively wait for the next letter to display). This difference in the nature of the cue might lead to the reinforcement of memory.

CONCLUSION

In this paper, we focused on the use of tactile cues to support vocabulary learning. The tactile cue was a vibration presented to the finger that should be used on the keyboard, to type the next letter in the appropriate English word.

We performed an experiment comparing tactile and ordinary visual cues. The tactile cue was more effective than the visual cue in terms of retaining the new vocabulary after one week.

Our future work includes comparison of tactile cues with incomplete (vague) visual cues, and an examination of ways in which multiple cues might be combined and optimized.

REFERENCES

1. Oxford, R. and Crookall, D. Vocabulary Learning - A Critical Analysis of Techniques. *TECL Canada Journal/Revue TESL Du Canada*, 7 (2), March, 1990.

2. Bojinov, H., Boneh, D., Sanchez, D., Reber, P. and Lincoln, P. Neuroscience Meets Cryptography. *USENIX Security 2012*. August 8-10, 2012.

3. Huang, K., Starner, T., Do, E., Weinberg, G., Kohlsdorf, D., Ahlrichs, C. and Leibrandt, R. Mobile Music Touch - Mobile Tactile Stimulation for Passive Learning. *CHI 2010*, April 10-15, 2010.

4. Kim, D., Johnson, B., Gillespie, R.B. and Seidler, R. Role of Haptic Cues in Motor Learning, *IEEE World Haptics Conference 2013*, April 14-18, 2013.

Trainer: A Motion-Based Interactive Game for Balance Rehabilitation Training

Guanyun Wang[1], Ye Tao[1], Dian Yu[2], Chuan Cao[1], Hongyu Chen[1], Cheng Yao[1]

[1]Zhejiang University
Hangzhou, 310027, China
{guanyun, taoye, yaoch}@zju.edu.cn,
{chuancaoidesign, hongyu89}@foxmail.com

[2]Macquarie University
Sydney, Australia
eayudian@gmail.com

ABSTRACT

In physiotherapy, the traditional approach of using fixed aids to train patients to keep their balance is often ineffective, due to the tendency of people to lose interest in the training or to lose confidence in their ability to finish the training. A Trainer system is proposed on traditional physiotherapy treatment methods to allow patients to play qualified and immersive games with a mobile aid. Using RF localization and self-balancing technology, the system allows patients to control a vehicle with their sense of balance. This platform provides a series of game feedback interface which involves part-body motion in sitting manipulation therapy to make the rehabilitation more flexible and more effective. This paper reports the designing and the control of the Trainer, the experimental evaluations of the performance of system, as well as an exploration of the future work in detail. Our work is intended to improve the patient experience of the physiotherapy rehabilitation using games with instinctive ways of controlling mobile instruments.

Author Keywords

Balance training; game-based rehabilitation; video game; habitual actions

ACM Classification Keywords

H.5.2. Information interfaces and presentation (e.g., HCI): User Interfaces.

INTRODUCTION

Every year, many people, even in middle-aged, suffer from stroke worldwide both new and recurring, which can result in hemiparesis and coordination difficulties in postural control [1]. The rehabilitation methods available are mainly such physical therapies as the treatment of balance and mobility disorders and that of the fine motor skills training. However, these methods can result in the low interest or failure of the patients due to the ignorance in the psychological need of the patients. Our system (Figure 1) utilizes mobility gaming technologies to encourage patients to develop physical movement and balance training in virtual gameplay.

Additionally, such case studies as Exergame[2] and game-based stroke rehabilitation[3], have demonstrated that the use of visual somatosensory games is a help for motor ability recovery, and a promise for balance rehabilitation. We are exploring to make traditional physiotherapy more visible and sensible by taking it in the form of immersive and dynamic video games in our system. The patients need to use the habitual actions to control the center of the body weight so as to control the vehicle in order to complete the in-game tasks. Hence, their physiotherapy training is finished in these courses. In this paper, a motion-based interactive game system is presented to provoke the interest and persistence as well as balance in training.

Figure 1. The Trainer system allows patients to play qualified and immersive games by employing video game technology and an intelligent vehicle.

DESIGN AND IMPLEMENTATION

In Trainer system (Figure 2), our work translates the balance training into the gameplay with the aid of vehicle. It consists of three major parts, the playing area with a large space (this is not a permanent usage), a self-balancing vehicle in control to move around the playing area by shifting the user's center of gravity, and a projector-camera system placed at a certain height and connected to a real-time image feedback system to detect the movement and to give feedback. Based on this system, a computer controlled game interface were designed which is available in balance training.

UIST'14 Adjunct, October 5–8, 2014, Honolulu, HI, USA.
ACM 978-1-4503-3068-8/14/10.
http://dx.doi.org/10.1145/2658779.2658783

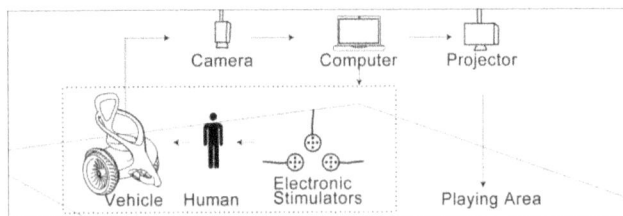

Figure 2. The Trainer system is built on a projector-camera program and an intelligent control program.

Motion Control

Different from the traditional body fixed aid, the mobile vehicle patient's manipulate becomes a controller of the patient's physical body in a virtual space, thus improving the physical therapy in muscular activity, and the body coordination in full-body play. The vehicle employed self-balancing technology to give control by shifting the center of gravity; there are 5 possible ways (forwards, backwards, rightwards, leftwards and steadily) to complete the in-game tasks, in a restricted way. If the patient's center of gravity maintains its original position, the vehicle will not move in any direction; while if he intuitively moves forward from the center of gravity, the vehicle will move forward (Figure 3). As a safeguard to prevent patients from falling over, the vehicle has a small wheel on both the front and the rear, thus achieving 3 point stability.

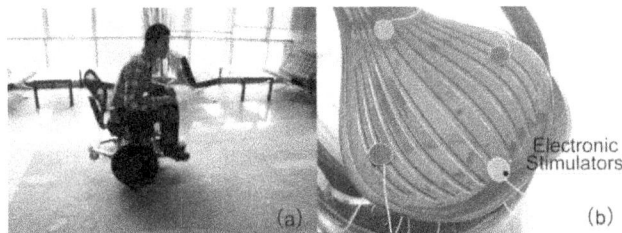

Figure 3. Trainer prototype: (a) Forward motion control; (b) electronic stimulators for feedback.

Movement Tracking

We use image processing software called Processing, coupled with RF localization technology provided by the video cameras, to mark out a playing area and track the movement of the vehicle within the playing area. We mark out the corners of the playing area by placing 4 blue triangles as reference points for the image acquisition. Through the successive images collected at different points of time, the system would be able to track the real-time movement.

Game Feedback

Two feedback programs are built to better facilitate the rehabilitation training. During the gameplay, the vehicle becomes a dynamic training aid to receive the body movement and serves as an electronic stimulator to adjuvant therapy. Four electronic stimulators (Figure 3) are embodied on the seat to give signs when the patients are in trouble. The red ones detect the movement forward and

backward, and accordingly, the black ones detect the movement leftward and rightward.

At this phase of the project, an Eating game has been created. Concept wise, it is similar to the classic mobile game Snake – the player tries to collect as much "fruits" while avoiding obstacles in the game. The game feedback is projected onto the ground in a visual way. Like the game Snake, once the fruit has been eaten, new fruit will appear at other locations, and a cycle repeats.

PRELIMINARY TEST

Preliminary tests were conducted with 8 patients (divided on average into two groups; one aged 25-40 in late recovery phase for balance disorder after accidents and, another aged 40-60 suffering from stroke). All patients were asked to complete 10 fruits in gameplay. We interviewed each participant after a stipulated period of study and found that there is a better motivation during the training in the patients with Trainer showed. Six of all claimed that the electronic stimulator was effective and beneficial in assisting correct the wrong directions. Two of aged 40-60 said that there is difficulty in completing tasks because the manipulation acclimatization took much time. They said that the system is effective in enhancing the confidence in completing the training task, and there still exist some difficulties in the control of the motion.

CONCLUSION AND FUTURE WORK

In this paper, we describe a motion-based interactive game system for physical rehabilitation to make physiotherapy more flexible and more received.

In the next stage, we intend to improve the control performance and to expand the game to allow multiplayer usage. This would introduce a social dimension to the rehabilitation process by allowing other people, such as other patients or the patients' family and friends, to participate in the training.

ACKNOWLEDGMENTS

The project supported by National Key Technology R&D Program during the Twelfth Five-year Plan Period (Grant No. 2012BAI34B00) and Provincial Key Laboratory of Service Robot.

REFERENCES

1. Shumway-Cook, A., Woollacott, M.H. *Motor control: Translating research into clinical practice*. Lippincott William & Wilkins Press, Philadelphia, USA, 2007.

2. Uzor, S., & Baillie, L. Investigating the long-term use of exergames in the home with elderly fallers. In *Proc. CHI 2014*, ACM Press (2014), 2813-2822.

3. Alankus, G., Proffitt, R., Kelleher, C., & Engsberg, J. Stroke therapy through motion-based games: a case study. ACM Transactions on Accessible Computing (TACCESS 2011), 4(1), 3.

SenseGlass: Using Google Glass to Sense Daily Emotions

Javier Hernandez   **Rosalind W. Picard**

MIT Media Lab

75 Amherst St., Cambridge, MA, 02142, USA

{javierhr, picard}@media.mit.edu

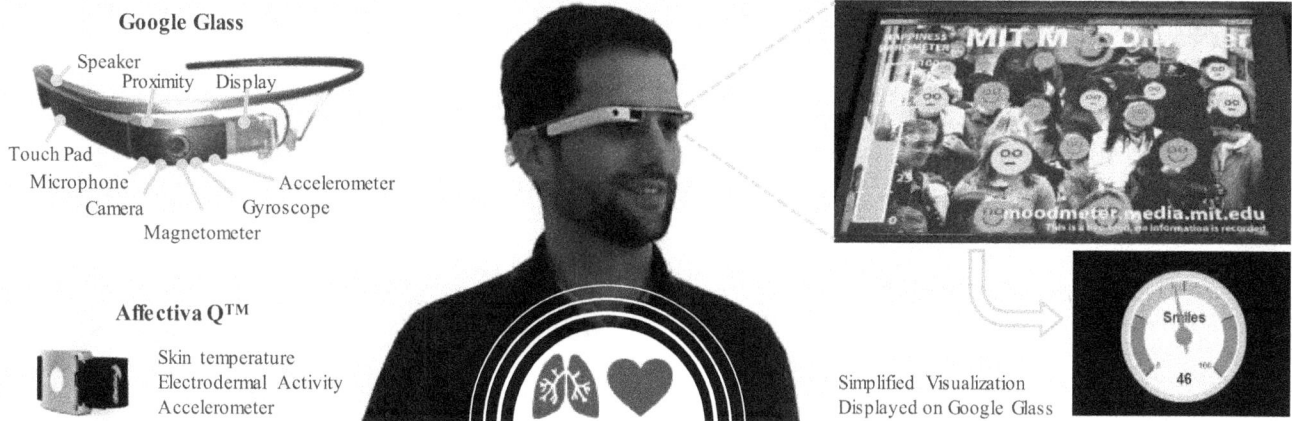

Figure 1. Sensors of Google Glass and wearable devices can help measure and visualize daily life emotions.

ABSTRACT

For over a century, scientists have studied human emotions in laboratory settings. However, these emotions have been largely contrived – elicited by movies or fake "lab" stimuli, which tend not to matter to the participants in the studies, at least not compared with events in their real life. This work explores the utility of Google Glass, a head-mounted wearable device, to enable fundamental advances in the creation of affect-based user interfaces in natural settings.

INTRODUCTION

Emotions play a very important role in our daily life. They not only help regulate important processes such as memory acquisition, attention and engagement, but also are fundamental to achieve successful social interactions. In order to create more natural and human-like interactions, researchers have focused on the creation of user interfaces that can measure and adapt to human emotions [4]. While most of the progress has been limited to controlled laboratory settings where emotions are easier to study, measuring and adapting to emotions during natural settings

UIST '14, Oct 05-08 2014, Honolulu, HI, USA
ACM 978-1-4503-3068-8/14/10.
http://dx.doi.org/10.1145/2658779.2658784

remains very difficult due to many challenges (e.g., uncomfortable sensors, unreliable ground truth data, uncontrolled environment) [5]. This work explores how Google Glass can help address some of the main challenges in the measurement, recognition and adaptation of real-life emotions, enabling fundamental advances for the creation of affect-based user interfaces in natural settings.

Affect Sensing

Google Glass (*Google Inc.*) is a commercial head-mounted wearable device equipped with several sensors (e.g., accelerometer, camera), connectivity capabilities (e.g., Bluetooth, WiFi), and a see-through display (see Figure 1). The device is designed to be worn like a pair of glasses, enabling gathering personal information of the wearer during daily activity. In a recent exploration [3], we have shown that motion sensitive sensors such as the accelerometer embedded in Glass can accurately capture subtle head motions due to the beating of the heart and respiration of the person, enabling comfortable measurement during sedentary activities in an office.

Glass can also be connected with existing state-of-the-art wearable devices that can comfortably monitor other relevant physiological signals. For instance, we have created a custom-made Android program that connects Glass with the Q^{TM} sensor (*Affectiva Inc.*) through Bluetooth and enables continuous measurement and visualization of the captured data. Being able to wirelessly collect different physiological parameters and have them automatically synchronized with the same device is critical for the understanding of emotions during natural settings.

Emotion Recognition

Once physiological data have been collected, learning methods need to be applied to infer the emotional states. When applying these methods, two critical challenges need to be addressed: obtaining reliable emotional ground truth and capturing the variability of natural settings.

To address the first challenge, researchers traditionally request people to self-report their emotional levels on the phone [5]. However, participants do not always hear phone notifications and/or find the process of fetching the phone slow and emotionally disruptive. Due to the convenient location of the Glass see-through display and the multi touchpad, participants can be more aware about the notifications and reduce the reporting time, yielding more frequent and reliable emotional ground truth data.

Another critical challenge is the large variability and unpredictability of natural settings where many different events can yield similar physiological responses. For example, several kinds of activities – physical, emotional, and cognitive, can elicit physiological stress and across some channels of measurement the stress signatures may look the same. In order to clearly disambiguate the source of the physiological responses, contextual information is needed. Some of our previous work has explored how cellphone data such as GPS, Bluetooth, calendar and caller activity logs can provide rich contextual information for stress measurement and reflection [1]. We have also explored the possibility of capturing rich visual context with a phone hanging from the neck [2], offering the possibility of not only capturing relevant features such as the number of people in front of the camera, but also their emotional responses. Knowing the dynamics of how those faces are smiling or not, for instance, can help discriminate between positive and negative situations. As Glass is equipped with all the previous sensors, it enables capturing a wide gamut of insightful contextual information. In order to start exploring some of the possibilities, we connected Glass with custom-made smile recognition software [1], allowing real-time detection, counting, and visualization of surrounding smiles (see right of Figure 1).

Visualizing and Adapting to Emotions

The form factor of Glass enables unobtrusive real-time visualization of affective information, which can potentially empower the wearers to change their behavior and better influence certain emotional states. When displaying the average intensity of the smiles of people, for example, users can increase their awareness and provide more control over certain situations. For instance, during a public speaking scenario, the speaker may not be able to look at every face of the audience. However, by displaying aggregated metrics such as the average intensity of smile on the see-through display, the speaker could know when the audience is losing engagement and appropriately modify the speech. Similarly, people with visual impairments and/or nonverbal expression interpretation challenges could benefit from real-time technologies to help them sense the emotional responses of others and reduce the uncertainty and stress associated with social interactions.

Capturing and processing continuous affective information in real-time also enables providing timely and gentle emotion management interventions. For instance, Glass is able to display a breathing guide (a line that rises and falls, slowly, guiding the user towards deep in- and out-breaths), once the sensor detects increased levels of relaxation, the display can fade away. This intervention is very similar to traditional biofeedback exercises, which are widely used for emotion regulation. However, Glass offers the possibility of comfortably and unobtrusively delivering the intervention when most needed, *in situ*, for example when dealing with computer problems that pop up during paper deadlines.

CONCLUSIONS

Combining state-of-the-art biosensors with Google Glass technology promises to advance the creation of affect-based user interfaces. We have started building prototypes and feel obligated to also mention limiting factors. For instance, battery and storage space highly constraint the sensors that can be simultaneously recorded. Furthermore, important privacy concerns are raised when monitoring information of others and/or transmitting affective information over the wireless. Our research has begun exploring the potential implications of such technologies and is performing research studies that quantitatively and qualitatively analyze the advantages and limitations of such approaches.

ACKNOWLEDGMENTS

This material is based upon work supported by Google, NSF CCF-1029585, and the MIT Media Lab Consortium.

REFERENCES

1. Ayzenberg, Y., Hernandez, J., Picard, R. W. FEEL: Frequent EDA and event logging, a mobile social interaction stress monitoring system. In *Proc. of Extended Abstracts of CHI*, (2012), 2357-2362.

2. Hernandez, J., Hoque, M. E., Drevo, W., Picard, R.W., Mood Meter: counting smiles in the wild. In *Proc. of Ubicomp*, (2012), 301-310.

3. Hernandez J., McDuff D., Fletcher R., Picard, R. W., Inside-Out: Reflecting on your inner state. In *IEEE PERCOM Workshops*, (2013), 324-237.

4. Hernandez J., Li Y., Rehg J., and Picard R. W. Physiological parameter estimation using a head-mounted wearable device. Submitted for publication.

5. Picard R. W. *Affective Computing*. MIT Press, Cambridge, MA, USA, 1997.

6. Wilhelm F. H., Grossman P. Emotions beyond the laboratory: theoretical fundaments, study design, and analytic strategies for advanced ambulatory assessment. In *Biological Psychology*, 84, 3, (2010), 552-569.

A Text Entry Technique for Wrist-worn Watches with Tiny Touchscreens

Hyeonjoong Cho
Korea University
Sejong City, South Korea
raycho@korea.ac.kr

Miso Kim
Korea University
Sejong City, South Korea
shineblack@korea.ac.kr

Kyeongeun Seo
Korea University
Sejong City, South Korea
chemd111@korea.ac.kr

ABSTRACT

We consider a text entry technique for wrist-worn watches with inch-scale touchscreens. Most of the watches which are commercially available, for example, Galaxy Gear, Omate, etc., have around 1.5-inch touchscreens that is too small for the shrinked Qwerty keyboard. Moreover, the virtual button-based techniques determine input-letters by distinguishing touched locations on touchscreens which continuously demands a user to carefully touch certain locations. Thus, they are not suitable to tiny-touchscreen devices in mobile environment. Instead, the proposed text entry technique allows a user to touch almost anywhere on the touchscreen for text entry by determining input-letters based on drag direction regardless of touched location. We implemented the proposed method on a commercial watch with 1.54-inch touchscreen for validating its feasibility.

Author Keywords

Text entry; wrist-worn watch; smart watch; touchscreen;

ACM Classification Keywords

H.5.2. Input devices and strategies

INTRODUCTION

Wearable technologies recently gain public attention as the next market-dominant devices after smart phones. Various wearable devices including watches, glasses, bracelets, jewelry, have attempted to penetrate into the market [1]. An intrinsic demand for those wearable devices is that they should be lightweight and small enough to be unobtrusive in daily life. Thus, it hinders use of large or middle-sized touchscreens, *i.e.*, 4~7 inches, for the wearable devices. The restricted touchscreen devices are sometimes designed to be operated by recognizing human voice. However, even though voice input allows expressive and effective interaction, it could be problematic in noisy environments and raise privacy issues in public spaces [2]. On the other

hand, other wearable devices utilize small touch-enabled area for subtle gestural input, *e.g.*, the touch area on Google glasses, tiny touchscreen of Galaxy gear. These areas are large enough for simple touch gestures, *e.g.*, tap, flick, etc., but they are too small to type with Qwerty keyboard. Not only the restriction in size but also the well-known fat finger problem incurs significant inconvenience with the miniaturized Qwerty keyboard.

There have been a few commercially available text entry methods for those devices, e.g., *Minuum*, *Swipe*, *Fleksy*[3,4,5]. They all heavily rely on automatic spell correction that sometimes may incur difficulty particularly in typing passwords, URLs, etc. In academia, Oney *et al*. proposed *ZoomBoard* that uses iterative zooming to enlarge tiny Qwerty keys to comfortable size [6]. They used $16mm \times 6mm$ keyboard and achieved an average speed of 9.3 words per minute with acceptable accuracy. However, the virtual button-based techniques in principle determine input-letters by distinguishing touched locations on touchscreens, which continuously demands a user to carefully touch certain locations.

We propose *DragKeys* for wrist-worn watches with tiny touchscreens. DragKeys allows a user to touch almost anywhere on the touchscreen since it determines input-letters by distinguishing drag directions regardless of touched locations. It sets a user free from careful touch of correct locations in mobile environment.

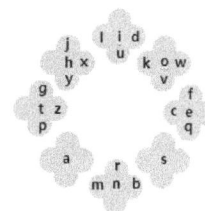

Figure 1. DragKeys on a write-worn watch with a 1.54-inch touchscreen and its key array

DESIGN

DragKeys has a key array that is circularly arranged around the text cursor, as shown in Figure 1. The key array is designed to continuously follow the text cursor as the typing progresses. DragKeys hierarchically contains two levels of key arrays and each level contains eight keys at most. A user enters a character by dragging the corresponding key to the text cursor but the user does not

UIST '14 Adjunct, Oct 05-08, 2014, Honolulu, HI, USA.
ACM 978-1-4503-3068-8/14/10.
http://dx.doi.org/10.1145/2658779.2658785

need to directly touch the keys. Figure 1 presents the key array of DragKeys designed for English. At most, five letters are assigned to each key in the first level. For instance, 'e', 'c', 'q', and 'f' are assigned to the same East key. To enter 'e', users generate a dragging gesture toward the West until the corresponding key reaches the text cursor in the middle of the keys. A user can enter 't', 'a', 'o', 'i', 'n', 's', and 'h' in the same way. Entering the other characters requires a few more gestures. To enter 'q', as shown in Figure 2, a user generates the first dragging gesture toward the West until the corresponding key reaches the text cursor. When it does so, the key is divided into the second-level keys around the text cursor again. A user then generates a second dragging gesture toward the North until the key corresponding to 'q' reaches the text cursor. Note that the gesture for entering 'q' is a single stroke with a single inflection.

The frequency of the English letters and our heuristic are considered to allocate letters to the keys. For example, frequently used letters, i.e., 'e', 't', 'a', 'o', 'i', 'n', 's', and 'h', are placed in the middle of the first-level keys such that a single linear dragging gesture is sufficient to enter them. After allocating the eight letters, the other 18 letters are also allocated based on our heuristic, for example, allocating a letter in order to make the dragging gesture to enter the letter resemble the letter shape.

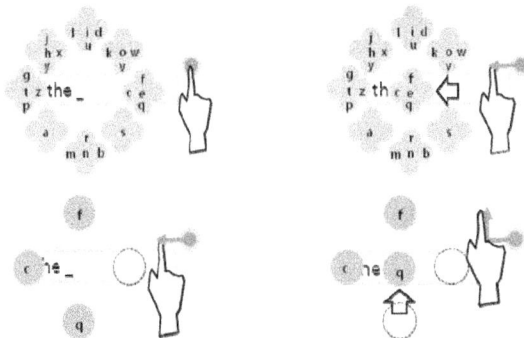

Figure 2. Sequence of entering 'q' with DragKeys

Kurtenbach *et al.* showed that consecutive off-axis marking gestures are difficult to perform accurately [7], and we therefore do not permit second-level off-axis dragging gestures. In addition, we consider that a single-stroke gesture consisting of two linear drags with no inflection is more difficult than one with a single inflection owing to a potential ambiguity. A light tapping gesture is designed to enter a 'space', and starting a dragging gesture with a double tap was designed to enter many other special letters. Two finger drag is also used to enter 'back space', etc.

IMPLEMENTATION AND FEATURES

We implemented DragKeys on a commercial wrist-worn watch, Goophone Smart Watch, with 1.54 inch touchscreen. Users can enter English alphabet, numbers, symbols, etc.

Since the key array of DragKeys is designed to superimpose and chase the text cursor, it leads the visual attention of users to where the text is actually being entered. This feature helps users focus more on what they are writing than on the positions of their fingertips as with Qwerty. DragKeys spatially separates its visual key array from the gesture sensing part. While users see their sentences when typing, their text entry gestures are read anywhere in the tiny touchscreen. Eventually after learning, this leads DragKeys to eyes-free text entry since a user can generate proper directional gestures relying on their proprioception without any visual feedback.

Additionally, two well-known problems of soft keyboards are inherently avoidable, *i.e.*, a finger occlusion problem in which a touching finger occludes other buttons on a soft keyboard, and a fat finger problem in which small buttons on the soft keyboard of a small touchscreen are hard to accurately touch with thick fingers. Finally, the multiple levels of key arrays that DragKeys may include are all centered on the text cursor. Thus, it spatially occupies a constant space rather than expanding its spatial occupation for a multilevel selection like in traditional pie menus[8].

CONCLUSION

We introduced DragKeys, a text entry technique for wrist-worn watches with tiny touchscreens. DragKeys allows a user to touch anywhere on the tiny touchscreen for typing. It is different from the tradition virtual button-based text entry techniques that continuously require users to carefully touch predefined locations on the touchscreens. Our future work includes running several user tests in various configurations with our current implementation to evaluate its performance in text entry speed, error rates, etc.

ACKNOWLEDGMENTS

This research was supported by BK21+ Prog., S. Korea

REFERENCES

1. Weiser.M. The computer for the 21st century. *SIGMOBILE Mob. Comput. Commun.* Rev. 3, 3(July 1999), 3-11.

2. Sawhney,N., Schmandt,C. Nomadic radio: speech and audio interaction for contextual messaging in nomadic environment. *ACM Trans. Comput.-Hum. Interact.* 7,3(2000), 353-383.

3. Minnum keyboard. http://minuum.com/

4. Swype keyboard. http://www.swype.com

5. Fleksy keyboard. http://fleksy.com

6. Oney, S., Harrison, C., Ogan, A., Wiese, J. Zoomboard: A diminutive Qwerty soft keyboard using iterative zooming for ultra-small devices, *CHI 2013*

7. Kurtenbach, G., Buxton, W., The limits of expert performance using hierarchic marking menus, *INTERACT'93 and CHI'93, ACM*, 1993, p. 482–487.

8. Callahan, J., Hopkins, D., Weiser, M., Shneiderman, B., An empirical comparison of pie vs. linear menus, *SIGCHI, ACM*, 1988. p. 95–100.

Understanding the Design of a
Flying Jogging Companion

Florian 'Floyd' Mueller   **Matthew Muirhead**

Exertion Games Lab

RMIT University

Melbourne, Australia

{floyd, matt}@exertiongameslab.org

ABSTRACT

Jogging can offer many health benefits, and mobile phone apps have recently emerged that aim to support the jogging experience. We believe that jogging is an embodied experience, and therefore present a contrasting approach to these existing systems by arguing that any supporting technology should also take on an embodied approach. In order to exemplify this approach, we detail the technical specifications of a flying quadcopter that has successfully been used with joggers in order to explore the design of embodied systems to support physical exertion activities. Based on interviews with five joggers running with our system, we present preliminary insights about the experience of jogging with a flying robot. With our work, we hope to inspire and guide designers who are interested in developing embodied systems to support exertion activities.

Author Keywords

Jogging; running; quadcopter; multirotor; drone; robot; exertion; sports; whole-body interaction; exergames

ACM Classification Keywords

H.5.2. [Information Interfaces and Presentation]: User Interfaces - Miscellaneous.

INTRODUCTION

Jogging has many health benefits and many people find it an engaging experience. In response, mobile phone apps have emerged that aim to support the jogging experience, for example the Nike+ app that reports to joggers how fast they ran. We note that these apps primarily focus on reporting athletic performance achievements and see an opportunity to explore alternative interactive technologies

Figure 1. We built a quadcopter for jogging outdoors

to support the jogging experience. In particular, we believe that jogging is an embodied experience [1] and that in consequence interactive systems aimed to support such activities should be designed with an embodied perspective in mind. In response, we present the technical details of a custom-made quadcopter for jogging as a result of having built and tested six quadcopters. Furthermore, we also present preliminary insights gained from having interviewed five joggers running with our system about their experience.

RELATED WORK

Prior work already demonstrated that a quadcopter could be used to support athletes [2], however, the objective of this prior system was to capture athletes' actions with an attached camera rather than investigate the interaction between the robotic system and the athlete (the objective of the study in this paper). The idea to support joggers with a quadcopter is also not new: an AR.Drone has been previously used to demonstrate the idea as a design concept [3], however, we found the hardware platform is not suitable for a formal user study. We are aiming to support not only indoor, but outdoor jogging, hence developed our own quadcopter system according to our requirements to suit a study with joggers outdoors [Fig. 1].

TECHNICAL DETAILS

After having custom-built six quadcopters in various configurations and sizes, we found the following system the best compromise between performance, safety, stability and outdoor flight characteristics [Fig. 2]: our current prototypal system consists of a Safeflight Quadcopter 500mm frame, Gemfan Carbon/Nylon 10 inch propellers and Sunnysky x2212 980kv brushless motors. The flight controller is a 3DR Pixhawk/PX4 controller (redundant STM32 microcontrollers) with ST Micro L3GD20 gyroscope, LSM303D accelerometer and magnetometer, Invensense MPU6050 accelerometer/gyroscope and MS5611 barometer. It also includes an off-board uBlox GPS and HMC5883 Magnetometer and has a 915MHz Telemetry link to a laptop running APM Planner 2.

Figure 2. The final design of the custom-built quadcopter.

PRELIMINARY INSIGHTS

We present preliminary insights based on five joggers running with our system for a minimum of 20 min each. Participants were casual joggers (jogging 1-4 times a month) and were given the opportunity to jog with the system beforehand in order to determine a pace that they found suitable. We used this to set up the speed of the quadcopter and laid out a jogging route in the shape of an approximate square over even terrain. We sent the route and speed to the quadcopter beforehand and the participants were free to jog with the quadcopter in any way they wanted and for how long they wanted. Immediately afterwards, while the joggers were still exhausted, we interviewed them about their experience.

We found so far that, firstly, jogging with a flying robot can be an engaging experience. Participants found jogging with the system an intriguing setup that motivated them to keep going. Participants reported that they could see the potential

of using such a setup to complement their jogging routine, but also to motivate them to run more often and even faster. They also found their runs to be more "fun" thanks to the quadcopter. Secondly, participants reported how running outdoors with the quadcopter, with the chance of being seen by other people, added to the excitement of running. This was surprising for us, as we expected apprehension of engaging with such a new setup in public, in particular in regards to the often negative connotation of drones in the media. Thirdly, the joggers reported that initially their focus was on the quadcopter, however, the novelty effect wore off quickly once they got tired, as their increasing exhaustion required them to refocus on the act of jogging itself. In particular, participants noted that the quadcopter became simply "a partner in the periphery". Fourthly, participants said that "who is in control" became an important question for them. On the one hand, the jogger is in control of the jogging experience, whilst on the other hand, the quadcopter determines the route (and the user-set speed). However, the jogger can regain control of the pace by cutting corners. Furthermore, because there is a perceived risk of the quadcopter dropping out of the air, the joggers run near, but not under the quadcopter, hence the system is determining where joggers are running explicitly (by means of the route), but also implicitly (by means of flying). As a result, the issue of control emerged for us as an intriguing theme for the design of robotic exertion systems.

DISCUSSION AND CONCLUSION

We presented a flying quadcopter aimed at supporting the jogging experience together with preliminary insights from casual joggers running with the system outdoors. This case study serves to exemplify our approach of investigating embodied systems to support exertion activities. Our contribution is two-fold: firstly, we provided the technical details about our system that successfully worked as jogging companion outdoors, which demonstrates the feasibility of our approach. Secondly, we presented preliminary feedback from joggers in order to construct an understanding of how such robots should be designed. Ultimately, with our work, we hope to inspire and guide designers who are interested in developing embodied systems to support exertion activities.

ACKNOWLEDGEMENTS

We thank all supporters of this work including the Australian Research Council Fellowship DP110101304.

REFERENCES

1. Dourish, P. *Where the Action Is: The Foundations of Embodied Interaction.* Boston, USA: MIT Press, 2001.
2. Higuchi, K., Shimada, T. & Rekimoto, J. Flying sports assistant: external visual imagery representation for sports training. In *Augmented Human*, 2011, ACM, 1-4.
3. Mueller, F., Graether, E. & Toprak, C., Joggobot: jogging with a flying robot. In *CHI'13 Extended Abstracts*, ACM, 2845-28

AirPincher: A Handheld Device for Recognizing Delicate Mid-air Hand Gestures

Kyeongeun Seo
Korea University
Sejong city, South Korea
chemd111@kroea.ac.kr

Hyeonjoong Cho
Korea University
Sejong city, South Korea
raycho@korea.ac.kr

ABSTRACT

We propose *AirPincher*, a handheld device for recognizing delicate mid-air hand gestures. AirPincher is designed to overcome disadvantages of the two kinds of existing hand gesture-aware techniques such as wearable sensor-based and external vision-based. The wearable sensor-based techniques cause cumbersomeness of wearing sensors every time and the external vision-based techniques incur performance dependence on distance between a user and a remote display. AirPincher allows a user to hold the device in one hand and to generate several delicate mid-air finger gestures. The gestures are captured by several sensors proximately embedded into AirPincher. These features help AirPincher avoid the aforementioned disadvantages of the existing techniques. It allows several delicate finger gestures, for example, rubbing a thumb against a middle finger, swiping with a thumb on an index finger, pinching with a thumb and an index finger, etc. Due to the inherent haptic feedback of these gestures, AirPincher eventually supports the eyes-free interaction. To validate AirPincher's feasibility, we implemented two use cases, i.e., controlling a pointing cursor and moving a virtual 3D object on the remote screen.

Author Keywords

Hand gesture recognition; hand-held device

ACM Classification Keywords

H.5.2 [information interfaces and presentation]: User Interfaces – Input devices and strategies.

INTRODUCTION

Among different body parts, the hand is the most effective, general-purpose interaction tool due to its dexterous functionality in communication and manipulation [2]. Hand gesture-aware recognition utilized wearable sensors such as data gloves and external video cameras [3]. Data gloves utilize sensors embedded into gloves to read hand and finger gestures. The close proximity between hands and sensors enable recognizing various delicate hand poses and movements. However, they require extensive calibration, restrict natural hand movement, and are often very expensive [3]. *FingerPad* is a nail-mounted device that turns the tip of the index finger into a touchpad using wearable magnetic sensors [1]. Despite their capability of detecting delicate finger gestures, the cumbersomeness of wearing them every time is unavoidable.

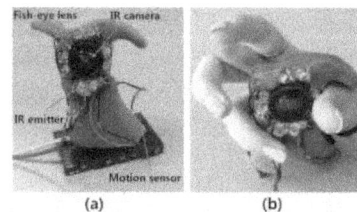

Figure 1. (a) A prototype of AirPincher, (b) User hand posture

On the other hand, hand gestures recognition based on external video cameras represents a promising alternative because of its potential to provide more natural, unencumbered, non-contact interaction [2]. Currently, several commercialized depth cameras, e.g., Kinect, provide three-dimensional visualization of objects, which allows barehanded control. A drawback of these approaches is that the performance of distinguishing small gestures depends on the distance between a camera and a user [3]. Additionally, the performance can be affected by a user pose, e.g., lying down. The hand gesture recognition also needs complex classification algorithms.

In order to alleviate those drawbacks of both approaches, we consider a new form factor, a graspable device embedded with a low-cost IR camera, IR emitters on each sides of the camera, a fisheye lens in front of the camera, and a low-cost motion sensor. The proposed device, *AirPincher*, allows a user to easily hold the device in one hand, to generate several finger gestures, e.g., pinching, rubbing, swiping etc., with a user's thumb, index and middle fingers of the holding hand. These gestures inherently offer haptic feedback and eventually support eye-free interaction. In addition, the close proximity between AirPincher and a user hand makes its performance independent from movement of the other body parts, e.g., lying down, walking. It allows a simple gesture recognition algorithm that robustly tolerates contextual noise.

UIST'14 Adjunct, October 5–8, 2014, Honolulu, HI, USA.
ACM 978-1-4503-3068-8/14/10.
http://dx.doi.org/10.1145/2658779.2658787

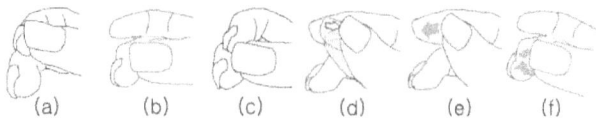

Figure 2. (a) Index finger pinch, (b) Middle finger pinch, (c) Index and middle finger pinch, (d) Double pinch (e) Swipe (f) Rubbing

AIRPINCHER DESIGN

Available gestures

The pinch gesture provides highly natural haptic feedback and instant availability[1]. Our hand is able to quickly bring a thumb and a forefinger together and apart and additionally, the tactile feedback from our pinch fingers makes us ensure whether the pinch is performed or not[4]. AirPincher supports several variations of the pinch gesture, as shown in Figure 2. Figure2 (a) and (b) shows a pinch with a thumb and an index finger and a pinch with a thumb and a middle finger, respectively. Figure2 (c) shows a pinch with a thumb, an index finger and a middle finger. Figure2 (d) is a double pinch corresponding to the double click of a mouse. Figure2 (e) shows a swiping thumb on an index finger. Figure2 (f) shows a rubbing thumb against a middle finger. These gestures can be mapped to various interfacing commands for current computers, e.g., left, right and double clicks, drag, scroll, mode switch, etc. Especially, Figure2 (f) shows the potential use of AirPincher as a mid-air touchpad for precise and stable 2D control of a pointing cursor. Furthermore, these gestures can be extended by combining them with output of the embedded motion sensor, such as the angular posture.

Implementation

Figure 1 shows our prototype of AirPincher and a user's holding hand. The IR camera and IR emitters are used to detect the pinch gesture of a user's holding hand and the motion sensor is used to measure the angular posture of AirPincher based on the roll, pitch and yaw angles. Its shape is designed to maintain IR camera to view the gestures of three fingers while a user holds the device. A fisheye lens is added to maximize the view angle of IR camera. As Figure 3 (a) shows a camera-captured image of a thumb and a middle finger, IR emitters help the fingers distinct from their background under different environmental light. After binarizing the images as in Figure 3 (b)-(h), gestures are recognized by a simple image processing algorithm. For example, a bundle of vertical lines only consisting of white pixels are established for Figure 3 (b)-(h). Based on the number of the lines that exceeds a predefined threshold, a pinch gesture occurrence is detected. According to the average of horizontal position of white vertical lines, the pinch gestures are classified into 3 kinds as shown in Figure3 (b)-(d). Subsequently, each pinch gesture is classified further. The index finger pinch is divided into a single pinch, a double pinch and a swipe, considering the duration of the pinch and the horizontal positional change of white vertical lines. The middle finger pinch is divided into a simple pinch and a rubbing using the

similar algorithm. In order to move a pointing cursor using the rubbing gesture, both horizontal and vertical movements of the rubbing need to be read. The horizontal movement is determined by the horizontal positional change of the white lines. The vertical movement is determined by the width of the thumb in the captured image, which is measured by counting the number of the white pixels on the top edge. These simple hardware and algorithm of AirPincher are advantageous to guarantees low power consumption and real-time gesture recognition.

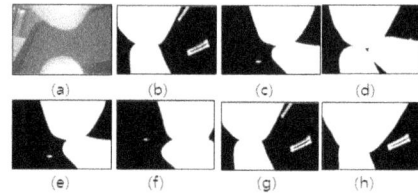

Figure 3. (a) Image captured from IR camera, (b) Middle finger pinch, (c) Index finger pinch, (d) Index & middle finger pinch, (e)-(f) Swipe, (g)-(h) Rubbing

Use cases

We implemented two use cases with AirPincher, controlling a pointing cursor and moving a virtual 3D object on the screen. A pointing cursor is controllable using rubbing, swiping, and pinching gestures. A user can also control a virtual 3D object using a pinch gesture together with the motion sensor output. More detailed demonstration is provided in our supplementary video clips.

CONCLUSION

We propose AirPincher, a handheld device for recognizing delicate hand gestures with a simple algorithm and a low-cost hardware. The design of AirPicher aimed at recognizing several hand gestures made by the user's thumb, index, and middle fingers. Our future work includes evaluating its performance in various configurations by conducting comprehensive user studies.

ACKNOWLEDGEMENTS

This work was supported by BK21+ Prog. funded by Ministry of Education, Science and Technology in S. Korea.

REFERENCES

1. CHAN, Liwei, et al. FingerPad: private and subtle interaction using fingertips. In Proc. *UIST 2013*. ACM Press (2013). 255-260.

2. EROL, Ali, et al. Vision-based hand pose estimation: A review. *Computer Vision and Image Understanding* (2007), 108.1: 52-73.

3. SUAREZ, Jesus; MURPHY, Robin R. Hand gesture recognition with depth images: A review. In *proc. RO-MAN*. IEEE(2012). 411-417.

4. Wilson, A. D. Robust computer vision-based detection of pinching for one and two-handed gesture input. In *Proc. UIST2006*. ACM Press (2006). 255-258.

Contelli: A User-Controllable Intelligent Keyboard for Watch-Sized Small Touchscreens

Taik Heon Rhee, Kwangmin Byeon, Hochul Shin

Samsung Electronics Co., Ltd.

129 Samsung-ro, Yeongtoung-gu, Suwon-si, Gyeonggi-do 443-742, Korea

{taikheon.rhee, km.byeon, darkblue}@samsung.com

Figure 1. *Contelli*, a user-controllable intelligent keyboard, allows a user actively determine a text entry mode according to the duration of key-tapping. (a) Automatic replacement mode: a string with short-tapped letters (e.g. 'gangnam') is automatically replaced into a suggested word (e.g. 'hangman'), the most probable one from the keyboard's lexicon. (b) Manual input mode: a string (e.g. 'gangnam') remains as typed when every letter is long-tapped. Each long-tapped letter is displayed in red.

ABSTRACT

Intelligent keyboards aid fast text entry by correcting user's erroneous input, but there is a big problem that a user always has to watch and judge of their suggestion results. *Contelli*, a user-*con*trollable in*telli*gent keyboard, monitors the duration of each key-tapping, and analyzes the possibility of mis-typing only for short-tapped letters. A long-tapped letter is regarded as a precise input and excluded in the process of candidate generation from a lexicon. Using *Contelli*, a user may actively 'control' the intelligent keyboards. S/he may type ordinary words quickly on watch-sized small touchscreens. Also, s/he may input a word as typed without switching off the automatic replacement or performing additional actions for the replaced result. In addition, long-tapping a part of a string reduces the number of replacement candidates, which contributes the more precise word replacement for highly erroneous input typed on small touchscreens.

Author Keywords

Contelli; user-controllable intelligent keyboard; intelligent keyboards; automatic word replacement; auto-correction

ACM Classification Keywords

H.5.2. [Information Interfaces and Presentation]: User Interfaces – Input devices and strategies

UIST'14 Adjunct, October 5–8, 2014, Honolulu, HI, USA.
ACM 978-1-4503-3068-8/14/10.
http://dx.doi.org/10.1145/2658779.2658788

INTRODUCTION

Intelligent keyboards, supported by automatic word-replacement or word-correction methods, are one of the most promising solutions to improve the efficiency of text entry on small touchscreens [1]. However, there is a big problem that a user always has to watch and judge of their suggestion results. On most commercial intelligent keyboards, an additional area is given to display the current input or suggested replacements, [2] or special swipe gestures can be used to make corrections [3]. As a result, a user may edit or change the decision of the intelligent keyboards, but s/he cannot 'control' the level of intelligence of the keyboards directly.

In this paper, we propose *Contelli*, a user-*con*trollable in*telli*gent keyboard. It monitors the duration of each key-tapping, and analyzes the possibility of mis-typing only for short-tapped letters. A long-tapped letter, which may be supported by a zooming UI, is regarded as a precise input and excluded in the process of candidate generation from a lexicon.

Using *Contelli*, a user may actively 'control' the intelligent keyboard. S/he may type ordinary words quickly on watch-sized small touchscreens with assistance from automatic word replacement function. Also, s/he may input a word as typed without switching off the function or performing additional actions for the automatically replaced result.

In addition, *Contelli* can contribute the more precise word replacement. A user may increase the accuracy of automatic replacement by just long-tapping a part of a string. This reduces the number of replacement candidates, since only ones with the same letters per each long-tapped letter's position can remains in the candidates.

CONCEPT AND IMPLEMENTATION OF CONTELLI

The main concept of *Contelli* is illustrated in Figure 1. Basically, as shown in Figure 1(a), when a user types a series of letters and a delimiter (e.g. space, enter) quickly with short-tapping, the string is automatically replaced into the most probable word from the keyboard's lexicon. On the other hand, as shown in Figure 1(b), s/he may input a word as typed by long-tapping every letter. It would be helpful when s/he wants to input out-of-vocabulary words, such as proper nouns, neologisms or foreign words.

Figure 2 describes another concept of *Contelli*. By designating a part of a string as precise input, a user can provide a hint for more precise word replacement. When a user often mis-types a certain word (e.g. 'rocket' → 'ticket' in Figure 2(a)), s/he may 'pin' a part of a string not to be replaced into other letters by long-tapping. By rejecting unwanted candidates which have different letters from the ones in the pinned positions, s/he can actively control the range of candidates.

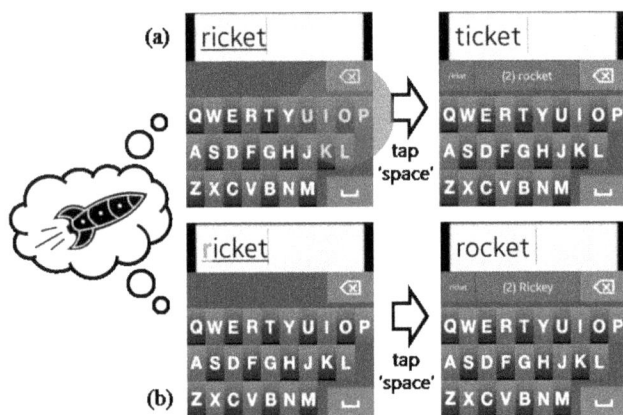

Figure 2. A user can provide a hint for more precise word replacement on *Contelli*. (a) A mis-typed text (e.g. 'ricket') may be replaced into not the intended word (e.g. 'rocket') but another one (e.g. 'ticket'). The red circle stands for the estimated average contact surface area of an index finger in proportion to the screen. (b) By long-tapping a part of a string (e.g. the first letter 'r'), the accuracy of automatic replacement is increased by rejecting unwanted candidates (e.g. ones not starting with 'r').

This concept is effective when the size of the keyboard is very small and the degree of erroneous input is higher. For example, the screen size of our implementation target Samsung Galaxy Gear is 3.0cm × 3.0cm (see Figure 3(a)). Considering the average width of the index finger is 1.6 to 2.0 cm for most adults [4] (see the red circle in Figure 2(a)), the small key size may cause more various types of erroneous input than those in smartphones. To input an exact letter on a small area, a zooming UI has been implemented as shown in Figure 3(b). In the experiment, the time threshold to distinguish between short and long press was set to 0.15 second.

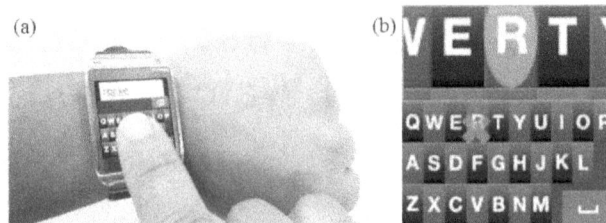

Figure 3. *Contelli* implementation on a watch-sized device. (a) Size comparison of *Contelli* with the actual hand and finger. (b) A screenshot of the zooming UI above the keyboard area. The blue cross denotes the actual touch point, which is not displayed on the touchscreen.

A preliminary experiment comparing with a commercial product [5] has shown that *Contelli* is useful for watch-sized small touchscreens. All of the six participants succeeded to type 20 words including five neologisms faster with the proposed keyboard than with the commercial one (see Figure 4). All of them expressed that the concepts of *Contelli* might be useful on watch-sized small touchscreens (4 'strongly agree' and 2 'agree').

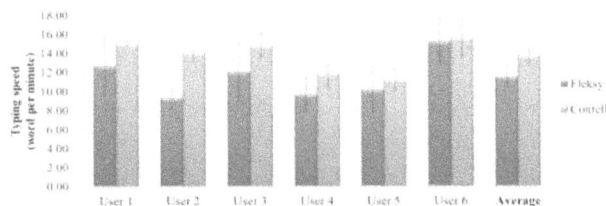

Figure 4. Typing speed comparison result (with 95% CI).

CONCLUSION AND FUTURE WORK

We proposed *Contelli*, a user-controllable intelligent keyboard for watch-sized small touchscreens which causes various types of erroneous input. A user may type any kinds of words whether it is included in a lexicon or not. Moreover, s/he can actively control the range of candidates by pinning a part of a string. We believe that these concepts would be highly effective for languages with more words or larger word variations than English, such as Chinese, Japanese or Korean.

REFERENCES

1. Bi, X., Ouyang, T., Zhai S., Both complete and correct? Multi-objective optimization of touchscreen keyboard, In *Proc. CHI 2014*, ACM Press (2014), 2297-2306.

2. Kocienda. K., Ordin, B., Method, system, and graphical user interface for providing word recommendations, U.S. Patent No 8,074,172 (2011).

3. Eleftheriou, K., User interface for text input, U.S. Patent Application 13/747,700 (2013).

4. Dandekar, K., Balasundar, B.I., Srinivasan, M.A., 3-D finite-element models of human and monkey fingertips to investigate the mechanics of tactile sense, J. Biomechanical Engineering 125, 5 (2003), 682-691.

5. Fleksy for Samsung Galaxy Gear 1, http://fleksy.com

G-raffe: An Elevating Tangible Block Supporting 2.5-D Interaction in a Tabletop Computing Environment

Jun-Gu Sim
CIDR Lab, Dept. of
Industrial Design,
KAIST, Yuseong-gu,
Deajeon, 305-701,
Republic of Korea
jungu.sim@kaist.ac.kr

Chang-Min Kim
CIDR Lab, Dept. of
Industrial Design,
KAIST, Yuseong-gu,
Deajeon, 305-701,
Republic of Korea
peterkim12@kaist.ac.kr

Seung-Woo Nam
Interactive 3D Research
Lab, ETRI, Yuseong-gu,
Deajeon, 305-700,
Republic of Korea
swnam@etri.re.kr

Tek-Jin Nam
CIDR Lab, Dept. of
Industrial Design,
KAIST, Yuseong-gu,
Deajeon, 305-701,
Republic of Korea
tjnam@kaist.ac.kr

ABSTRACT

We present an elevating tangible block, G-raffe, supporting 2.5-dimensional (2.5-D) interaction in a tabletop computing environment. There is a lack of specialized interface devices for tabletop computing environments. G-raffe overcomes the limitation of conventional 2-D interactions inherited from the vertical desktop computing setting. We adopted a rollable metal tape structure to create up and down movements in a small volume of the block. This also becomes a connecting device for a mobile display to be used with the tabletop computer. We report on our design rationale as well as the results of a preliminary user study.

AUTHOR KEYWORDS

Tangible interface; spatial interaction; interface devices;

ACM CLASSIFICATION KEYWORDS

H5.2 user interfaces—input devices and strategies

INTRODUCTION

The tabletop computing environment is widely used in the development of multi-touch interfaces and large display technologies. In the tabletop computing environment, a user interacts with the computer horizontally. However, interface devices for tabletop computers are still similar to those of vertically used desktop computers. Few specific interface devices have been developed for the tabletop computing environment. Tabletop computing offers a new interaction space that intuitively integrates the real and digital worlds; we can put real world objects and associate them with the information on the display. In the meantime, multiple displays can be used together when overlapped on top of the tabletop display.

One way to improve tabletop interaction is to use tangible blocks. Tangible blocks offer new interaction techniques that

UIST'14 Adjunct, October 5–8, 2014, Honolulu, HI, USA.
ACM 978-1-4503-3068-8/14/10
http://dx.doi.org/10.1145/2658779.2658789

users can use to directly manipulate digital information. Examples include Lumino [1], Tangible bots [2], Relief [3], ZeroN [4],and CapStones [5], just to name a few. These research prototypes are passive and graspable devices supporting 2-D interactions. Although there are a few active blocks, expensive additional sensing equipment is necessary, decreasing the practicality. The potentials of horizontal interaction have not been fully explored.

We present a new tangible interface block, G-raffe, to efficiently adopt the features of the tabletop display. It allows users to use the mixed reality space above the tabletop display. As a tangible interface device, it can be used both for representation and control in 2.5-D space. It creates up and down physical movements with the least additional equipment of a rollable metal tape structure. Following, we will report on our design rationale and the results of a preliminary user study.

Figure 1. G-raffe, a tangible interface device providing 2.5-dimensional interaction above a tabletop display.

G-RAFFE

G-raffe is a tangible interface device, providing 2.5-D interaction above horizontal tabletop displays (Figure 1). It is a pointing device used with an elevated head piece that can display and manipulate spatial information. The up and down movement is made possible by a rollable steel ribbon structure that minimizes the size of the device. It is distinct from existing devices that require excessive sensing and actuating equipment.

The head part of G-raffe elevates according to the data linked in the contents and the location of the device on the tabletop display. Digital information is actively represented with physical feedback. The user can also directly manipulate the height to update associated data.

G-raffe was designed to support integrated use of multiple devices (e.g. tabletop computer with a smartphone). The information shown on the smartphone and tabletop screen is linked and updated in real time. G-raffe serves as a connecting and integrating device in the context where a user carries multiple devices.

APPLICATION

G-raffe can be applied in various contexts because it allows the use of mixed reality space on top of the tabletop display. For building site navigation (Figure 2), G-raffe can physically show the height of the location. An elevation view can be shown when the head height is adjusted. Annotation or floor-specific information can be added for different heights of a building.

G-raffe can also be used in educational applications (Figure 3). Biological information, such as from living animals or plants, can be actively shown on the height of a mountain or the depth of the sea, enhancing the engagement of child users.

Figure 2. Building site navigation application. Data mapping (left); developed application (right).

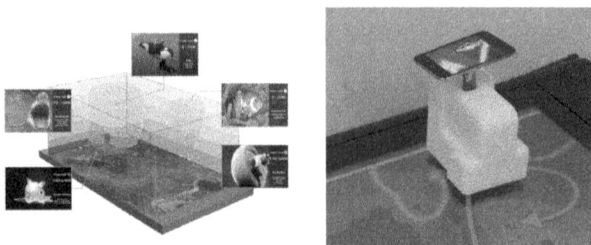

Figure 3. Biological education application. Data mapping (left); developed application (right).

PRELIMINARY USER STUDY

A preliminary user study was conducted to evaluate the usefulness of the device in different contexts and collect feedback on how to improve the device. Six college students participated in the study. Wacom CINTIQ 24HD Touch display was used as the tabletop computing setting. After a 10-minute tutorial session, participants freely used G-raffe for about 20 minutes according to three application scenarios: 3-D data navigation, building floor navigation, and site-specific biology content navigation.

Participants responded that G-raffe helped them to understand virtual spatial data more intuitively due to the physical activation. They appreciated that G-raffe made it possible to manipulate three-dimensional contents without bulky equipment like HMD or trackers. They considered the device engaging and playful because the information shown on the head part was actively updated according to the contents of the tabletop screen with physical movement.

Several limitations of the device were also found. Most notable was the unstable holding unit and the slow elevating speed. Also, delays between the tabletop screen and the mobile phone display were noted. Some of the participants felt uncomfortable that the main body of G-raffe covers the screen space of the tabletop display.

CONCLUSION

In this paper, we presented a tangible block providing a new user experience in a tabletop computing environment' G-raffe, a compact tangible interaction device with a height-controlling feature. Application scenarios and preliminary user study were also introduced. G-raffe can be a new type of active interface device for the tabletop computing environment, efficiently integrating three-dimensional information. We expect G-raffe can be applied in various contexts, including educational software, navigation systems, and data visualization in tabletop computing environments.

REFERENCES

1. Baudisch, P., Becker, T., & Rudeck, F. (2010). Lumino: Tangible blocks for tabletop computers based on glass fiber bundles. *Proc. of CHI, 10,* 1165-1174.

2. Pedersen, E. W., & Hornbæk, K. (2011). Tangible bots: Interaction with active tangibles in tabletop interfaces. *Proc. of CHI, 11,* 2975-2984.

3. Leithinger, D., et al. (2011). Direct and gestural interaction with relief: A 2.5-D shape display. *Proc. of ACM symposium, 11,* ACM Press, 541-548.

4. Lee, J., et al. (2011). ZeroN: Mid-air tangible interaction enabled by computer controlled magnetic levitation. *Proc of ACM symposium, 11,* 327-336.

5. Chan, L., et al. (2012). CapStones and ZebraWidgets: Sensing stacks of building blocks, dials, and sliders on capacitive touch screens. *Proc of CHI 12,* 189-2192.

Building Implicit Interfaces for Wearable Computers with Physiological Inputs: Zero Shutter Camera and Phylter

Tomoki Shibata, Evan M. Peck, Daniel Afergan, Samuel W. Hincks, Beste F. Yuksel, Robert J.K. Jacob

Tufts University

Medford, MA, 02155, USA

{tshibata,epeck02,afergan,shincks,byukse01,jacob}@cs.tufts.edu

ABSTRACT

We propose implicit interfaces that use passive physiological input as additional communication channels between wearable devices and wearers. A defining characteristic of physiological input is that it is implicit and continuous, distinguishing it from conventional event-driven action on a keyboard, for example, which is explicit and discrete. By considering the fundamental differences between the two types of inputs, we introduce a core framework to support building implicit interface, such that the framework follows the three key principles: Subscription, Accumulation, and Interpretation of implicit inputs. Unlike a conventional event driven system, our framework subscribes to continuous streams of input data, accumulates the data in a buffer, and subsequently attempts to recognize patterns in the accumulated data – upon request from the application, rather than directly in response to the input events. Finally, in order to embody the impacts of implicit interfaces in the real world, we introduce two prototype applications for Google Glass, *Zero Shutter Camera* triggering a camera snapshot and *Phylter* filtering notifications the both leverage the wearer's physiological state information.

Author Keywords

implicit interface; wearable computing; Google Glass; brain-computer interface; BCI; fNIRS

ACM Classification Keywords

H.5.m. Information Interfaces and Presentation (e.g. HCI): Miscellaneous

INTRODUCTION

With both the rise of wearable computing devices and physiological sensors, the integration of sensing technology into wearables is becoming increasingly common. However, despite the advertised potential, there are only a few existing applications to date that leverage this input to ease interaction. When compared to stationary computers, wearables tend to have advanced but limited communication channels to/from

wearers. For example, Google Glass, a head mounted wearable device, offers two main interaction methods: touch gestures on the side bar and voice commands, but does not come with a conventional keyboard or mouse input. Behind the advent of wearable technology era, it is a challenge to design interfaces by taking advantages of having physiological inputs as additional communication channels.

To address this challenge, we build implicit interfaces which have the potential to augment conventional interaction styles. Implicit interfaces take the wearer's physiological signals as input and adapt to the wearer's present physiological state. In this way wearable computers can have the ability to *passively* act on the behalf of the user on a moment-to-moment basis by responding the wearer's physiological state, which is unlike the conventional Human-Computer Interaction in which explicit action initiates system response. Unlike explicit inputs, which are discrete commands by the user, such as typing on a keyboard, implicit physiological inputs are contiguous and may or may not require its immediate utilization. Because of the fundamental difference between the two types of inputs, a mechanism to accommodate implicit inputs is essential for implementing implicit interfaces.

This paper presents our core framework for building implicit interfaces, based on three principles: 1) *Subscribing or receiving passive sensor information*, 2) *Accumulating or holding implicit input*, and 3) *Interpreting the wearer's state*. The purpose of introducing this framework is to ease the implementation of implicit interface applications. We then present two prototype applications for Google Glass that make use of this framework - *Zero Shutter Camera* and *Phylter*, which both leverage the wearer's brain state information.

RELATED WORK

We have been studying Brain-Computer Interfaces (BCI) with using functional near-infrared spectroscopy (fNIRS), measuring hemodynamic changes happening in the prefrontal cortex. In a recent study, Afergan et al. showed a physiological interface making changes to a system when detecting periods of extended high or low workload can keep users engaged [1]. In this paper, we propose a method for abstracting the process to deal with passive physiological inputs, originally implicit brain input considered in our preliminary BCI study. We introduce three key principles for utilizing physiological input from any sensor in implicit user interfaces.

CORE FRAMEWORK WITH THREE KEY PRINCIPLES

In this section, we consolidate a core framework aiming to accommodate implicit input. The core framework adhere to the three key principles:

1) Subscription: Ability to continuously receive information since implicit physiological input is a stream of information. (Client-Server architecture over a Bluetooth, IP-based or even wired connection would be applicable to achieve this.)

2) Accumulation: Ability to hold the received information for a certain duration in order to allow pattern recognition over recent past data.

3) Interpretation: Ability to recognize the wearer's present physiological state based on the accumulated information when the wearable computer asks. (Since there may be more than one implicit channel, this ability is also responsible to encompass all implicit input channels.)

In order to illustrate the impact of our core framework in implicit interactions between wearable and wearer, we next introduce the two prototypes built on its foundations: *Zero Shutter Camera* and *Phylter* for Google Glass.

Zero Shutter Camera

Zero Shutter Camera is a native Google Glass application that takes the prediction of the wearer's state as input and triggers a camera snapshot at special moments. *Zero Shutter Camera* determines when to take pictures by continuously monitoring the wearer's physiological state over a Bluetooth connection. Figure 1 represents the implicit interaction flow, invoked by the application passively responding to the wearer's current physiological state. To test the application, we used our real-time brain monitor [2] as input.

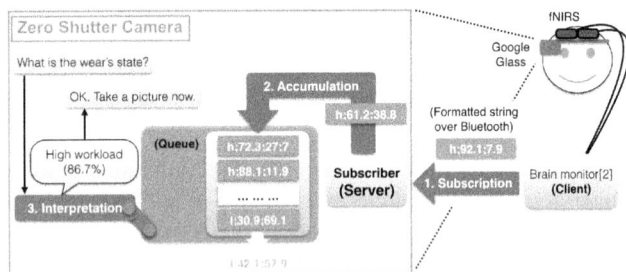

Figure 1. Zero Shutter Camera Framework. The introduced core framework 1) *subscribes* **continuous state classification data as the formatted string, 2)** *accumulates* **at least 10 [sec] of the immediate data in the queue, and 3)** *interprets*, **when the application asks, by reporting the quantified confidence value [%] of the wearer being in a high or low workload state by averaging the accumulated data. Finally, if the application understands the wearer is in high workload state with a confidence value above a heuristic threshold, then takes a picture for the wearer.**

We emphasize that the *Zero Shutter Camera* is *not* a direct control to push the shutter button by the brain. Instead, it passively takes pictures for the wearer based on the wearer's physiological state via an implicit communication channel. Because physiological state changes from moment to moment, not only can the *Zero Shutter Camera* be used in daily life as a life-log, it comes into its own in situations where the wearer is having situation disability - a circumstance where a non-disabled person is considered to be having temporal but critical disability due to the immediate context. For instance, the application would be most beneficial for police officers or medical doctors who are dealing with emergency situations where both hands are preoccupied.

Phylter

Without an intelligent protocol for timing and filtering content, notifications by wearable devices can easily distract wearers. Aiming to mitigate the issue, *Phylter* is an intermediate software between notification senders and Google Glass to schedule the delivery of notifications by using predictions of the wearer's state as input. We tested *Phylter* with our real-time brain monitor [2] as input. *Phylter* assesses the interruptibility of the user based on wearer's current brain state, ultimately deciding if she has the cognitive resources available to handle a notification of a known level of importance.

Phylter treats the implicit brain input in exactly the same way as *Zero Shutter Camera* by following the introduced core framework, except that implicit physiological information is conveyed over an IP-based connection. *Phylter*'s decision making logic is that whenever *Phylter* receives a notification from a notification sender, inspecting the wearer's current state. If the wearer has high cognitive workload with a heuristic threshold value, then *Phylter* blocks the notification; otherwise, delivers it to Google Glass.

Although we demonstrate two prototypes that take wearer's brain state as input, they can be easily modified to integrate other types of physiological input as long as they follow the introduced core framework.

CONCLUSION

Incorporating our three key principles (Subscription, Accumulation and Interpretation), we introduced the core framework to support implementing implicit interfaces for wearable computers. We presented two prototypes built on the foundation of the core framework for Google Glass, *Zero Shutter Camera* and *Phylter*, and illustrated their implicit interactions between wearable and wearer. We believe that the use of physiological input for implicit interfaces serves as an appropriate stepping-stone to an era in which wearable computers are not only worn by humans but actually become a part of the body.

NOTES

Zero Shutter Camera is made open source located at `https://github.com/zshiba/zero-shutter-camera`.

We thank NSF (IIS-1065154 and IIS-1218170) and Google for supporting this research.

REFERENCES

1. Afergan, D., Peck, E. M., Solovey, E. T., Jenkins, A., Hincks, S. W., Brown, E. T., Chang, R., and Jacob, R. J. Dynamic difficulty using brain metrics of workload. In *Proc. CHI 2014* (2014).

2. Girouard, A., Solovey, E. T., and Jacob, R. J. Designing a passive brain computer interface using real time classification of functional near–infrared spectroscopy. *IJAACS 6*, 1 (2013), 26–44.

PoliTel: Mobile Remote Presence System that Autonomously Adjusts the Interpersonal Distance

Masanori Yokoyama
NTT Service Evolution
Laboratories
Kanagawa, Japan
yokoyama.masanori@lab.ntt.
co.jp

Masafumi Matsuda
NTT Communication
Science Laboratories
Kyoto, Japan
matsuda.masafumi@lab.ntt.
co.jp

Shinyo Muto, Naoyoshi Kanamaru
NTT Service Evolution Laboratories
Kanagawa, Japan
{muto.shinyo,
kanamaru.naoyoshi}@lab.ntt.co.jp

ABSTRACT
Mobile Remote Presence (MRP) system that uses a smart device such as smartphone and tablet pc as video conferencing equipment is getting popular. There are varieties of smart devices, and the appearance of a smart device varies from one to another. We assumed that the appropriate interpersonal distance for an MRP system varies depending on the appearance of the smart device. To confirm our assumption, we conducted a preliminary experiment. The result of the experiment suggested that the value of the proper interpersonal distance increases as the video size increases. It is known that the task load of the remote operator of the MRP system increases if the operator is forced to manually control the MRP system to keep the interpersonal distance to the appropriate level, which adversely affects the quality of the communication through MRP. To resolve the problem, we propose PoliTel, a novel MRP system which autonomously adjusts the interpersonal distance according to the appearance of the smart device by controlling the position or video size of MRP, and allows the operator to concentrate more on the conversation with the person facing to the MRP system.

Author Keywords
Telepresence; proxemics; interpersonal distance; semi-autonomy; human robot interaction

ACM Classification Keywords
H.5.2. Information interfaces and presentation: User Interfaces – Interaction styles

INTRODUCTION
Mobile Remote Presence (MRP) system consists of video conferencing equipment and a device which carries the video conferencing equipment. Recently, MRP system that

uses specified smartphone and tablet pc as video conferencing equipment [1] is getting popular. In the near term, the MRP system that can incorporate various models of smart devices will come on the market. There are varieties of smart devices, and the appearance of a smart device varies from one to another. It is suggested that the appearance of the MRP system affects the characteristics of the communication through MRP system [2]. Among several features which characterize the communication through MRP system, we especially focused on the interpersonal distance, the distance between person and MRP system [3], since it is known that the distance between the persons greatly affects the quality of the communication. We assumed that the appropriate interpersonal distance (shown in Figure 1) for an MRP system varies depending on the appearance of the smart device. The task load of the remote operator of the MRP system will increase if the operator is forced to manually control the MRP system to keep the interpersonal distance to the appropriate level, because it is difficult to drive the MRP system delicately using the controller [3]. In this work, we report the result of a preliminary experiment which investigates the relation between the appearance of the smart device incorporated into the MRP system and the proper interpersonal distance for the MRP system. Based on the result of the experiment, we propose PoliTel (Polite Telepresence system), a novel MRP system which autonomously adjusts the interpersonal distance according to the appearance of the smart device by controlling the position or video size of the MRP system.

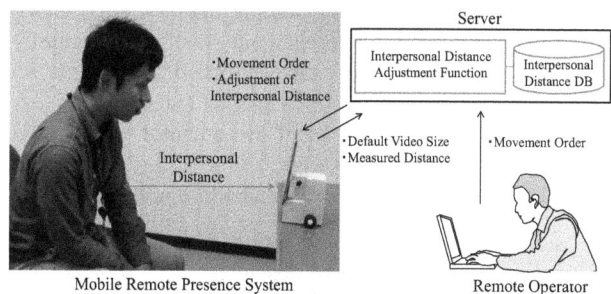

Figure 1. System Overview of PoliTel.

INTERPERSONAL DISTANCE FOR MRP
We conducted a preliminary experiment to confirm that the appropriate interpersonal distance for an MRP system

varies depending on the appearance of the smart device. The appearance of the smart device includes the display size and video size. We hypothesized that the interpersonal distance for the MRP system is affected only by the video size. In this experiment, we prepared two smart devices (10 inch display and 5 inch display), and tested the following experimental conditions: For 10 inch display, (a) face occupies full screen, (b) upper body occupies full screen, (c) upper body occupies half the area of the full screen, and for 5 inch display, (d) face occupies full screen, (e) upper body occupies full screen. In this experiment, nine male volunteer speakers (ages 26-42) speak their favorite things to another three male volunteers (ages 24-30) in separate room through the MRP system. For each experimental condition, the speakers went through a round of 5 tasks. The speakers are asked to place the chair on their satisfied position in front of the MRP system by themselves before sitting down on the chair and start to speak. All of the participants were explained about the aim of this experiment after the experiment. The number of pixels between the speakers and MRP system on the video that was shot by fixed camera was measured. One pixel was compatible with 2mm of real size. Figure 2 shows 9 speaker's mean and standard deviation of the interpersonal distance. As expected, the tendency that the mean of the interpersonal distance on bigger video size conditions was bigger than that on smaller video size conditions was observed.

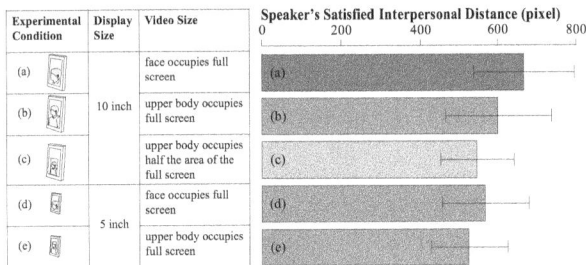

Figure 2. Mean of Interpersonal Distance in Each Experimental Condition.

POLITEL

In view of the result of the preliminary experiment and the fact that the task load of the remote operator increases if forced to adjust the interpersonal distance manually, following requirements of semi-autonomous system are needed: (1) to adapt to various sizes of the smart devices, (2) to reduce of the task load of the operator of the MRP system arises from manually controlling the MRP system to keep the interpersonal distance to the appropriate level.

The semi-autonomous method that indicates additional information such as a map of obstacles and a trajectory of the free path was proposed [3], but it is suggested that the time to complete the task increased in the method. Consequently, previous method doesn't satisfy system requirement (2).

PoliTel has following features to fulfill the system requirements: (1) getting the information about the default video size of the smart device to adjust the interpersonal distance, (2) autonomously adjusting the interpersonal distance by controlling the position or video size of the MRP system and presenting no extra information for the operator. Figure 1 shows the system overview of PoliTel. The MRP system is loaded with range sensors to measure the distance between the obstacles and front/back side of MRP. The server has a DB that includes video sizes and the proper interpersonal distances. When the operator turns on the system, the server gets the information about the default video size from MRP system, and selects the proper interpersonal distance from the DB. The distance between the obstacles and front/back side of the MRP system is measured receiving a queue generated by detecting faces in the video taken by the front camera of the smart device. The distance measured by the front sensor is treated as the interpersonal distance. When the difference between measured distance and appropriate interpersonal distance exceeds the threshold, the server starts to adjust the distance. When the operator have not manipulated the system for a certain amount of time, the server judges that the operator has no intention to drive the MRP system, and adjusts the interpersonal distance by controlling the position of the MRP system. In the case that the distance required to be displaced for the adjustment is longer than the measured distance, or that the operator manipulates the MRP system frequently, the server adjusts the interpersonal distance by controlling the video size.

Interpersonal distance adjustment function of PoliTel allows the operator to concentrate more on the conversation with the person facing to the MRP system in the use case that the shop staff meets the client at the remote place.

CONCLUSION AND FUTURE WORK

We suggested that the value of the proper interpersonal distance increases as the video size increases by the preliminary experiment, and proposed PoliTel, a novel MRP system which autonomously adjusts the interpersonal distance by controlling the position or video size of the MRP system. Further work is needed to investigate whether the results arose from proxemics or visibility of the display, and to invent the algorism to select the proper way for the adjustment considering the cost and risk of each way.

REFERENCES

1. Romo: http://www.romotive.com

2. I. Rae, L. Takayama, and B. Mutlu, One of the gang: supporting in-group behavior for embodied mediated communication, in *Proc. of CHI*, pages 3091–3100, 2012.

3. A. Kristoffersson, S. Coradeschi, and A. Loutfi, A Review of Mobile Robotic Telepresence, *Advances in Human Computer Interaction*, page 1–17, 2013

Riding the Plane – Bimanual, Desktop 3D Manipulation

Jinbo Feng
The University of North
Carolina at Charlotte, USA
jfeng3@uncc.edu

Zachary Wartell
The University of North
Carolina at Charlotte, USA
zwartell@uncc.edu

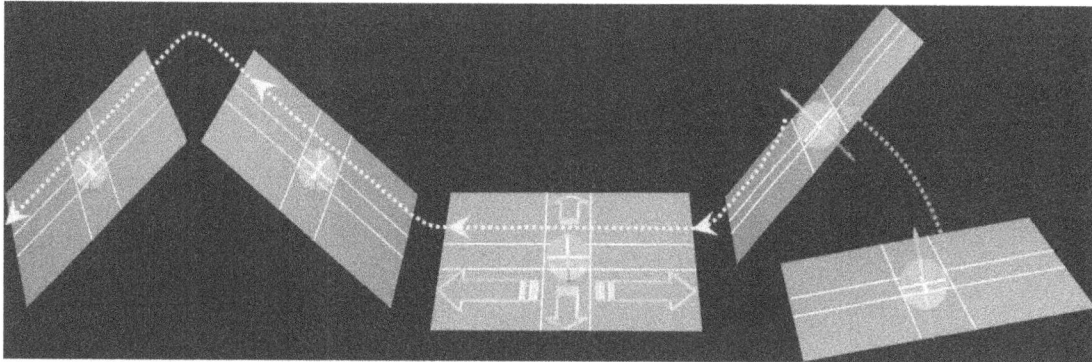

Figure 1. A possible dotted path of 3D cursor by moving perpendicular to (blue) and on (yellow) the cursor plane

ABSTRACT

A bimanual 7 Degree of Freedom (DOF) manipulation technique based on a hybrid 3D cursor driven by the combination of mouse and trackball is presented. This technique allows the user to move the cursor to the target location in 3D scene by following a conceived straight or curved path. In the pilot study, participants could learn the technique in a short time and perform the docking task steadily without physical fatigue.

Author Keywords

3D manipulation; Stereoscopic Virtual Environment; Docking test; 7 Degree of Freedom; 2D input device

ACM Classification Keywords

H.5.m. Information interfaces and presentation (e.g., HCI): User Interfaces; Input devices and strategies.

INTRODUCTION

Many 3D interaction techniques based on 2D input devices use virtual 3D widgets and convert 2D desktop gestures into the movements in 3D space driven by the cursor movement on the 2D screen plane [1]. Many of these manipulators require a relatively complicated combination of menu selections and keystrokes while still only allowing movement in fixed directions [2]. 3D input devices have a direct mapping between the physical and object movement which is more intuitive. However, 3D devices do not always outperform mouse based techniques for 3D tasks,

UIST'14 Adjunct, October 5–8, 2014, Honolulu, HI, USA.
ACM 978-1-4503-3068-8/14/10.
http://dx.doi.org/10.1145/2658779.2658792

such as 3D object placement [3]. In addition, missing physical support with isotonic 3D input, either free hand or held devices, introduces greater arm fatigue.

We present a bimanual technique using a mouse and 3DOF trackball for 3D spatial interaction. The devices control a translucent 3D cursor made of sphere embedded in a square. The trackball controls the cursor orientation while mouse motion moves the cursor parallel (or perpendicular) to the plane embedding the square. We describe the technique's use in a 7 DOF (pose + scale) docking task and discuss early evaluations.

METHODOLOGY AND IMPLEMENTATION

Usually, mouse cursor is restricted on the screen plane and users have used to the mouse – cursor movement mapping even there is an almost $90°$ angle between their moving directions. We assume it would be easier to understand the mapping if the angles are smaller than 90 degrees (Fig .2).

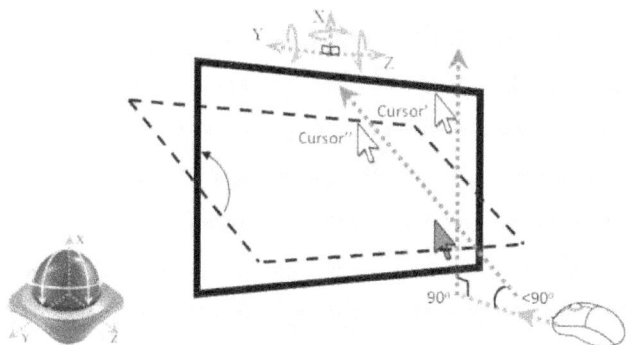

Figure 2. 3DOF trackball and cursor movement in planes

Thus, we created a 3D hybrid cursor which has a constraint cursor plane and restricted the default cursor movement on this plane (which could also enhance depth perception [4]) instead of the screen plane. Then, the cursor could slide to any location of the 3D environment by changing the tilt angle of the plane. Also, a spherical core which always locates at the center of the cursor plane indicates the cursor location and rotation center of the cursor plane.

The attitude of the cursor plane is controlled by a trackball (Fig. 2) which could rotate along all 3 Cartesian axes and map the rotation directly to the plane rotation. The cursor plane always rotates along the same absolute world axis as the rotation axis of the trackball despite its attitude. For instance, in Fig. 2, the trackball and cursor plane have the same Cartesian axes, if we rotate trackball along X axis (white cursor), both dotted and solid planes will rotate along X axis with the same direction (light blue cursor).

The cursor translation is restricted on the cursor plane driven by standard mouse with the motion direction following rules analogous to resolution of forces (Fig. 3).

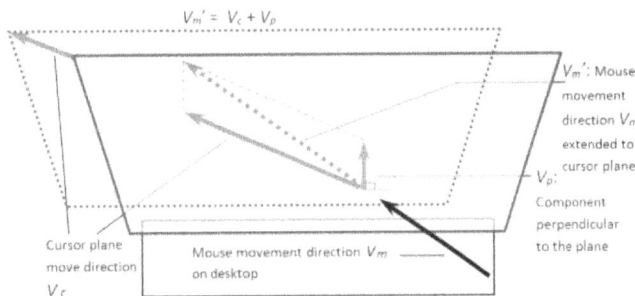

Figure 3. Movement mapping between mouse and cursor plane motion directions in a Top-down perspective view

When the mouse is moved in a direction V_m on the desktop (Fig. 3), the direction of the motion is extended directly onto the cursor plane location (V_m') and resolved into a perpendicular component V_p to the cursor plane and a component V_c on it. By default, we assume the hybrid cursor can only be translated on the cursor plane with the direction of V_c. When the right mouse button is clicked, the cursor translates in the perpendicular component direction V_p. The magnitude of cursor translation is same as the displacement of mouse on desktop (Position Control). The user could move the mouse while rotating the trackball to approximate a curved path in 3D space (Fig. 1).

To manipulate an object in the virtual environment, the user places the spherical core inside the target, then, the target movement is attached to the cursor movement. The object scaling is controlled by the mouse wheel.

PRELIMINARY USER STUDY

The experiment uses a desktop VR setup with Nvidia 3D Vision for stereo display. Software is based on OSGVE [5] and Microsoft Raw Input. A translucent docking box of fixed size is shown at the center of the screen with a random orientation for each trial. Three target boxes with yellow frames with different sizes are located at random positions above a checkerboard ground plane (Fig. 4). Each box face has a unique color. The user selects each target box and aligns it with the docking box matching like colored faces via translation, rotation and scaling. Each target box vertex must be within 0.84 cm [6] of the corresponding docking box vertex.

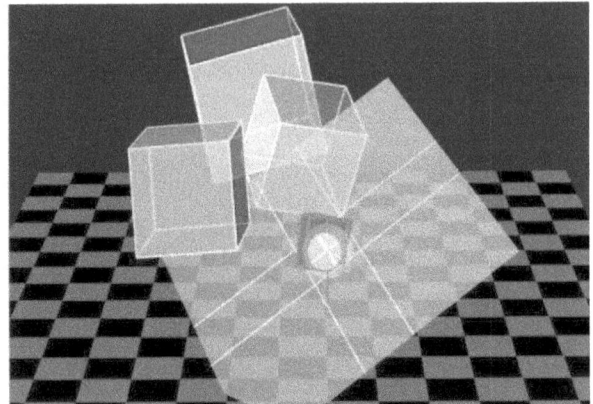

Figure 4. Docking task environment

We ran a pilot student with 3 students from Architecture and Mechanics. After averaged 10 trials, they achieved a 40 second completion time for docking a single box. Subjectively they rated the rotation as intuitive and enjoyed "flying" the cursor in 3D scene. Other 2 users achieved completion times in 15 seconds after 40 minutes training.

CONCLUSIONS AND FUTURE WORKS

This poster presents a bimanual, desktop 3D manipulation technique that could possibly be used for geometric modeling and other applications. We performed an initial pilot study. We are planning a comparative study that will include other manipulation techniques using 2D and 3D input technologies.

REFERENCES

1. Blender Manual, Manipulators: http://wiki.blender.org/index.php/Doc:2.6/Manual/3D_interaction/Transform_Control/Manipulators.

2. Eric Allan Bier. Skitters and jacks: interactive 3D positioning tools. In *Proc.* I3D '86, ACM Press (1986), 183-196.

3. François Bérard, Jessica Ip, Mitchel Benovoy, Dalia El-Shimy, Jeffrey R. Blum and Jeremy R. Cooperstock. Did "Minority Report" Get It Wrong? Superiority of the Mouse over 3D Input Devices in a 3D Placement Task. In *Proc.* INTERACT '09, 400-414.

4. Zhai, S., Buxton, W., and Milgram, P. The partial-occlusion effect: utilizing semitransparency in 3D human-computer interaction. ACM TOCHI '96, Vol. 3, No. 3. 254-284.

5. Suma Evan, osgVirtualEnvironment. http://osgve.sourceforge.net/.

6. Zhai, S. and Milgram, P. Quantifying coordination in multiple DOF movement and its application to evaluating 6 DOF input devices. In *Proc* CHI 1998, 320–327.

Hairlytop Interface: A Basic Tool for Active Interfacing

Shuhei Umezu   **Masaru Ohkubo**   **Yoshiharu Ooide**   **Takuya Nojima**

Graduate School of Information Systems, University of Electro-Communications

1-5-1, Chofugaoka, Chofu, Tokyo, 182-8585 JAPAN

{s.umezu, marchalloakbow, y.ohide}@vogue.is.uec.ac.jp, tnojima@nojilab.org

ABSTRACT

The Hairlytop Interface is a high scalability interface composed of hair-like units called smart hairs. The original version of the smart hair comprised a shape-memory alloy, drive circuits, and a light sensor. Simply placing the smart hair above a light display device enabled each smart hair to be bent and controlled by modulating the intensity of light from the display. Various prototypes of the Hairlytop Interface have been created to show its high flexibility in configuration. This flexibility should help users to develop their own moving interfaces.

Author Keywords

Smart hair; Hairlytop Interface; shape-memory alloy; soft actuator; haptic; surface display; smart material interface.

ACM Classification Keywords

H.5.2 [**Information interfaces and presentation**]: User Interfaces – *Interaction styles*

INTRODUCTION

Many animals use their hair/fur to communicate their emotional state. For instance, bristled hair often indicates anger, excitement, or surprise. Similarly, a cluster of filament-like materials, such as hair and carpet pile, has sufficient potential to act as a human-machine interface if its shape is controllable as for animals. The Hairlytop Interface, which is a collection of such filament-like material, called "smart hair", is a system originally based on this concept [4]. Comprising a shape-memory alloy (SMA), drive circuits, and light sensor, a smart hair placed over a conventional light display such as LCD enables it to be controlled through changes in the intensity of light.

One of the main characteristics of the Hairlytop Interface is its high degree of flexibility in configuration. The generic structure of the smart hair is quite simple allowing various types of smart hairs to be easily developed. This flexibility

UIST '14 Adjunct, Oct 05-08 2014, Honolulu, HI, USA
ACM 978-1-4503-3068-8/14/10.
http://dx.doi.org/10.1145/2658779.2658793

should help users to develop a variety of original moving interfaces. Plentiful variations provide lots of different modes of interactivity.

RELATED WORK

A collection of soft, filamentary materials is often used for creating various types of interfaces. Nakajima et al. developed FuSA2, a graphic display consisting of optical fibers [2]. This system offers a soft surface to the touch, like a coating of fur, and provides visual feedback by stroking, tearing, and other actions. However, it is not shape controllable. The fur interface by Furukawa et al. is an active fur interface [1]. Using vibration motors, their system offers controlled bristling, but this interface requires motors to control every piece of fur, and hence causes low flexibility in configuration. Nakayasu et al. developed next a system called "plant", which is an application of their proposed motion display [3]. The display is composed of sparsely integrated SMA-based units. Each unit is fixed tightly to a frame, but its configuration is not easy to change.

BASIC STRUCTURE OF THE HAIRLYTOP INTERFACE

The basic structure of the Hairlytop Interface (**Figure 1**) is a collection of smart hairs. The SMA of each hair is covered with a flexible tube and connected to the drive circuit incorporated with a light sensor. The amount of bending of the SMA integrated flexible tube can then be controlled through light intensity. In this original version, a conventional LCD display is used to provide the controlling modulation signals of light.

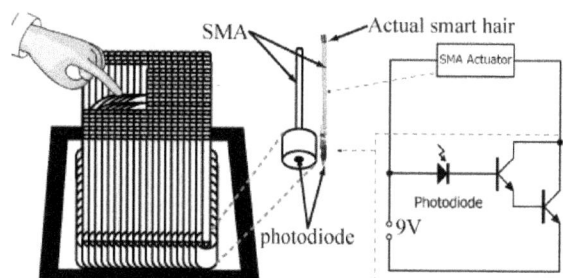

Figure 1. Illustration of the Hairlytop Interface, smart hair, and its basic drive circuitry.

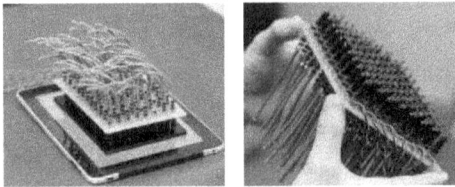

Figure 2. Photos of the Hairlytop Interface

(Left: atop a LCD; Right: view of light sensors)

VARIATIONS OF THE HAIRLYTOP INTERFACE

Furry decoration

To improve its appearance, a furry decorated version of a smart hair was developed (Figure 3). By covering the original smart hair with fur for handcrafts, the original, lawn-like appearance becomes a furry animal-like appearance common to many domestic and wild animals (Figure 4). This appearance should help the Hairlytop Interface to be used as an emotive communication medium as with animals.

Figure 3. Furry decoration of a smart hair.

Figure 4. Original version of the Hairlytop Interface (a-1, a-2), and a furry-decorated version (b-1, b-2).

Variations of control signals

As the basic structure of the smart hair is simple, it is easy to change sensors. In consequence, various kinds of signals can be used to control its movements. The left panel of **Figure 5** shows a prototype that uses a line signal from a tablet. In this version, the smart hair represents a dog's ear, which can express in its movements emotions such as joy and sadness. To control the bending of the smart hair, different frequencies within a sound signal are generated periodically.

Figure 5. Hairlytop interfaces controlled by acoustic signals.

The right panel shows another prototype that uses an acoustic signal. In this version, any musical instruments, or even handclapping, can be used to control the amount of bending of the smart hair. Using sound to control the Hairlytop Interface makes its design much easier for the casual user.

Block-like structure to improve their composition

When considering situations where thousands of smart hairs are used, block-like smart hairs might be more suitable (Figure 6). Although a smart hair does not need a signal wire, a power cable is necessary. In this situation, connecting power cables is a bothersome task. This block-like structure helps users to join and separate thousands of smart hairs. In the figure, SMA is installed on top of a black box. Inside the box, basic drive circuits are inserted. A silver tape attached to the surface of the box is used to supply the current. Thus, a simple contact between blocks enables power to be supplied. Additionally, four magnets are mounted in the box and used to couple and decouple one box from another. This function should make re-configuring boxes much easier.

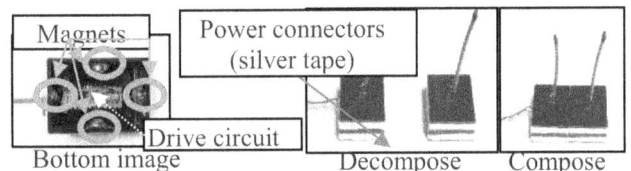

Figure 6. Prototype of block-like smart hairs.

CONCLUSION

Various prototypes of the Hairlytop Interface are described to highlight their high flexibility in configuration. The smart hairs have ample potential as a fundamental unit that could form various user-interactive interfaces. In future work, we shall continue to develop such interfaces with a view to broaden their application.

REFERENCES

1. Furukawa, M., Uema, Y., Sugimoto, M., and Inami, M. Fur interface with bristling effect induced by vibration. *Procs of the Augmented Human*, (2010), Article No. 17.

2. Nakajima, K., Itoh, Y., Tsukitani, T., et al. FuSA2 touch display: a furry and scalable multi-touch display. *Procs of the ACM International Conference on Interactive Tabletops and Surfaces*, (2011), 35–44.

3. Nakayasu, A., Tomimatsu, K. SMA motion display: plant. *Procs of the ACM SIGGRAPH Posters*, (2010), no. 29.

4. Ooide, Y., Kawaguchi, H. and Nojima T. An assembly of soft actuators for an organic user interface. *Procs of the ACM UIST*, (2013).

Speeda: Adaptive Speed-up for Lecture Videos

Chen-Tai Kao, Yen-Ting Liu, Alexander Hsu

Computer Science Department

Stanford University

{chentai, eggegg, kzm}@stanford.edu

ABSTRACT

Increasing the playback speed of lecture videos is a common technique to shorten watching time. This creates challenges when part of the lecture becomes too fast to be discernible, even if the overall playback speed is acceptable. In this paper, we present a speed-up system that preserves lecture clearness in high playback rate. A user test was conducted to evaluate the system. The result indicates that our system significantly improves user's comprehension level.

Author Keywords

MOOC; playback; speed

ACM Classification Keywords

H.5.2. User Interfaces: User-centered design

INTRODUCTION

Increasing popularity of Massive Open Online Course (MOOC) has resulted in a variety of user behaviors intended to boost study efficiency. Using higher playback speed is a common technique to save precious watching time, as long as the overall lecture remains understandable. However, due to fluctuating speaking rate, sometimes it becomes impossible to understand video segments where the speaker talks fast. Also, there exists room to accelerate video segments with little information (e.g. long pauses) to further save time. These problems inevitably lower both study efficiency and quality.

Several works focused on video and audio summarization [1] [5], using techniques including time compression and pause reduction. However, crucial information may be missing in video summaries, making the lecture inconsistent. Smart-Player [2] achieved adaptive video fast-forward based on the complexity of current scene and predefined semantic events. In this manner, users were able to scan through video faster without missing areas of interest. While the work considered video complexity, it did not exploit speech features, which rendered the lecture impossible to listen.

In this paper, we propose that the playback speed should be dynamically adjusted based on instantaneous syllable density.

UIST '14, Oct 05-08 2014, Honolulu, HI, USA

ACM 978-1-4503-3068-8/14/10.

http://dx.doi.org/10.1145/2658779.2658794

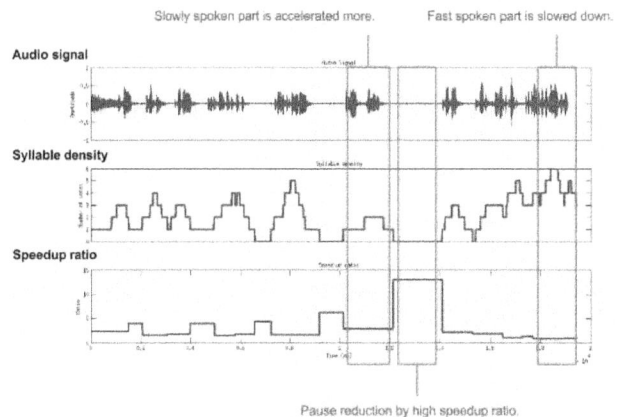

Figure 1. An audio sample processed by Speeda. Top to bottom: The original audio signal; instantaneous syllable density; speed-up ratio of each clip. Note that the speed-up ratio is calculated inversely proportional to the speaking rate, which is indicated by syllable density.

That is, video segments with few syllables should be accelerated more, and vice versa. Consequently, playback time can be minimized while the lecture remains clear enough to understand.

We introduce Speeda, a video speed-up system that implements this concept. With wide adoption of MOOC videos, Speeda is able to save large amount of learning time and boost learning quality simultaneously.

SYSTEM DESIGN AND IMPLEMENTATION

To ensure every part of the video is discernible, the speed-up ratio is made inversely proportional to the syllable density. See Figure 2 for architecture of Speeda, which we explain below.

First, syllables detected by Harma's method [4] are used for segmentation, generating lots of *clips*. There are two kinds of *clip*, where a *segment* contains several syllables, and a *pause* has none. For every *segment*, the speed-up ratio is determined by its average syllable density as follows:

$$\text{speedup ratio} = \text{desired speed} \times \frac{\text{segment's syllable density}}{\text{video's syllable density}}.$$

All *pauses* are sped up to have 0.2 seconds, which is short but good enough for breaking in sentences. Now the speed-up ratio of all segments and pauses are determined, we speed

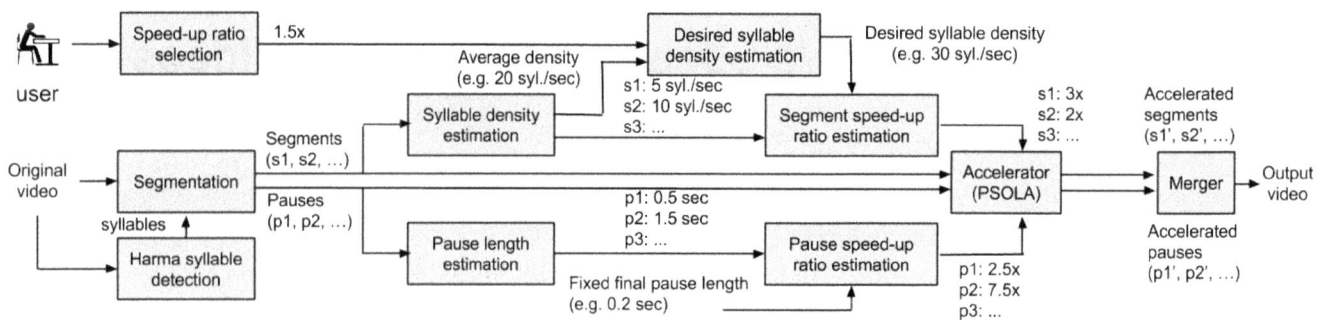

Figure 2. The Speeda system. Given the desired speed, Speeda calculates each clip's speed-up ratio and accelerates the video accordingly.

up each clip accordingly by Pitch Synchronous Overlap and Add (PSOLA) [3], a time stretching technique that changes speed of an audio signal without affecting its pitch. We then concatenate all the clips to generate the output video. Figure 1 gives an example of a 10-second speech sample processed by Speeda.

EVALUATION AND RESULT

Our research question was whether video generated by Speeda improves user's comprehension level compared to normal speed-up video of the same length. To answer the question, we picked a TED talk video no participant has watched before. The talk was about ethics, reducing the bias of participant's prior knowledge. Both the standard 2x speed-up version and an Speeda version were generated and had the same length. Lasecki et al. [6] used comprehension test to evaluate the impact of various video caption systems on students' comprehension level. Similar method was adopted here to evaluate Speeda.

10 students participated our user study (5 females, age ranged from 19 to 35). All of them had experience watching MOOC videos, spending 1-3 hours per week in average. Participants were randomly divided into two groups. We conducted a between-subject study, where one group watched normal speed-up video, and the other watched the Speeda version. After that, we asked 6 comprehension questions, with score ranging from 0-6, which was the number of questions correctly answered.

We found comprehension improvement for users who watched the Speeda version. A t-test comparing the comprehension score of the control (normal speed-up, mean = 2, std. dev = 0) to the scores with the treatment condition (Speeda speed-up, mean = 3.6, std. dev = 1.1402) is significant (t(-3.1379) = 0.03492, p¡.05).

DISCUSSION

The study result indicates that Speeda improves comprehension. Surprisingly, our method is not overwhelmingly favored by all participants. Some reported that the video sped up by Speeda sounds slightly unnatural. How to improve the video quality requires further exploration.

Although the video content accelerated by Speeda were better understood, note-taking under such high playback speed was still stressful, as suggested by some feedback. This can be expected, given that the lecture time is drastically compressed. It thus highlights the potential to explore how to pause lectures adaptive to its context.

CONCLUSION

In this paper we presented a speed-up system that plays lecture fast and clear, by using syllable density to dynamically determine the speed-up ratio. We believe that the proposed system has several strengths. First, fast spoken parts are slowed down, greatly boosting learning quality. Second, slowly spoken parts are accelerated even more, saving precious watching time. Lastly, as shown by a user study, Speeda significantly enhanced user's comprehension level.

REFERENCES

1. Arons, B. Speechskimmer: A system for interactively skimming recorded speech. *ACM Trans. Comput.-Hum. Interact. 4*, 1 (Mar. 1997), 3–38.

2. Cheng, K.-Y., Luo, S.-J., Chen, B.-Y., and Chu, H.-H. Smartplayer: User-centric video fast-forwarding. In *Proceedings of the SIGCHI Conference on Human Factors in Computing Systems*, CHI '09, ACM (New York, NY, USA, 2009), 789–798.

3. Gold, B., Morgan, N., and Ellis, D. *Speech and Audio Signal Processing: Processing and Perception of Speech and Music*, 2nd ed. Wiley-Interscience, New York, NY, USA, 2011.

4. Harma, A. Automatic identification of bird species based on sinusoidal modeling of syllables. In *Acoustics, Speech, and Signal Processing, 2003. Proceedings. (ICASSP '03). 2003 IEEE International Conference on*, vol. 5 (April 2003), V–545–8 vol.5.

5. He, L., Sanocki, E., Gupta, A., and Grudin, J. Auto-summarization of audio-video presentations. In *Proceedings of the Seventh ACM International Conference on Multimedia (Part 1)*, MULTIMEDIA '99, ACM (New York, NY, USA, 1999), 489–498.

6. Lasecki, W. S., Kushalnagar, R., and Bigham, J. P. Helping students keep up with real-time captions by pausing and highlighting. In *Proceedings of the 11th Web for All Conference*, W4A '14, ACM (New York, NY, USA, 2014), 39:1–39:8.

Structured Handoffs in Expert Crowdsourcing Improve Communication and Work Output

Alex Embiricos, Negar Rahmati, Nicole Zhu, Michael S. Bernstein
Stanford University
{embirico, negar, nicolez, msb}@cs.stanford.edu

ABSTRACT

Expert crowdsourcing allows specialized, remote teams to complete projects, often large and involving multiple stages. Its execution is complicated due to communication difficulties between remote workers. This paper investigates whether structured handoff methods, from one worker to the next, improve final product quality by helping the workers understand the input of their tasks and reduce integration cost. We investigate this question through 1) a "live" handoff method where the next worker shadows the former via screen sharing technology and 2) a "recorded" handoff, where workers summarize work done for the next, via a screen capture and narration. We confirm the need for a handoff process. We conclude that structured handoffs result in higher quality work, improved satisfaction (especially for workers with creative tasks), improved communication of non-obvious instructions, and increased adherence to the original intent of the project.

Author Keywords

Expert crowdsourcing; crowdsourcing; CSCW;

INTRODUCTION

Many professional, complex projects are split and structured into interdependent tasks [4]. As a result, there is a salient need to enhance crowd collaboration among experts[3]. However, most existing crowdsourcing platforms assume that work will be carried out independently, resulting in additional time and labor incurred during moderation, integration and bugfixing [5]. The expert crowdsourcing model introduces complications in coordination and conflict [5] which is similar to coordination neglect in traditional organizations [2].

This paper introduces lightweight, structured handoffs to minimize coordination neglect, through person-to-person, i.e. "live" and artifact-to-person, i.e. "recorded" methods. These are applied to remote, expert crowdsourced projects that require technical and creative expertise. We hypothesize that having a formalized structure of handing off the task from one worker to the next will help workers understand the form

UIST'14 Adjunct, October 5–8, 2014, Honolulu, HI, USA.
ACM 978-1-4503-3068-8/14/10.
http://dx.doi.org/10.1145/2658779.2658795

and function of their task input, reduce integration costs, and prevent downstream errors.

STUDY DESIGN

This study manipulated the web design and implementation process. 16 participants worked to build 6 newsfeed webpages. We designed our task to: 1) have precedence and relevance to the crowdsourcing community, 2) have open ended solutions which leave room for creative license, 3) be challenging enough to assess technical capability/shortcomings, 4) require communication of different areas of expertise among workers, and 5) be sequential since sequential task decompositions are more scalable than parallel setups[1].

In the "live" scenario, the experimenter "authors" the task, and hands off the requirements to the designer through a live conference and screen share. Both then interface together for a desired amount of time in activities of their choosing. The author then leaves the call and the designer proceeds with the work. Once the designer indicates completion, he/she then performs the same screen sharing and video conferencing step with the developer.

The "recorded" scenario consists of screen and audio recording as the method of handoff, so the previous worker is not required to be present for the next. Designers make a short screen capture video (1-5 minutes) with voiceover for the developer. Designers are encouraged to navigate the design flow, show inspirational websites, voice general intentions, etc.

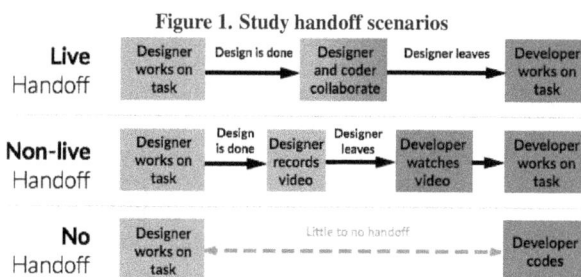

Figure 1. Study handoff scenarios

Since all scenarios entail two roles, a designer and a developer, we strove for conformity during hiring. We recruited designers on Stanford campus and developers via oDesk.

Procedure

Two methods, one live and the other recorded, are refined and tested. In addition, there is a control group given the same task but no instructions for performing the handoff, to simulate the existing standard in crowdsourcing. Two runs are performed for each method, each with one front-end designer and one front-end developer (see Figure 1).

The designer is given a very rough idea of what to wireframe from the author, i.e. the experimenter. The control scenario experts were simply given the authors' original instructions and open access to the work done by previous workers. All project-related materials are shared via Google Drive and workers are given uniform access.

RESULTS AND DISCUSSION

16 participants successfully carried out their roles in the 6 projects to completion. These participants have unique survey answers, and comprise of 6 different newsfeed designs and front-end code.

H1: Handoffs help the workers understand the form and function of the input of their tasks

In general, users found that time spent doing live and recorded handoffs were "valuable" or "somewhat valuable". Under all test scenarios, we found that all workers indicated valuable time spent when learning about the work already done.

We assessed user experience in various aspects. On a scale from −1 to 1, the developers' satisfaction of information received was 0.8 in the handoff scenario and 1.0 in the no handoff scenario. On the other hand, the designers' satisfaction was 0 in the handoff scenario and −1 in the control scenario. We found that while developer satifaction were unchanged by the handoffs, the designers responded more positively in the handoff condition.

This suggests that for creative tasks such as design, it is important to have handoffs to convey quality information. This result is further validated by worker comments in the survey: a designer in the handoff condition found that "The instructions were very long," whereas a designer in the non handoff requested that we "make [the] author guideline more sophisticated."

We coded assessments of designers' wireframes and developers' code. The best compliance of developer's work to designer's intent was seen with the live handoff. Both designers for the "live" handoff scenario intended for simple and minimal interfaces, which were reflected in their final HTML layout. Author handoffs and instructions explicitly state "minimialist" desires. In the control case, the exact lines of designers' wireframes were rigidly followed. We derive the insight that: in handoffs, workers were able to better perpetuate the minimalistic, newsfeed-like design intention from author, to designer, and finally to the developer.

H2: Handoffs reduce process losses and integration costs

"Live" handoffs helped developers ramp up to the design intent in an average of 1.5 minutes. From live chat logs, we know both trials averaged 10 minutes of interaction. The 1.5 minute in ramp-up time in the live scenarios indicate time that developers spent independently assessing previous work.

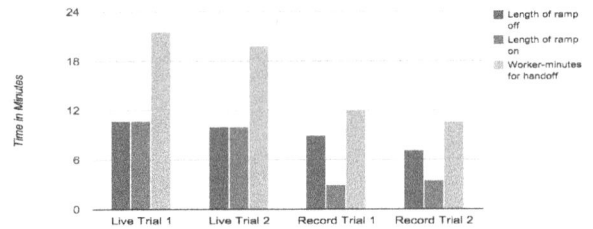

Figure 2. Lengths of time used by workers for handoff

Thus they found the getting up to speed process less frustrating than the control group, who spent an average of 7.5 minutes reading instructions and wireframes. The "recorded" handoff participants reported the highest ramp-up times, averaging 8 minutes across 4 people.

An average of 10 minutes were spent for live handoffs (see Figure 2). In the "recording" scenario, the previous worker spent more time making the video. But the subsequent worker spent significantly less time ramping up to the designer's work. We venture to extrapolate that, should creating the videos become more convenient, the total time for the "record" handoffs will further decrease.

CONCLUSION

We found that integrating handoffs in expert crowdsourcing produced better results. Live and recorded handoff methods led to more work output and higher quality work than no handoffs. For remote experts with flexible schedules, the live handoff method proves most effective. For the common case, when workers cannot agree on a time to meet, the recorded method provides an alternatively effective improvement. Future work should consider and implement the introduced handoff techniques in expert crowdsourcing platforms such as Foundry[5].

REFERENCES

1. André, P., Kraut, R. E., and Kittur, A. Effects of simultaneous and sequential work structures on distributed collaborative interdependent tasks. In *Proceedings of the 32nd annual ACM conference on Human factors in computing systems*, ACM (2014), 139–148.

2. Heath, C., and Staudenmayer, N. Coordination neglect: How lay theories of organizing complicate coordination in organizations. *Research in organizational behavior 22* (2000), 153–191.

3. Kittur, A. e. a. The future of crowd work. In *Proceedings of the 2013 conference on Computer supported cooperative work*, ACM (2013), 1301–1318.

4. Malone, T. W., and Crowston, K. The interdisciplinary study of coordination. *ACM Computing Surveys (CSUR) 26*, 1 (1994), 87–119.

5. Retelny, D., e. a. Expert crowdsourcing with flash teams. *27th annual ACM symposium on User interface software and technology* (2014). (in press).

LightWeight: Wearable Resistance Rehab Visualization

Zane Cochran,
Brianna Tomlinson
Georgia Institute of Technology
School of Interactive Computing
85 Fifth Street, Atlanta, GA, 30308
zrcochran3@gatech.edu,
btomlin@gatech.edu

Dar-Wei Chen
Georgia Institute
of Technology
School of Psychology
654 Cherry Street,
Atlanta, GA, 30332
darwei.chen@gatech.edu

Kunal Patel
Georgia Institute of Technology
School of Computer Science
266 Ferst Drive
Atlanta, GA 30332-0765
kpatel333@gatech.edu

ABSTRACT

People recovering from arm injuries are often prescribed limits to the amount of strain they can place on their muscles at a given point during the recovery process. However, it is sometimes difficult for them to know when a given activity creates strain in excess of these limits. To inform this process, we have developed a prototype, the LightWeight, and describe it here. The aim of the LightWeight is to inform users of the strain on targeted muscles as the activity occurs, and to display the relationship of that strain to the aforementioned limits. LightWeight is embedded within a compression sleeve that measures muscle strain through conductive fabric and EMG while displaying that information through an intuitive circular LED display.

Author Keywords

Wearable technology, User Interface, rehabilitation, human factors.

ACM Classification Keywords

H.5.2 [Information interfaces and presentation]: User interfaces – Prototyping.

INTRODUCTION

After injuries, student-athletes often undergo drastic lifestyle changes as they are not only unable to physically exert themselves at their usual high levels of performance, but also struggle with performing simple daily tasks. Regular sessions with trainers are often implemented as part of the rehabilitation process for these student-athletes.

Student-athletes are also often prescribed lifting restrictions for their activities outside of rehabilitation (e.g. limits on the amount of weight they can lift, push, or pull). However,

UIST '14 Adjunct, Oct 05-08 2014, Honolulu, HI, USA
ACM 978-1-4503-3068-8/14/10.
http://dx.doi.org/10.1145/2658779.2658796

they are not always well informed as to whether a given activity, such as opening a door, strains their muscles past their prescribed limits. Furthermore, because of this lack of knowledge, they are sometimes hesitant to do anything that might create muscle strain anywhere close to their limit and can sometimes experience muscle atrophy from low levels of exertion. A device that conveys this knowledge of muscle strain is the prototype presented here, and although the target user group here is student-athletes recovering from injuries, other potential users that could find this device useful include a variety of post-surgery patients and those working in occupations that require a significant amount of lifting or risk of overexertion.

PROTOTYPE DESIGN

The LightWeight is made of two main parts: A) A sport compression sleeve (Figure 1) embedded with conductive fabric electrodes, which is connected to a nearby electromyography (EMG) amplifier, and B) A circular array of sixteen individually-addressable RGB LED pixels to display muscle strain. The sleeve, which is made to be breathable and to shield the user from the electronics, is placed around the targeted muscle group to measure strain and relay that information to the user via the LED display.

When the device is turned on, the pixels in the LED display light up in sequence to orient the user to the display; similar activity occurs when the device is synchronized with the user's smartphone. Users will also be able to track progress and data through the LightWeight phone application when the two are paired (Figure 2).

Typically during rehabilitation and training sessions, users are not only prescribed an upper lifting restriction, but a lower one as well (to prevent the aforementioned muscle atrophy). These limits are displayed proportionally along the circular array of LEDs, informing the user of the desired muscle strain limitations. These lights are reconfigurable so that the display can adapt to changing prescribed lifting restrictions as the recovery process continues. These limits are shown distinctively in blue on the LED display (Figure 3); the other pixels fill the spaces in between the limits. The colors of those pixels change depending on the user's muscle strain relative to the limits: too little strain (yellow; Figure 4), an appropriate amount (yellow plus green; Figure 5), or too much (yellow, green, and red, with haptic

Fig. 1 Student athlete wearing the LightWeight sleeve.

Fig. 2 LightWeight mobile app tracking user data.

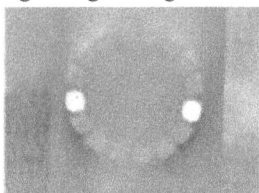

Fig. 3 Calibration Lights   Fig. 4 Strain below limit

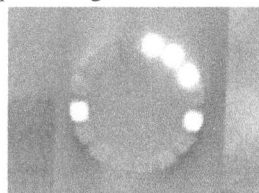

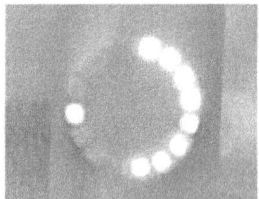

Fig. 5 Strain within limit   Fig. 6 Strain above limit

feedback also provided in upper portion of sleeve; Figure 6). These colors were chosen because their meanings are roughly equivalent to those of the colors on standard American stoplights (Nielsen, 1993, "Consistency and standards," para. 1): green denoting "proceed," yellow denoting "caution," and red denoting "stop." Similarly, the orientation of the circular array is set such that it can be read much like a standard analog clock: no weight (12 o'clock), lower limit (3 o'clock), and upper limit (9 o'clock) (Nielsen, 1993, "Match between system and the real world"). These design features will allow users to interpret output from the device in a way that is consistent with conventions learned from the outside world.

DISCUSSION

The next step to improving the LightWeight is to perform user evaluation/testing. Initial testing will focus on training mode because the device requires more attention from users there than in everyday mode. Due to various problems of testing the device on injured student-athletes (e.g. logistics, sample size, interruption of recovery schedules), tests will be carried out with healthy students as participants. The tests for participants will include lifting objects and performing workout activities while interpreting device feedback regarding muscle strain relative to prescribed lifting restrictions. Participants will also have the opportunity to provide feedback about the LightWeight's usability, comfort, and phone application.

To test the viability of the system, a set of user tests will determine not only users' weight perception accuracy with the device, but also measure how well users are able to interpret the information it provides. During the study, participants will place items of unmarked weight onto a segmented line drawn on the floor according to how heavy they believe the item to be. The segmented line will be divided into 16 equal portions, and markers will indicate on the line where the user's recommended lower and upper limits occur. Immediately after picking up a weighted item, users will place each one on the line relative to how much they think it weighs in relation to their recommended limits. For example, a user that believes an item is just under the upper limit may place the item left of and relatively close to the upper limit marker. This procedure eliminates the need for participants to remember multiple weights (and therefore getting them mixed up when reporting the weights) and more easily allows them to show understanding of the weights' relative order (important if user already knows generally what some reference weights feel like). The participants will be evaluated based on the average distance each placed weight is from the known, correct position on the line.

CONCLUSION

The LightWeight informs users of muscle strain, whether it occurs during rehabilitation or daily life, using intuitive design embedded within a comfortable athletic sleeve. Formal participant experiments in the future will test the practicality and display design of the device, spurring the next stages of improvement for the LightWeight.

ACKNOWLEDGMENTS

The authors would like to thank Dr. Lauren Wilcox, Carla Gibson, and the staff at the Georgia Tech Sports Medicine and Rehabilitation Clinic for their contributions to the development of this prototype.

REFERENCE

1. Nielsen, Jakob. (1993). *Usability Engineering.* Academic Press, Cambridge, MA

Push-Push: A Two-Point Touchscreen Operation Utilizing the Pressed State and the Hover State

Jaehyun Han, Sunggeun Ahn, Geehyuk Lee
HCI Lab, KAIST
291 Daehak-ro, Yuseong-gu,
Daejeon, Rep. of Korea
{jay.jaehyun, topmaze88, geehyuk}@gmail.com

ABSTRACT

A drag operation is used for many two-point functions in mouse-based graphical user interfaces (GUIs), but its usage in touchscreen GUIs is limited because it is mainly used for scrolling. We propose Push-Push as a second two-point touchscreen operation that is not in conflict with a drag operation. We implemented three application scenarios and showed how Push-Push can be used effectively for other two-point functions while overlapping drag operations are used for scrolling.

Author Keywords

Touch interface; Pressure; Hover; Two point operation.

ACM Classification Keywords

H5.2 [Information interfaces and presentation]: User Interfaces. - Input devices and strategies.

INTRODUCTION

A drag operation has been an important operation in mouse-based GUIs. For instance, a drag operation is used for many two-point functions, such as moving an icon, selecting a range of text, drawing a rectangle to select multiple objects, moving a slider bar, and so on. A drag operation is also important in touchscreen GUIs, but its usage is limited compared with that of mouse-based GUIs because a drag operation is primarily used for scrolling, and cannot be directly used for other two-point functions. Using a drag operation for other functions usually requires a mode change, e.g., using a time out. For example, in an Android GUI, using a drag operation to select a range of text requires a mode change with a timeout. As two-point functions are equally important in touchscreen GUIs, we propose that we need an additional two-point operation that is not in conflict with a drag operation. With such an additional two-point operation, one will be, for example, able to move an application icon while scrolling to other pages on a smartphone main screen.

In order to find a new two-point operation, we paid our attention to the rich design space of recent new touchscreen

UIST'14 Adjunct, October 5–8, 2014, Honolulu, HI, USA.
ACM 978-1-4503-3068-8/14/10.
http://dx.doi.org/10.1145/2658779.2658797

technologies with force sensing and proximity sensing [1, 2, 5]. With additional touch states, there can be many possible different two-point operation designs. Figure 1 illustrates one of them, called Push-Push, that we are investigating in the current study. It is assumed that a touchscreen has four states: out (out of sensing range), hover (within proximity sensing range), touched, and pressed states. A Push-Push is represented by a thick red line; two points are selected when it enters a pressed state. A Push-Push is cancelled if it leaves the hover state before it selects an end point.

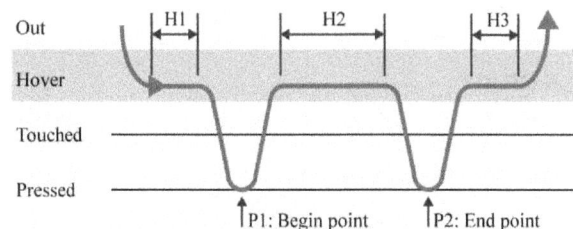

Figure 1: A sequence of a Push-Push operation

We considered the following two main requirements in the design of Push-Push. First, a new two-point operation should not be in conflict with a drag operation. At first, we considered a click-and-drag operation, but this did not allow an overlapping drag operation for scrolling. We also considered dragging in the pressed state, but this was a laborious operation [4]. During a Push-Push operation, one can use a drag operation to scroll the page, as long as the finger does not leave the hover zone. Second, a new two-point operation should enable precise selection of two points with a "fat" finger. Precise selection with a finger is difficult, and this is why touchscreen GUIs use a text-selection widget with adjustment handles. In a Push-Push operation, as shown in Figure 1, hover periods, H1 and H2, can be used for fine adjustment of selections at P1 and P2 without occlusion by the finger. In addition to meeting the two main requirements, we noted that Push-Push has a space to accommodate a subsequent action, such as menu selection which often follows a two-point operation. A context menu may be shown in H3 if a user does not pass the hover zone but dwells in it. In this poster, we present three application scenarios of Push-Push, and show the result of a user study that we did to see if it would meet the aforementioned basic requirements.

PUSH-PUSH APPLICATIONS

We implemented the following three application scenarios: selecting texts, selecting multiple items, and moving an icon. We used Galaxy Note 3 as it is capable of proximity sensing. For force sensing, we attached four force sensitive resistors (FSRs) on the back of the device following [3].

In the first scenario, one can select text with Push-Push as shown in Figure 2a. The first and the second pushes mark the start and end positions of a text selection. A text cursor appears when the finger enters the hover zone so that one can adjust the cursor position before a push action. A context menu appears after the second push. The cursor and the context menu disappear when the finger leaves the hover zone. In the second scenario, a 5 x 3 image matrix appears on the screen. One can draw a selection box using Push-Push to select/deselect multiple images as shown in Figure 2b. In addition, one can select/deselect an individual image by tapping. The third scenario consists of four pages with icons as shown in Figure 2c. One can pick an icon with the first push, and drop it with the second push. Between the two pushes a shaded icon follows the finger indicating a moving state. In this state, one can turn the page using a flick or drag gesture.

USER STUDY

We conducted an experiment to study the efficacy of Push-Push scenarios compared with traditional counterparts without Push-Push (Push-Push vs. Traditional). We used Android applications (Gmail, Gallery, and Widget pages) as the reference designs for the traditional counterparts. Three experimental tasks corresponding to the three application scenarios were: A) selecting text between a green character and a red character, B) selecting images from a green image to a red image, and C) moving a green icon to a red rectangle.

Eight graduate students participated in the study (1 female, 1 left-handed, mean age 26). They were instructed to use the index finger while holding the device in the non-dominant hand. They repeated 15 trials for each of the three tasks in the two conditions (90 trials in total). We generated task instances randomly, but the same task set was used for both conditions. The order of the two conditions was counterbalanced among participants. Each participant had a five-minute practice session for each task, and then a main session, which took about an hour.

As shown in Table 1, the mean completion times of the Push-Push condition was significantly smaller than that of the Traditional condition in all of the three tasks. The error rates in all of the three tasks showed no significant difference. The results showed the potential of Push-Push, but we also found problems in the current Push-Push design. For instance, the error rate with Push-Push seemed large in task C. We observed that participants sometimes left the hover zone accidentally while performing a flick gesture to turn the page. Another problem was that the context menu in task B seemed to interfere with the subsequent selection operations. Also, in task A, some pointing errors occurred when the width of the

character was very small (< 2 mm). We expect that most of these problems will be handled in the next design iteration.

We observed that no accidental push gesture occurred while they perform tapping or drag gestures. Many participants favored pointing in the hover state since it reduced occlusion problem. Some participants mentioned that aiming the character in the hover state was a little more difficult than aiming in the touch state. A few participants felt fatigue at the finger and wanted to use the thumb instead.

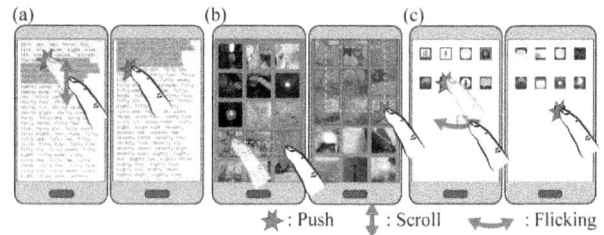

Figure 2: The three application scenarios of Push-Push

	Task A		Task B		Task C	
	CT*	ER	CT*	ER	CT*	ER
Push-Push	5.4	10.8	4.6	5.0	3.5	10.8
Traditional	7.0	7.5	5.0	2.5	4.5	3.3

Table 1: The mean completion time (CT, sec) and the mean error rate (ER, %) (* indicates p < 0.05, paired t-test).

CONCLUSION

We proposed Push-Push as a second two-point touchscreen operation that is not in conflict with a drag operation. We showed the feasibility of Push-Push by implementing application examples and comparing them with traditional touchscreen counterparts. We also found the problems of the current Push-Push design, and immediate future work is improving Push-Push based on the results of the user study. The main goal of the current study is to characterize the rich design space of a touchscreen augmented by both a pressed state and a hover state.

ACKNOWLEDGMENTS

This work was supported by the IT R&D program of MKE/KEIT. [KI10041244, SmartTV 2.0 Software Platform]

REFERENCES

1. Apple Inc., Frustrated Total Internal Reflection and Capacitive Sensing, US Patent, US20140092052 A1.

2. Samsung Inc., Air-View Functions on Galaxy Series, http://www.samsung.com/us/support/howtoguide/N0000004/13142/159745

3. Heo, S., and Lee, G., ForceDrag: Using Pressure as a Touch Input Modifier. In Proc. OzCHI (2012), ACM Press, 204-207.

4. Lee, S. and Lee, G., Design of Interaction Techniques for Clickable Touch Screens, Ph. D. Thesis (2012), KAIST.

5. Rosenberg, I., and Perlin, K., The UnMousePad: An Interpolating Multi-Touch Force-Sensing Input Pad. ACM Trans. Graph. 28, 3, (July 2009).

Slack-Scroll: Sharing Sliding Operations among Scrolling and Other GUI Functions

Eunhye Youn, Geehyuk Lee
HCI Lab, KAIST
Daejeon, Rep. of Korea
{yeh1989, geehyuk}@gmail.com

ABSTRACT

Sliding is one of the basic touchscreen operations, but is mainly used for scrolling in mobile touchscreen GUIs. As a way to share sliding operations among scrolling and other GUI functions, we propose Slack-Scroll. We implemented two application scenarios of Slack-Scroll, and asserted their feasibility in a user study. All participants could accept and adapt well to the new techniques enabled by Slack-Scroll.

Author Keywords

Slack-Scroll; dragging; scrolling; touchscreen interaction.

ACM Classification Keywords

H5.2 [Information interfaces and presentation]: User Interfaces. - Input devices and strategies.

INTRODUCTION

Sliding, moving in contact with the screen, is an essential component of touchscreen operations. One can slide to move a file to a folder, to select an item in a pie-menu, to make a single-stroke gesture, to adjust a selection point before taking-off, and so on. In practice, however, sliding is not being utilized for these GUI functions because sliding is primarily used for scrolling, which is a particularly important GUI function in a small-screen device, such as a smartphone. For this reason, one usually has to do a mode-switching first before using sliding for other functions. For example, one has to use a time-out before starting to use sliding to move an icon on the Android GUI and the iOS GUI alike. Scrolling is important in a touchscreen GUI, but sliding is an operation that is too basic to be used for scrolling only.

Our question at this point was "Can scrolling share sliding with other functions?" Scrolling may not need all of the possible forms of sliding. To answer this question, we collected trajectory data from a user study and analyzed the features of sliding operations for scrolling. One of the observations in the analysis was that the range of sliding is relatively long – sliding for less than 5mm was not common

when it was for scrolling. This led us to consider the concept of "Slack Scroll", which we explain with a state diagram in Figure 1. When one touches the screen, the system enters the Slack state, from which it may go to the Scroll state if the touch movement satisfies a scroll-on condition (e.g., moving for more than 5mm), and may go to the Scan state if the touch movement makes a scroll-off gesture (e.g., making a U-turn before satisfying the scroll-on condition). As the state names imply, sliding is for scrolling in the Scroll state only, and can be used for other functions in the Slack state and the Scan state. The Trans state is for allowing clutching while scrolling. Complex the state-diagram may look, the net result is that sliding to scroll now have some amount of slack before it is engaged to scrolling.

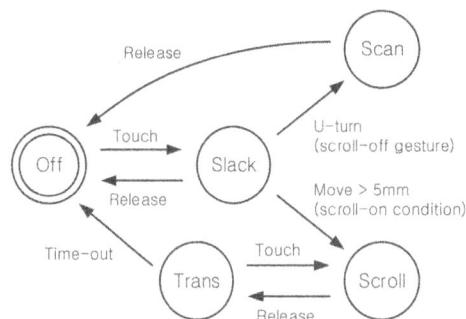

Figure 1: The state-transition diagram of Slack-Scroll.

In this poster, we present a few interaction examples that are made possible by Slack-Scroll. In addition, we report user feedback about the new interaction techniques collected in a user study.

SLACK-SCROLL APPLICATIONS

We implemented two Slack-Scroll application scenarios, A and B, as shown in Figure 2. In scenario A, users can use a take-off strategy for selecting a small target [1] because they can adjust a touch point for some amount before activating scrolling. This is an example of application scenarios utilizing the Slack state. In scenario B, users can make a small gesture, such as a U-turn gesture, to enter the Scan state and continue with a menu selection with scrolling turned off. This is an example of application scenarios utilizing the Scan state. A transition to the Scan state will usually trigger a function, such as a context menu, as shown in Figure 2b, and moving a selected icon. Once in the Scan state, one may continue with any gestures, such as marking menu gestures [2].

UIST'14 Adjunct, October 5–8, 2014, Honolulu, HI, USA.
ACM 978-1-4503-3068-8/14/10.
http://dx.doi.org/10.1145/2658779.2658798

FEASIBILITY TEST

We conducted a user study to examine the feasibility of the two scenarios. First, we wondered if users would be able to utilize the Slack state for pointing adjustment. Second, we wondered if it would be easy for users to make a small gesture to enter the Scan state. Also, we wondered if users would not be disturbed by the small slack before scrolling.

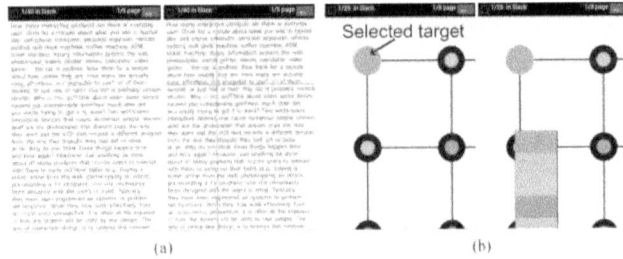

Figure 2: (a) Scenario A – small target selection, and (b) Scenario B – context menu invocation.

Experiment A was for scenario A with six participants (1 female, average age 24.3, all right-handed). The task was to select 40 text targets in a long page (about 3 screens long). Participants performed 5 instances of the task with or without Slack-Scroll (Slack vs. Default condition). The order of the two conditions was counterbalanced. In the Slack condition, participants could adjust pointing due to Slack-Scroll. In the Default condition, participants could not adjust pointing once the finger touches the screen. Participants performed the tasks with the index finger while seated. They were given sufficient practice time before the experiment.

The numbers of trials per target in experiment A are shown in Figure 3b. There was a significant difference between the two conditions (paired t-test, $t(5) = 2.678$, $p < .05$). The amounts of pointing adjustment in the Slack condition is shown in Figure 3a, where the average distance of the adjustments was around 1.5mm (SD = 1.21mm). This asserts that participants could utilize the 5mm slack effectively for adjusting pointing without incurring accidental scrolling.

Experiment B was for scenario B with six participants (1 female, average age 25.7, all right-handed). The task was to change the color of 25 targets in a large page (2.5 x 2 screen size) using a context menu. Participants performed 8 instances of the task with or without Slack-Scroll. The order of the two conditions was counterbalanced. In the Slack condition, participants could use any small gesture with a quick turn, which they felt comfortable, to invoke a menu. In the Default condition, participants had to use a time-out (500ms) to invoke a menu. Other conditions were the same as in experiment A.

The rate of an unintended scrolling in experiment B was around 2.67%. Three participants used a v-shape gesture, two used a circular gesture, and one used a swaying gesture,

similar to MicroRolls [3], in order to invoke a menu. There was a significant difference in completion time between the two conditions (paired t-test, $t(5) = 8.016$, $p < .0001$), as shown in Figure 3c. The main reasons for this difference are thought to be the time-out operations in the Default condition and the continuity of the gesture (from invoking a menu to selecting a color) in the Slack condition.

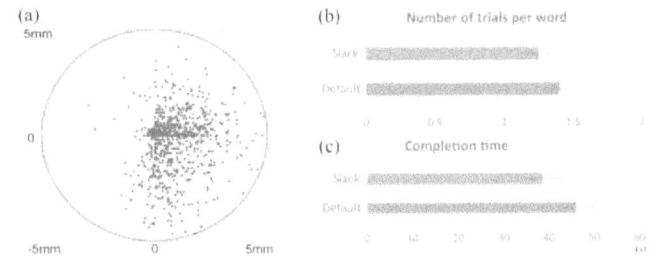

Figure 3: (a) The distribution of pointing adjustments in exp. A, (b) average number of trials per target in exp. A, and (c) average completion time in exp. B.

In the post-experiment interview, all participants answered they did not feel any difference in scrolling actions between the two conditions. Also, they all liked Slack-Scroll. In task A, they agreed that the take-off selection method would be beneficial especially for small targets. One participant said that he felt comfortable because he did not make many mistakes when using take-off technique with Slack-Scroll. In experiment B, they all liked Slack-Scroll especially because they did not need to wait 500ms to invoke a menu.

CONCLUSION

We proposed the concept of Slack-Scroll, and showed its potential benefit in a user study with two application scenarios. Immediate future work is 1) to improve the scroll-off gesture and the scroll-on condition based on empirical data and 2) to quantify the effect of Slack-Scroll on the usability of a touchscreen GUI.

ACKNOWLEDGMENTS

This work was supported by the IT R&D program of MKE/KEIT. [KI10041244, SmartTV 2.0 Software Platform]

REFERENCES

1. Potter, R. L., Weldon, L. J., and Shneiderman, B. Improving the accuracy of touch screens: an experimental evaluation of three strategies. In Proc. CHI 1988.

2. Kurtenbach, G., and Buxton, W. Issues in combining marking and direct manipulation techniques. In Proc. UIST 1991.

3. Roudaut, A., Lecolinet, E., and Guiard, Y. MicroRolls: expanding touch-screen input vocabulary by distinguishing rolls vs. slides of the thumb. In Proc. CHI 2009

FlickBoard: Enabling Trackpad Interaction with Automatic Mode Switching on a Capacitive-sensing Keyboard

Ying-Chao Tung[1], Ta-Yang Cheng[1], Neng-Hao Yu[2], Mike Y. Chen[1,3]

[1]National Taiwan University, [2]National Chengchi University, [3]Research Center for Information Technology Innovation, Academia Sinica

tony61507@gmail.com, jimmy@jomican.com, jonesyu@nccu.edu.tw, mikechen@csie.ntu.edu.tw

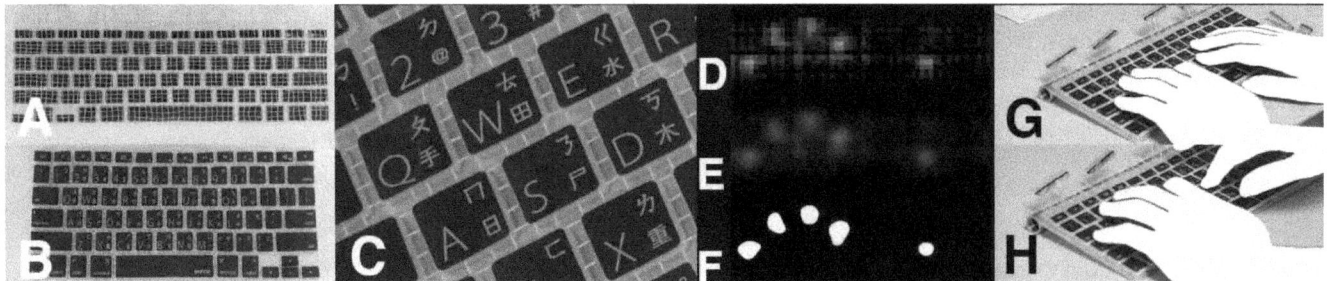

Figure 1. We present a keyboard cover with capacitive touch sensing capability which automatically disables itself while typing. Sensing wires are embedded into a typical keyboard cover (A), the modified cover is then put on an off-the-shelf keyboard (B). The sensing grid is all over the keyboard with 0.5cm grid size (C). This results in a low-resolution raw intensity image when hands are near the surface of the keyboard (D). The image is then processed to obtain touched areas (E+F). The raw image can also be used to robustly recognize whether user wants to type on the keyboard (G) or to control cursor with touchpad (H) using a machine learning-based classifier.

ABSTRACT

We present FlickBoard, which combines a trackpad and a keyboard into the same interaction area to reduce hand movement between separate keyboards and trackpads. It supports automatic input mode detection and switching (ie. trackpad vs keyboard mode) without explicit user input. We developed a prototype by embedding a 58x20 capacitive sensing grid into a soft keyboard cover, and uses machine learning to distinguish between moving a cursor (trackpad mode) and entering text (keyboard mode). Our prototype has a thin profile and can be placed over existing keyboards.

Author Keywords

Keyboard; Touchpad; Co-located input devices;

ACM Classification Keywords

H.5.2. Information Interfaces and Presentation (e.g. HCI): User Interfaces

INTRODUCTION

Operating GUI system requires both pointing devices and text input devices. However, most of the commercially available computers put these two devices at two adjacent

UIST'14 Adjunct, October 5–8, 2014, Honolulu, HI, USA.
ACM 978-1-4503-3068-8/14/10.
http://dx.doi.org/10.1145/2658779.2658799

positions, which requires hand repositioning while switching between two devices. Past works[1, 3, 5] tried to solve this problem by enabling touch sensing capability on the keyboard. In this work we take a step further to make the sensing layer that is easy to be added on the off-the-shelf keyboards. Furthermore, the key issue of the dual functional keyboard is how to automatically switch the pointing mode to the typing mode and vice versa. To our knowledge, this issue has not been solved yet. We present FlickBoard, a keyboard cover with capacitive touch sensing capability. We use this keyboard film to collect user's data and design an automatically mode switching algorithm between co-located touchpads and keyboards based on users' intention.

RELATED WORK

Previous research has shown that co-locating two devices together will improve user performance[1]. However, the integrated device still requires manual mode switching to avoid false triggering of pointing device. ThumbSense[4] tried to implement an automatic input mode switching for keyboard by maintaining a state machine controlled by touchpad and keyboard event. Althouth it helps users keep their fingers on the home row, it still requires users to move their thumb onto the touchpad. Longpad[2] has shown that a larger touchpad can enable more possibilities for interactions. TypeHoverSwipe[5] implemented a modified keyboard recognizes in-air hand gestures and obtains coarse finger position. Some new interaction techniques for in-air and on-surface gesture on keyboard are explored. The depth map generated by infrared range finder is fast and stable, but the finger position obtained by the system is too rough to control mouse cursor because the sensors were interspersed between the keycaps. Capacitive sensing, in contrast, can obtain higher resolution image under this condition.[3]

SYSTEM OVERVIEW

Our system consists of three parts: 1) capacitance-to-digital converters, 2) sensing film, 3) graphical recognition system and 4) automatic mode switching predictor

Sensing Cover

We built a capacitive sensing grid on a keyboard cover. The modified cover was placed over Apple keyboard. We connect ground end to the body of Apple keyboard to stabilize the readings. The grid consists of 58 vertical and 20 horizontal 30#AWG cooper wires. With mutual capacitance sensing technique, each cross point of vertical and horizontal wires can be a single sensing point, so the system can capture a 58x20 frame. The sensing resolution could be higher if the conductive pattern is directly printed on the cover. With this modified cover, we can add touch sensing capability to a standard mechanical keyboard without modifying it.

Capacitance To Digital Converters(CDC)

To measure the change of capacitance value of the sensor grid, we referenced WireTouch's design[1] and designed a customized CDC. The main idea of this design is to measure the delay of the signal passed through sensor. First we generate square wave with a programmable clock generator. Connect the square wave signal to the vertical wires of the sensor grid through demultiplexers. We can raster scan through all the 58 vertical wires by selecting through channels. 20 OP-Amps are connected to the horizontal wires of the sensor grid, amplifying the weakened and delayed signal. We measure the phase shift of the amplified signal compared to the original square wave by sending it into an analog switch as control signal. The switch is connected to an RC low-pass filter. Finally, we measure the output voltage of RC low-pass filter, which has positive correlation to the mutual capacitance of the selected cross point. The whole system can be designed to be smaller and portable. Currently the CDC can scan a 58x20 frame at 20 Hz.

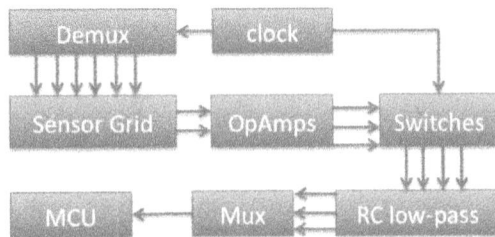

Figure 2. CDC circuit diagram.

Graphical Recognition System

Sensor values are organized as a 58x20 pixel image, each pixel has 10 bit resolution. Collected image is subtracted with background signal level collected when system is started. The image will be linearly scaled to 464x160 pixels, and apply Gaussian filter on the image. Finally, the system detects blobs in the processed image as touched points. (Figure 1.F)

[1]WireTouch `http://www.wiretouch.net/`

Automatic Mode Switching Prediction

We also implemented Motion Signature[5] to recognize whether user is trying to use pointing device or not. Since the sample rate is relatively lower (20Hz) compared to the original condition(325Hz), we reduced the referenced frames to only 10 frames in the process of building motion history image(MHI). Finally, we classify the MHIs with Random Decision Forests(RDF), the same classifier used in TypeHoverSwipe[5]. We designed a user study to collect training data and validate our system. The aim of task design is to simulate the circumstance of text processing: ,1) Type some text in the editing area, 2) Select a part of text and Change the font face. 3) Type another words, 4) Insert a picture with button in the tool bar and drag the picture to the appropriate position. 5) Continue typing. The ground truth of training data for RDF model is obtained by a foot pedal act as mode switch operated by participant. Collecting ground truth with foot pedal can avoid interfering with participants' hand posture while operating.

PRELIMINARY RESULTS

We have tested our prototype with a small training dataset(7 minutes of single user's training data at 15 Hz frame rate.) and the result looks promising. In a 5 fold cross validation, the overall accuracy of RDF is 99.56%, rounded to two decimal places. We will recruit more users to validate our system in the future.

CONCLUSION

In this work, we designed a keyboard add-on that is easy to install to enable touch capability on the regular keyboard. Base on the preliminary test, we can automatically detect user's intention of switching between pointing and typing. We plan to perform a formal user study and system evaluation in the following months. The proposed touch sensing technique has higher resolution over the previous works, it can also be used for bimanual multitouch gestures.

ACKNOWLEDGEMENTS

This study was partially supported by the National Science Council, Taiwan, under grant NSC102-2221-E-004-004.

REFERENCES

1. Fallot-Burghardt, W., Fjeld, M., Speirs, C., Ziegenspeck, S., Krueger, H., and Läubli, T. Touch&type: A novel pointing device for notebook computers. NordiCHI '06, ACM (New York, NY, USA, 2006), 465–468.

2. Gu, J., Heo, S., Han, J., Kim, S., and Lee, G. Longpad: A touchpad using the entire area below the keyboard of a laptop computer. CHI '13, ACM (New York, NY, USA, 2013), 1421–1430.

3. Habib, I., Berggren, N., Rehn, E., Josefsson, G., Kunz, A., and Fjeld, M. Dgts: Integrated typing and pointing. In *INTERACT 2009*, T. Gross, J. Gulliksen, P. Kotz, L. Oestreicher, P. Palanque, R. Prates, and M. Winckler, Eds., vol. 5727 of *Lecture Notes in Computer Science*. Springer Berlin Heidelberg, 2009, 232–235.

4. Rekimoto, J. Thumbsense: Automatic input mode sensing for touchpad-based interactions. In *CHI '03 Extended Abstracts on Human Factors in Computing Systems*, CHI EA '03, ACM (New York, NY, USA, 2003), 852–853.

5. Taylor, S., Keskin, C., Hilliges, O., Izadi, S., and Helmes, J. Type-hover-swipe in 96 bytes: A motion sensing mechanical keyboard. CHI '14, ACM (New York, NY, USA, 2014), 1695–1704.

Traceband: Locating Missing Items by Visual Remembrance

Farshid Tavakolizadeh
Multimedia University
Cyberjaya, Malaysia
email@farshid.ws

Jiawei Gu
Baidu Inc.
Beijing, China
gujiawei@baidu.com

Bahador Saket
University of Arizona
Tucson, AZ 85716 USA
saket@cs.arizona.edu

ABSTRACT

Finding missing items has always been troublesome. To tackle the hassle, several systems have been suggested; yet they are inflexible due to excessive setup time, operational cost, and effectiveness. We present Traceband; a lightweight and portable bracelet, which keeps track of every targeted commonly used object that a user interacts with. Users can find the location of missing items via a web-based software portal.

Author Keywords

Finding missing items; bracelet; image matching; life logging; Traceband

ACM Classification Keywords

C.3 Special-purpose and application-based systems: Real-time and embedded systems.

INTRODUCTION

Locating daily used objects is a serious concern for both youth and elderly due to absentmindedness or perceptual problems [6]. We often lose objects, we forget where we keep or leave them. Looking for an object could get very frustrating especially if we have no lead on where to start.

Several systems introduced novel methods to tackle lost finding scenarios. Ueoka et al. [7] proposed a head mounted vision interface system that continuously records videos from the user viewpoint. The system searches through videos for predefined items and if there is a match, it assigns the portion of video to that item. WristSense is a wrist-worn device that utilizes an accelerometer to detect hand gestures and trigger a camera [2]. Hand gestures should be trained at a previous stage by wearing an additional head mounted camera, performing each desired gestures and labeling. A system by Nakada et al. [5] requires attaching RFID tags to commonly used objects.

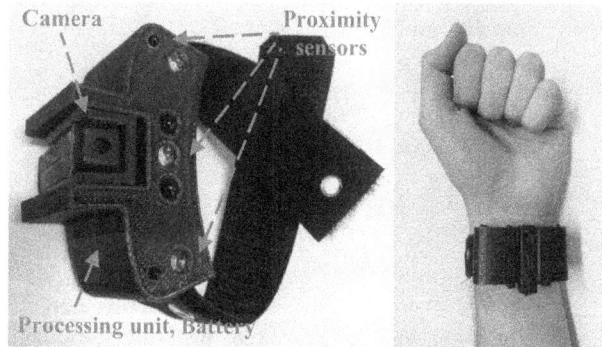

Figure 1. The bracelet consists of three proximity sensors, a camera, rechargeable Li-Ion batteries, a custom processing board, and transmission module.

It then detects them using RFID readers and ultrasonic position detectors mounted at the environment. Another work utilizes a wearable RFID reader to detect the tagged objects [1]. Although many of these solutions were innovative and successful, they were not efficient (e.g. excessive trainings, memory usage, battery life constrains) [2, 7], or flexible (e.g. improper camera position for capturing placement of objects) [7], or visually desirable (e.g. multiple devices in every room, attaching active RFID tags to commonly used objects) [1, 5].

While previous approaches were helpful, alternative methods can enhance the experience. To assist users in locating their missing items, we present Traceband.

SYSTEM DESIGN

Figure 1 shows the prototype. It consists of a proximity sensing module that detects status of wearer's hand with regards to any surface. Approaching or distancing a surface triggers the camera to capture frames of the front space for five seconds (up to 10 fps). We make sure that recorded photos are clear using a metric for blurriness [3]. Furthermore, we apply Chi-Square test on their histograms to filter near-duplicates.

Each set of photos is sent wirelessly to a server which compute their ASIFT keypoints [4, 8] and compares them with archived personal items. Personal items are archived at a previous setup stage using an independent web-based software (Figure 2). The server records an incoming log photo only if it is related to a match among archived personal items. We consider a photo as 'related' if it is followed or preceded by a matching photo within a range of 15 frames. An unrelated photo could be a result of proximity changes to a surface without detecting any personal items. Each related set of photos is assigned to the personal item as the most recent matching group.

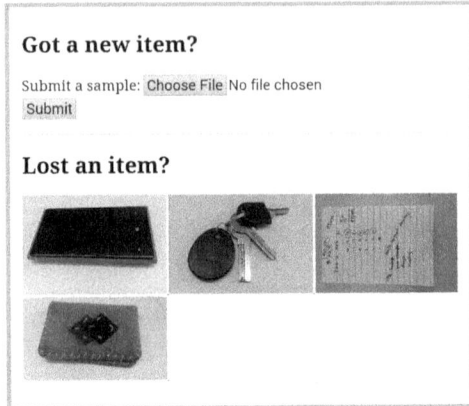

Figure 2. Traceband website. Users can archive new personal items, or search for lost ones.

Matching and visualization of archived photos

To find a lost object, the user can directly open the webpage (Figure 2) and click on the archived photo of that object. Once the user clicks on one of the archived photos, the server loads the most recent group of frames assigned to that item. The sequence is displayed in reverse time order with matches bolder than others; see Figure 3.

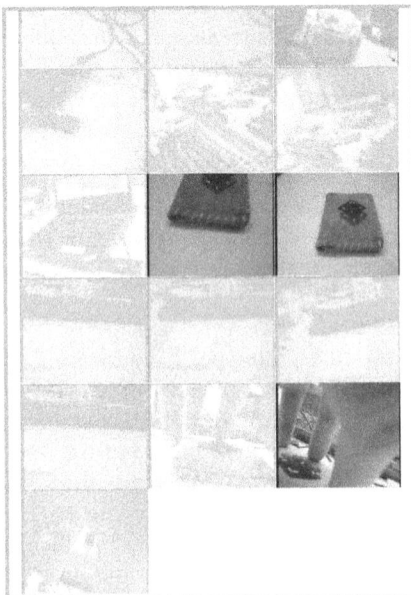

Figure 3. Results of searching the cup. The images containing the match are highlighted. Other images complement the matches to help in quick remembrance of missing object's location.

CONCLUSION AND FUTURE WORK

We introduced a novel system to facilitate object finding by picturing where it was left behind. It is a compact and lightweight design that can be embedded into the current smartwatches form-factor. We have tested our system in various daily scenarios, holding different objects. Since we only took distinct and related scenes, less processing and time were spent on computation of image feature. This also helped in effective usage of memory, faster retrieval and display of a concise sequence of scenes. The arrangement (Figure 3) helped testers to quickly identify the location of matched items.

This work will be further developed to increase the matching rate on objects with slight flat features. We also plan to add infrared capturing system to enhance the operation in poor lighting conditions and darkness.

ACKNOWLEDGMENTS

We thank all people who volunteered in the system testing and video production. Moreover, we thank Dr. Shendong Zhao and Dr. Taku Hachisu for providing constructive comments on previous versions of this document. The authors have no affiliation with brand names, logos, and products used for testing the system and video shooting.

REFERENCES

1. Fishkin, K.P., Philipose, M. and Rea, A. Hands-on RFID: wireless wearables for detecting use of objects. In Proc. ISWC '05, 38-41.

2. Maekawa, T., Kishino, Y., Yanagisawa Y. and Sakurai, Y. WristSense: Wrist-worn Sensor Device with Camera for Daily Activity Recognition. In Proc. PERCOM '12, 510-512.

3. Marziliano, P., Dufaux, F., Winkler, S. and Ebrahimi, T. A no-reference perceptual blur metric. In Proc. ICIP '02, vol. 3, 57–60.

4. Morel, J.M. and Yu, G. ASIFT, A new framework for fully affine invariant image comparison. SIAM Journal on Imaging Sciences, 2(2):438-469 (2009).

5. Nakada, T., Kanai, H. and Kunifuji, S. A support system for finding lost objects using spotlight. In Proc., MobileHCI '05, 321-322.

6. Tenney, Y. J. Ageing and the misplacing of objects. British Journal of Developmental Psychology, 2(1):43-50 (1984).

7. Ueoka, T., Kawamura, T., Kono, Y. and Kidode, M. I'm Here!: A Wearable Object Remembrance Support System. In Proc. MobileHCI '03, 422-427.

8. Yu, G. and Morel, J.M. A fully affine invariant image comparison method. In Proc. ICASSP '09, 1597-1600.

Tangential Force Input for Touch Panels Using Bezel-Aligned Elastic Pillars and a Transparent Sheet

Yuriko Nakai, Shinya Kudo, Ryuta Okazaki, Hiroyuki Kajimoto

The University of Electro-Communications

1-5-1 Chofugaoka, Chofu, Tokyo 182-8585, Japan

{yuriko, kudo, okazaki, kajimoto}@kaji-lab.jp

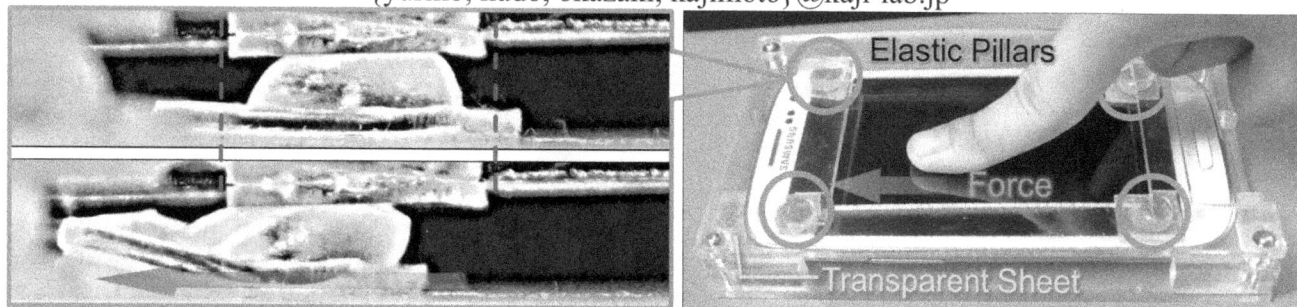

Figure 1 Appearance of the new structure enables tangential force input for touch panel

ABSTRACT

This research aims to enable tangential force input for touch panels by measuring the tangential force. The system is composed of a plastic sheet on a touch panel, urethane pillars on the panel that are aligned at the four corners of the bezel, and a case on top of the pillars. When the sheet moves with a finger, the pillars deform so that a tangential force can be obtained by measuring the movement of the finger. We evaluated the method and found that the system showed realistic force sensing accuracy in any direction. This input method will enable development of new applications for touch panels such as using any part of the touch panel surface as joysticks, or modeling virtual objects by deforming them with the fingers.

Author Keywords

bezel; shear deformation; tangential force; touch panel; elastic pillar;

ACM Classification Keywords

H.5.2. Input devices and strategies, Haptic I/O, Interaction styles

INTRODUCTION

We interact daily with portable devices using touch operation. Today's touch panels employing capacitive sensing can simultaneously detect the position and contact area of the user's fingers, and the latter information can be regarded as a pressing force. On the other hand, force sensing is limited to a vertical direction. This led us to

develop a measurement scheme that can sense tangential force on the touch panel with a simple non-powered method using only a transparent gel layer [1]. This paper is a follow-up of the previous work, suggesting a new structure as shown in Figure 1, leading to more robust omnidirectional force sensing.

RELATED WORK

Harrison and Hudson placed joysticks between the display and touch panel to obtain a shear force [1]. Vlack et al. developed GelForce [3], which used transparent gel with embedded color markers and a camera. They captured displacement of the markers and obtained the force vector distribution by solving the inverse problem. These research studies realized 3 DoF force sensing on touch surfaces, but they required special electrical components such as joysticks or cameras, which limited their practical use. Heo and Lee proposed a method of distinguishing between the drag operation and tangential force by measuring the contact area (vertical force) and the speed of the touch movement [4]. The method needed no additional hardware. However, the authors mentioned they observed that the distinction between tangential force and drag operation was quite difficult to achieve, especially in the case of a forward direction.

We previously developed a measurement scheme which can sense tangential force on the touch panel using a transparent gel layer [1]. The displacement of the finger is mechanically amplified so that force sensing becomes more accurate, compared to the case without the gel layer. However, we found that there was a tradeoff between touch sensitivity and tangential force sensing accuracy, which depended on the thickness of the gel layer. This is because the thicker gel leads to greater finger movement and easier detection of the tangential force, while also leading to reduced touch sensitivity because the gel is an electrical insulator. In other words, vertical force sensing (that requires touch area size sensing), and tangential force sensing, were incompatible.

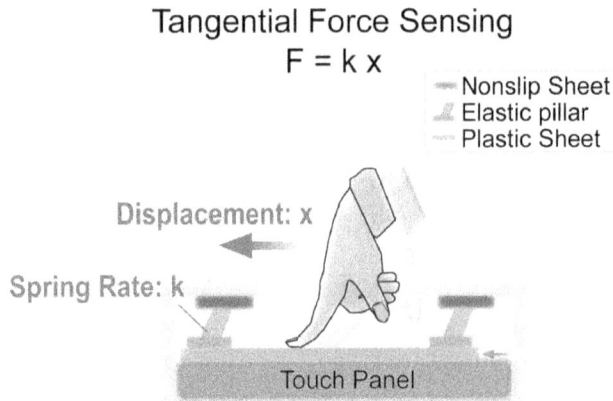

Tangential Force Sensing
$F = k\,x$

— Nonslip Sheet
▟ Elastic pillar
⎯ Plastic Sheet

Displacement: x

Spring Rate: k

Touch Panel

Figure 2 Components of new Structure and System for sensing tangential force

METHOD

The new structure we developed looks similar to a smart phone case (Figure 1). Elastic pillars (6mm thick urethane cushion pad, 30 ASKER C) are sandwiched between nonslip sheets attached to the reverse side of the top layer and a plastic sheet (0.2 mm thick) on a touch panel (Figure 2). Figure 2 also shows the operation of the device. Users touch the touch panel via the plastic plate. When a tangential force is applied, the elastic pillars deform with a shear strain. The maximum displacement is about 5 mm in all directions. The deformation is detected as the touch position displacement by the standard function of the touch panel. This displacement is considered to be approximately proportional to the tangential force, assuming linear elasticity.

This new structure is more durable than our previous one because there is no direct vertical pressure from the finger to the elastic body. Furthermore, the thin plate does not hinder touch sensing, which makes vertical and horizontal force sensing compatible.

EVALUATION

The evaluation system consisted of a smartphone with a capacitive touch panel (GT-I9300, SAMSUNG) mounted on a 3 DoF force sensor (DSA-03A, Tec Gihan Co., Ltd.). The participants were six laboratory members (age: 21-26, five males and a female). They were asked to place the index fingers of their dominant hands at the center of the touch panel, and to gradually increase the tangential force. We also asked them to input force from 200 gf to 1000 gf by observing the value on a PC monitor. The directions of force were front, back, right and left, and we obtained two sets of data simultaneously; the displacement of their fingers on the touch panel and the tangential force measured by the 3 DoF force sensor. The experiments on vertical force sensing were conducted with the same setup,

by obtaining the change in the contact area of their fingers and the vertical force.

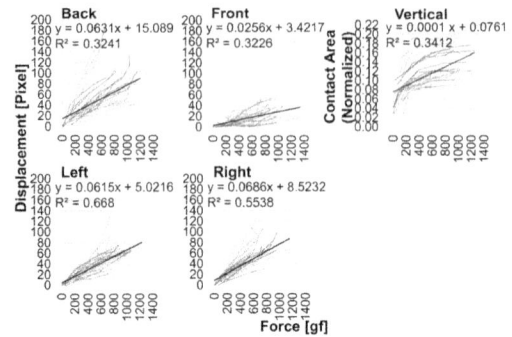

Figure 3 Relationship between the tangential forces and finger displacement or the change in the contact area

The results are shown in Figure 3. The horizontal axis is the actual force and the vertical axis is the finger displacement (tangential force case) or contact area size (vertical force case). Overall, correlation coefficients of all graphs are not high, probably because the displacement depends on each finger's softness. However, we also observe that correlation coefficients of tangential force sensing are comparable with that of vertical force sensing that has already been used in many applications in existing touch panels. We believe that this implies that we achieved 3DoF force sensing with acceptable accuracy.

CONCLUSIONS

We have proposed a new measurement scheme that can sense tangential force on the touch panel with a simple non-powered method using a soft gel layer. In this study, we suggested a new structure which replaced the gel layer with urethane pillars and a plastic sheet. It improved not only durability, but also the vertical force sensing accuracy without degrading of the tangential one. Our next step is to optimize design parameters such as elasticity of the pillars based on user study.

REFERENCES

1. Nakai, Y., Kudo, S., Okazaki, R., Kajimoto, H., Kuribayashi, H., Detection of Tangential Force for a Touch Panel Using Shear Deformation of the Gel, CHI EA '14 CHI '14 Extended Abstracts on Human Fact. In *Comp. Syst.* (2014), 2353-2358.

2. Harrison, C. and Hudson, S., Using Shear as a Supplemental Two-Dimensional Input Channel for Rich Touchscreen Interaction, CHI '12 Proc. SIGCHI Conf. on Human Fact. In *Comp. Syst.* (2012), 3149-3152.

3. Vlack, K., Mizota, T., Kawakami, N., Kamiyama, K., Kajimoto, H. and Tachi., GelForce: A Vision-based Traction Field Computer Interface, CHI EA '05 CHI '05 Extended Abstracts on Human Fact. In *Comp. Syst.* (2005), 1154-1155.

4. Heo, S. and Lee, G., Indirect shear force estimation for multi-point shear force operations. In CHI '13 Proc. SIGCHI Conf. on Human Fact. In *Comp. Syst.* (2013), 281-284.

Ethereal: A Toolkit for Spatially Adaptive Augmented Reality Content

Gheric Speiginer
School of Interactive Computing
Georgia Institute of Technology, Atlanta, GA USA
gheric.speiginer@gatech.edu

Blair MacIntyre
School of Interactive Computing
Georgia Institute of Technology, Atlanta, GA USA
blair@cc.gatech.edu

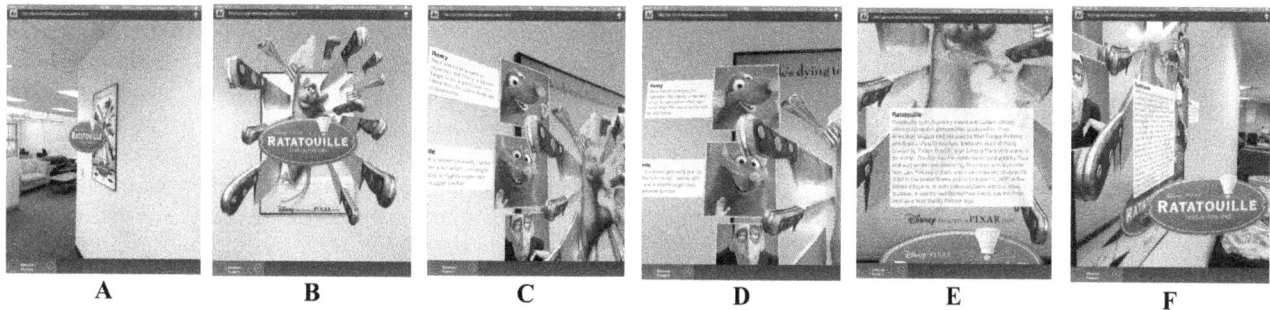

Figure 1: Alternate views of spatially adaptive AR content.

ABSTRACT
In this poster, we describe a framework and toolkit (Ethereal) for creating spatially adaptive content based on complex spatial and visual metrics in augmented reality, and demonstrate our approach with an illustrative example.

Author Keywords
Augmented Reality; Adaptive Information Presentation; UI Toolkits; Web-based Augmented Reality

ACM Classification Keywords
H.5.1 Multimedia Information Systems: Artificial, augmented, and virtual realities

INTRODUCTION
We are actively exploring two complementary approaches for supporting the effective presentation of complex media-rich content in AR environments. The *top-down* approach considers how AR systems can dynamically influence *global* composition of content. The *bottom-up* approach considers AR systems can dynamically influence *local* presentation of content. As we transition from individual AR applications to complex AR environments, both approaches are necessary. The bottom-up approach is the focus of the research reported here.

Our particular approach to supporting dynamic adaptive behavior in augmentations is inspired by the concept of Level of Detail (LOD) in 3D computer graphics. We generalize LOD as a multidimensional breakpoint state-machine to support adaptation effects based on complex and customizable metrics, beyond the usual distance or area metrics used in traditional LOD. Other AR researchers have leveraged the LOD concept. Diverdi's LOD interface concept describes AR applications that display data and interface widgets at discrete levels of detail [1]. Coelho's concept of Level of Error allows for adaptation to changing spatial accuracy and uncertainty in AR interfaces [3].

Related projects in the Ubicomp world include the context toolkit, a toolkit for designing context-aware applications [6], and the proximity toolkit, a toolkit for designing proxemic-aware interfaces [5]. Our work can also be framed as a toolkit for designing proxemic- and context-aware augmentations. While spatially adaptive AR is not new (one of the earliest AR papers describes a knowledge-based AR maintenance system capable of generating designs for laser printer maintenance based on the user's viewing position and the communicative intent of the maintenance step [2]), our primary contribution is a general-purpose framework for supporting the design of augmentations as complex spatially adaptive systems.

AR SPATIAL ADAPTIVITY FRAMEWORK

Augmentation
An augmentation is a unit of computer-mediated (virtual) content that is associated and integrated with a (physical) "place" in the real world (e.g., location, object, or person). Augmentations can be composed of arbitrarily complex combinations of 2D and/or 3D content and behaviors.

UIST'14 Adjunct, October 5–8, 2014, Honolulu, HI, USA.
ACM 978-1-4503-3068-8/14/10.
http://dx.doi.org/10.1145/2658779.2658802

Surface

A Surface is an abstraction for a rectangular region of 2D multimedia content, situated in 3D. Augmentations can be composed of surfaces and/or 3D content (such as 3D models, but also lines and other graphics). Surfaces have a width and height, position, rotation, scale, and density.

Spatial Design Metrics

For practical purposes, complex 3D spatial relationships must be expressed as simpler 2D visual relationships whenever possible. We have developed a variety of metrics meant for designers to use in order to construct adaptation effects based on these metrics. While some metrics are more intuitive than others, designers can experiment with them to develop an intuition for how they work.

Spatial Adaptation Effects

Spatial adaptation effects are the behaviors directly responsible for adapting the layout and/or contents of an augmentation in response to changing spatial relationships, represented by spatial design metrics. Spatial adaptation effects can be composed of and combined with each other in order to create more complex adaptation effects

Breakpoint Range

A Breakpoint Range is a generalization of the LOD concept; observing and reporting the state of a metric based on pre-specified boundaries, zones, hysteresis, and threshold values. These values are intentionally selected to produce desirable behavior. Some "trial and error" may be necessary to optimize behavior (particularly for hysteresis and threshold values), however such a workflow is common among motion graphics designers. Designers can combine Breakpoint Ranges in order to create more complex multidimensional breakpoint systems.

ETHEREAL TOOLKIT

The Ethereal toolkit is implemented in javascript, and integrates with the popular three.js library (a library that encapsulates 3D graphics functionality for the web) as well as the browser's Document Object Model (DOM). Ethereal is designed to support the dynamic adaptation of arbitrary virtual objects in the scene, with special support for Surface objects. In Ethereal, Surface objects extend from THREE.Object3D, and wrap native DOM elements in order to proxy transformations between the DOM and the THREE Scenegraph. In order to support complex animated transitions, we also created a plugin for the GreenSock Animation Platform (GSAP), a popular tool for motion media artists. Our GSAP plugin extends Ethereal's capabilities with GSAP's powerful tweening and timeline APIs. Applications built with Ethereal run in an updated version of Argon, a separate research project which exposes a subset of Qualcomm's Vuforia AR SDK (among other features) in a custom browser designed to support AR [4].

Figures 1 illustrates various views of a complex media-rich adaptive augmentation that we developed with Ethereal and GSAP in two days, and demonstrates, at a high level, how augmentations can dynamically adapt to the user's movements through the environment. (A) and (B) shows alternate views based on the user's distance and angle in relation to the poster. (A) shows how the movie title rotates to face the user at a large angle. (B) shows how the poster scales up, with an enlarged and centered title, when the user is far and looking directly at the poster. In (C) and (D), as the user gets close to the characters, additional information text slides into view if the character is near the center of the screen. Hysterisis and thresholds for each metric keeps the character's text momentary visible when the user looks away or between two characters. A metric based on relative direction between the camera and each character is used to shift the character left and right as the user changes their viewpoint, creating a parallax effect (notice the two mice images are shifted between (C) and (D)). (E) and (F) demonstrates how the horizontal density of the text region adapts at discrete breakpoints to keep the text legible at various viewing angles.

FUTURE WORK

Our current version of Ethereal is in use in a number of projects at our institution, and continues to evolve. We hope to provide additional functionality to make it easier to create complex content in AR. Our users are especially interested in having libraries of common patterns of breakpoints, metrics and adaptation effects that they can apply to their own projects. Finally, we are planning a qualitative study of designers, to both validate our current direction and inform our future work

ACKNOWLEDGMENTS

This material is based upon work supported by the National Science Foundation Graduate Research Fellowship Program under Grant No. DGE-1148903, and the GEM Fellowship. We would also like to thank Hafez Rouzati, Brian Davidson, and Jeff Wilson for their work on Argon2. The Argon2 project has been supported by Qualcomm, the GVU center, and GT IPaT.

REFERENCES

1. DiVerdi, S., Hollerer, T., and Schreyer, R. Level of Detail Interfaces. IEEE Computer Society (2004).

2. Feiner, S., MacIntyre, B., and Seligmann, D. Knowledge-based augmented reality. *Communications of the ACM 36*, 7 (1993), 53–62.

3. MacIntyre, B. and Coelho, E.M. Adapting to dynamic registration errors using level of error (LOE) filtering. (2000).

4. MacIntyre, B., Hill, A., Rouzati, H., Gandy, M., and Davidson, B. The Argon AR Web Browser and standards-based AR application environment. IEEE, 65–74.

5. Marquardt, N., Diaz-Marino, R., Boring, S., and Greenberg, S. The proximity toolkit: prototyping proxemic interactions in ubiquitous computing ecologies. *UIST '11:* (2011), 315.

6. Salber, D., Dey, A.K., and Abowd, G.D. The context toolkit: aiding the development of context-enabled applications. *CHI '99:* (1999), 434–441.

Reaching Targets on Discomfort Region Using Tilting Gesture

Youli Chang
Seoul National University
ylchang@hcil.snu.ac.kr

Sehi L'Yi
Seoul National University
shlyi@hcil.snu.ac.kr

Jinwook Seo
Seoul National University
jseo@snu.ac.kr

ABSTRACT

We present three novel methods to facilitate one hand targeting at discomfort regions on a mobile touch screen using tilting gestures; TiltSlide, TiltReduction, and TiltCursor. We conducted a controlled user study to evaluate them in terms of their performance and user preferences by comparing them with other related methods, i.e. ThumbSpace, Edge Triggered with Extendible Cursor (ETEC), and Direct Touch (directly touching with a thumb). All three methods showed better performance than ThumbSpace in terms of speed and accuracy. Moreover, TiltReduction led users to require less thumb/grip movement than Direct Touch while showing comparable performance in speed and accuracy.

Author Keywords

Touch screen; one-handed interaction; tilting gesture

ACM Classification Keywords

H.5.2 [Information interfaces and presentation]: User Interfaces - Input devices and strategies

INTRODUCTION & RELATED WORK

Large smartphones makes some parts of the screen unreachable when interacting with only one hand. It is difficult for a thumb to reach a far-target on a large screen while maintaining a safe one hand grip of the device. Since people prefer one hand interaction even when both hands are available [2], large screen sizes introduced a new set of challenges in one hand interaction design.

There have been several attempts to address this issue. ThumbSpace [3] utilizes a miniature semitransparent space placed in a comfortable region that maps relative positions of all components in the screen. Edge Triggered with Extendible Cursor (ETEC) [4] is another approach which makes use of an offset cursor. The cursor is triggered with a bezel swipe and moves faster than thumb's moving speed, which helps reach a target outside the thumb's range.

We noted that people use the strategy to tilt the devices towards the thumb, so that a far-target gets closer to their thumbs. GripSense [1] exploited such behavior to identify

UIST '14, Oct 05-08 2014, Honolulu, HI, USA
ACM 978-1-4503-3068-8/14/10.
http://dx.doi.org/10.1145/2658779.2658803

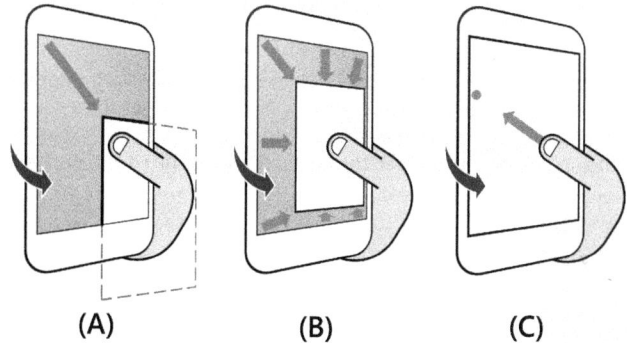

Figure 1. Three methods triggered with a tilting gesture are designed for reaching targets on discomfort regions. TiltSlide (A), TiltReduction (B), and TiltCursor (C).

the handedness of a user. We collected the magnitude of tilt when users directly touch targets on an 8x14 grid (Fig. 2), and confirmed that users actually tilt the device towards the thumb more when they have to touch targets farther away.

ONE-THUMB INTERACTION BASED ON TILTING

We designed three novel methods for one-handed target acquisition in large smartphones; TiltSlide, TiltReduction, and TiltCursor, to be triggered by a tilting gesture.

TiltSlide (TS) When a user tilts a device, the screen slides to the tilting direction (Fig. 1A). There are eight sliding directions; right-down, right, right-up, up, left-up, left, left-down, and down. The screen slides until any of the edges hit the center of the physical screen.

TiltReduction (TR) When a user tilts a device, the screen shrinks to fit in a customized comfort region (Fig. 1B). We determined the region as a rectangle that users draw by diagonally dragging their thumb (from top-left to bottom-right) while previewing shrunk sized screen. They were allowed to draw a rectangle repeatedly until they could comfortably reach the entire rectangle whose aspect ratio is maintained to that of screen to avoid distortion.

TiltCursor (TC) While a device is being tilted, a cursor appears on the position where the user starts a swipe gesture (Fig. 1C) and it moves faster than thumb to help reaching a far-target.

STUDY DESIGN

We hypothesized that our tilting methods will be faster than ThumbSpace, since ThumbSpace needs additional cognitive effort to determine the relative position of a target on the semitransparent space **(H1)**. Because the initial position of

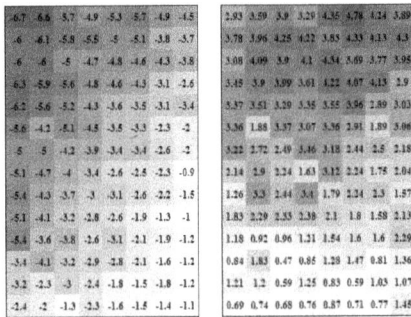

Figure 2. Gyroscope values for x-axis (left) and y-axis (right) when acquiring targets on screen. Negative values for x-axis denote tilting to the right, and positive values for y-axis denote tilting down. The darker the color, the more tilted the device.

the cursor is closer to the target compared to that of ETEC, TC will be faster than ETEC (**H2**). TR will be less accurate than DT and TS, since it reduces the target size when whole screen shrinks to fit to the comfort region (**H3**).

We conducted a user study to evaluate the three methods against DT (directly touching with a thumb), ThumbSpace [3] and ETEC [4]. We recruited 18 participants (10 females, 8 males, average age = 24, all right-handed). Participants held a large smartphone (Samsung Galaxy Note 3 with 5.7" screen) in their right hands and performed target acquisition tasks using each of six methods for 5 trials. One trial contained 30 target acquisition tasks with targets at randomly activated regions on an 8x14 grid ($7\ mm^2$ as target size) while maintaining the same total thumb-travel distance for each trial. We used a Latin Square design for eliminating ordering effects and completed the experiment with survey questionnaires.

RESULTS AND DISCUSSION

We analyzed results using a repeated-measures ANOVA and found significant effects for task completion time ($F_{5,85} = 24.59$, $p < .01$) and error rate ($F_{5,85} = 9.65$, $p < .01$). We used Bonferroni correction for post hoc analysis.

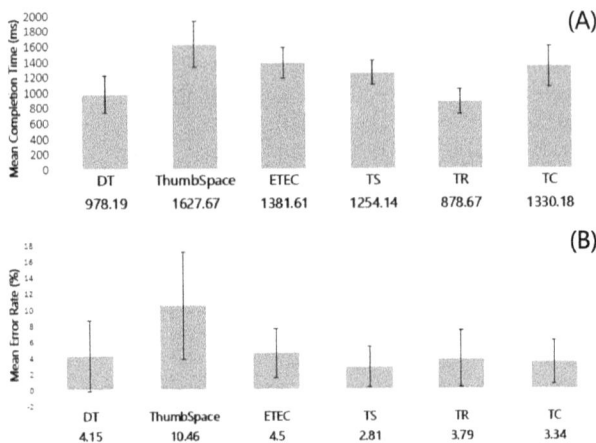

Figure 3. Mean completion time (A) and mean error rate (B) of all six targeting methods. Error bars denote standard deviation.

All three tilting methods (TC, TS, and TR) were significantly faster than ThumbSpace (all $p < .01$), confirming H1. We could not confirm H2 since TC showed no significant difference from ETEC. Other noteworthy result was that TR was significantly faster than ETEC ($p < .01$). Moreover, TR had no significant difference from DT, while other methods were significantly slower than DT. In terms of accuracy, ThumbSpace showed significantly more errors than all other methods ($p < .001$). TR did not have any significant difference compared to DT, rejecting H3.

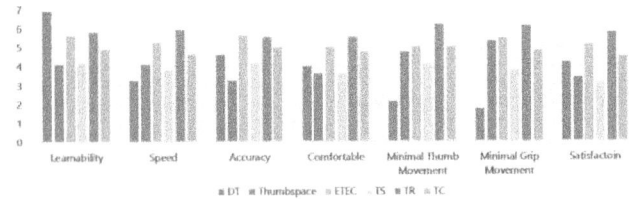

Figure 4. Questionnaire results (means)

Questionnaire results showed that TR had no significant difference from DT about learnability. In terms of thumb/grip movement, there were significant effect between DT and the other methods ($p < .001$). In summary, compared to DT, TR showed a promising result that it required less thumb/grip movement while showing comparable performance in speed and accuracy.

CONCLUSION

We proposed three methods to help reaching discomfort regions when using only one hand. We applied the tilting gesture to trigger our methods since the gesture is naturally used when reaching far-targets. We validated our methods through a user study by comparing other three related methods. All three methods showed better performance than ThumbSpace in speed and accuracy. Especially, TiltReduction led users to require less thumb/grip movement than Direct Touch without showing any significant differences in speed and accuracy.

ACKNOWLEDGEMENTS

This work was supported by the National Research Foundation of Korea (NRF) grant funded by the Korea government (MSIP) (No. 2011-0030813).

REFERENCES

1. Goel, M., Wobbrock, J.O., and Patel, S.N. GripSense: Using Built-In Sensors to Detect Hand Posture and Pressure on Commodity Mobile Phones. *Proc. UIST'12*.545-554.2012.

2. Karlson, A.K., Bederson, B.B., and Contreras-Vidal J.L. Understanding Single-Handed Mobile Device Interaction. *Tech report HCIL-2006-02.*

3. Karlson, A.K., Bederson, B.B., ThumbSpace: Generalized One-Handed Input for Touchscreen-Based Mobile Devices. *Proc. Interact'07*.324-339.2007.

4. Kim, S., Yu, J., and Lee, G. Interaction Techniques for Unreachable Objects on the Touchscreen. *Proc. OzCHI'12*.295-298.2012.

Integrating Optical Waveguides for Display and Sensing on Pneumatic Soft Shape Changing Interfaces

Lining Yao, Jifei Ou, Daniel Tauber, Hiroshi Ishii

MIT Media Lab

{liningy, jifei, dtauber, ishii}@media.mit.edu

ABSTRACT

We introduce the design and fabrication process of integrating optical fiber into pneumatically driven soft composite shape changing interfaces. Embedded optical waveguides can provide both sensing and illumination, and add one more building block to the design of designing soft pneumatic shape changing interfaces.

INTRODUCTION

PneUI [9] has been introduced as a mean to develop soft composite material that integrates both sensing and actuation mechanism. PneUI adds the I/O functionalities by compositing individual functional components (e.g. liquid metal for stretch sensing). As an alternative approach, we suggest that by adding optical fibers one can unify the I/O functionalities in one material. This simplifies the design and fabrication of PneUI material.

Our main contribution is: integration of optical waveguides into pneumatic shape changing interfaces to allow for shape and interaction sensing as well as general illumination and pixel displaying; documentation of the general fabrication and design process; two example applications.

RELATED WORK

Using optical fibers for illumination and sensing is a widely explored domain in HCI: sensing and illumination cloth [3,5], touch sensing on rigid surfaces[4,8], phycon recognition through fiber bundles [1,2], and customized sensors [6,7]. Our goal is to leverage previous work in the context of pneumatic shape changing interfaces. Rather than breaking new ground in the field of using optical fibers for displays in general, we try to demonstrate how broad and powerful the existing techniques are in the context of elastomer based shape changing UIs.

POINTS

Illumination

By embedding optical waveguides with their lengths perpendicular to the silicone surfaces, we can create elastic materials with pixelated displays. Figure 1 shows three samples with different original resolutions, and the

UIST'14 Adjunct, October 5–8, 2014, Honolulu, HI, USA.
ACM 978-1-4503-3068-8/14/10.
http://dx.doi.org/10.1145/2658779.2658804

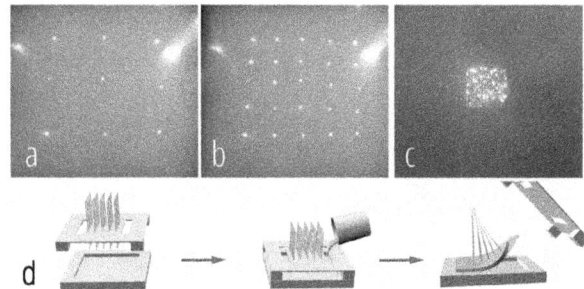

Figure 1: Pixelated displays with different resolutions.

general fabrication process.

Sensing: Hovering and Touch Sensing

We composite pairs of optical fibers into elastomer for touch sensing on deformable surfaces (Figure 2). This approach has been used for touch sensing on rigid surfaces [4,8]. When a finger touches one sensor pair, the IR source light travels through one fiber, is reflected by the finger, goes back through the other adjacent fiber and is sensed by the IR receiver at the end. We are able to tell the hover, touch, left and right swipe. Values below were measured with fibers with a diameter of 0.25mm.

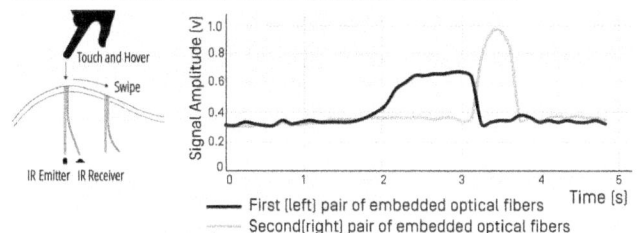

Figure 2: Sensor generated voltage changes during one swipe from the left to the right.

Application: Pneuxel

Inspired by the method introduced in PneUI [9] to create dynamic texture display, we developed Pneuxel to unify both dynamic haptic and visual display in one. While dynamic displays have been used to replace static images for public signs, most of the haptic-based signs for visually impaired users are static. Figure 3 shows when a "turn left" arrow is displayed, the cell units can be inflated column by column from the right to the left to convey the same information through haptic sensation.

Pneuxel is made of five by five individually controllable cells that can light up through an optical waveguide composite.

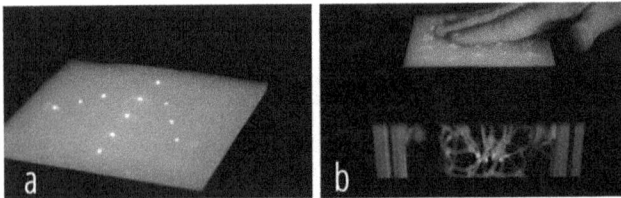

Figure 3: Pneuxel visual and haptic display

It can simulate variable degrees of expansion and contraction through pneumatic actuation (Figure 4). Pneumatic control platform contains one stationary air compressor, one stationary pumps and 50 3/2 solenoid valves.

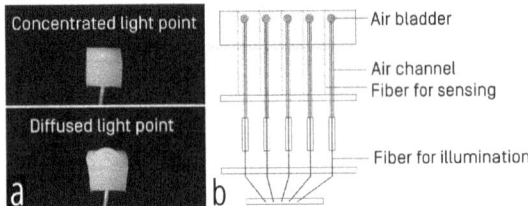

Figure 4: Assembly of each unit (a) and the system (b).

SURFACE

Illumination

To illuminate a certain pattern on an elastomeric surface, in addition to utilizing the aforementioned pixel approach, we can also design predefined patterns. By casting a clear silicone with a predefined shape into another translucent silicone, we can make the translucent part illuminated through light scattering. In this case, the single light source is guided by the section made with clear silicone (Figure 5).

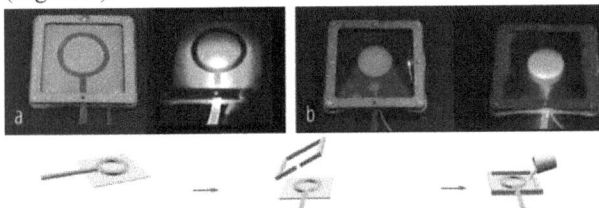

Figure 5: Light travels through transparent elastomer and illuminates other regions.

Sensing

This stretch sensor is designed by sensing the light loss traveling through the clear, elastic silicone when it is stretched (Figure 6). As the elastomer gets thinner, more loss is induced on the higher order modes.

Application: Self-Illuminating Lamp

To demonstrate the simplification achieved by the current approach, we rebuilt the lamp presented in PneUI [9] but with different sensing and illumination techniques. While the original PneUI lamp contains LED components soldered on copper tapes as well as liquid metal for sensing, the new lamp is fabricated by compositing two elastomers. The transparent elastomer guides light from the top through the whole body, as well as provides stretch sensing functionality (Figure 7). This makes the design more sturdy, cheaper and a lot easier to fabricate.

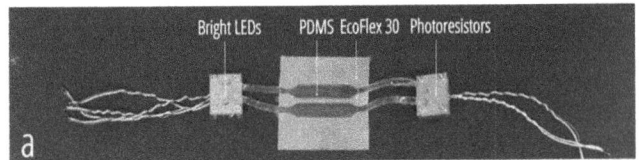

Figure 6: Customized stretch sensor.

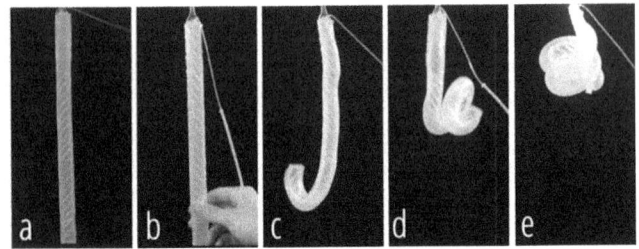

Figure 7: Improved shape changing lamp with only elastomer composite.

REFERENCE

1. Baudisch, P., Becker, T., and Rudeck, F. Lumino : Tangible Blocks for Tabletop Computers Based on Glass Fiber Bundles. *Proc. of CHI 2010*, ACM Press (2010), 1165–1174.

2. Fukuchi, K., Nakabayashi, R., Sato, T., and Takada, Y. Ficon: A Tangible Display Device for Tabletop System Using Optical Fiber. *Proc. of ITS 2011*, ACM Press (2011), 1.

3. Hashimoto, S., Suzuki, R., Kamiyama, Y., Inami, M., and Igarashi, T. LightCloth: Senseable Illuminating Optical Fiber Cloth for Creating Interactive Surfaces. *Proc. of CHI 2013*, ACM Press (2013), 603–606.

4. Jackson, D., Bartindale, T., and Olivier, P. FiberBoard: compact multi-touch display using channeled light. *Proc. of ITS 2009*, ACM Press (2009), 25–28.

5. Rantala, J., Hännikäinen, J., and Vanhala, J. Fiber Optic Sensors for Wearable Applications. *Personal Ubiquitous Comput. 15*, 1 (2011), 85–96.

6. Rudeck, F. and Baudisch, P. Rock-Paper-Fibers : Bringing Physical Affordance to Mobile Touch Devices. *Proc. of CHI 2012*, ACM Press (2012), 1929–1932.

7. Willis, K.D.D., Brockmeyer, E., Hudson, S.E., and Poupyrev, I. Printed Optics : 3D Printing of Embedded Optical Elements for Interactive Devices. *Proc. of UIST 2012*, ACM Press (2012), 589–598.

8. Wimmer, R. FlyEye : Grasp-Sensitive Surfaces Using Optical Fiber. *Proc. of TEI 2010*, ACM Press (2010), 245–248.

9. Yao, L., Niiyama, R., Ou, J., Follmer, S., Silva, C. Della, and Ishii, H. PneUI : Pneumatically Actuated Soft Composite Materials for Shape Changing Interfaces. *Proc. of UIST 2013*, ACM Press (2013), 13–22.

Towards Responsive Retargeting of Existing Websites

Gilbert Louis Bernstein
Stanford University
gilbert@gilbertbernstein.com

Scott Klemmer
UC San Diego
srk@ucsd.edu

ABSTRACT

Websites need to be displayed on a panoply of different devices today, but most websites are designed with fixed widths only appropriate to browsers on workstation computers. We propose to programmatically rewrite websites into responsive formats capable of adapting to different device display sizes. To accomplish this goal, we cast retargeting as a cross-compilation problem. We decompose existing HTML pages into boxes (lexing), infer hierarchical structure between these boxes (parsing) and finally generate parameterized layouts from the hierarchical structure (code generation). This document describes preliminary work on ReMorph, a prototype 'retargeting as cross-compilation' system.

Author Keywords

Responsive Design; Document Layout; Webpages; Retargeting

ACM Classification Keywords

H.5.2. User Interfaces: Screen Design

HOW BIG IS YOUR SCREEN?

Websites are being viewed on a increasing diversity of devices. Among U.S. adults, 46% own smartphones, 57% have laptops, 19% own an e-book reader, and 19% have a tablet computer[5]. Across different manufacturers and models, these devices saturate a continuum of screen size, aspect ratio, and resolution. However, most websites are designed with fixed size layouts, (in the vicinity of 960px) frustrating visitors on mobile devices.

To cope with the challenge of adapting to a wide range of devices, designers are adopting a suite of techniques and strategies known as "responsive design."[4] Responsively designed webpages maintain a single document, whose layout "responds" to the viewport size and resolution by making discrete changes in the layout of page elements. For instance, in a responsive design a grid of photos is handled by progressively decreasing the number of columns in response to narrower display widths. (By contrast, proportional scaling results in shrinking the individual photos, limiting the effective size adaptation to a narrower range of sizes)

UIST'14 Adjunct, October 5–8, 2014, Honolulu, HI, USA.
ACM 978-1-4503-3068-8/14/10.
http://dx.doi.org/10.1145/2658779.2658805

RETARGETING AS COMPILATION

ReMorph is a system for programmatically rewriting existing webpages, which we use to retrofit existing webpages with viewport-adaptive layouts. (i.e. responsive design)

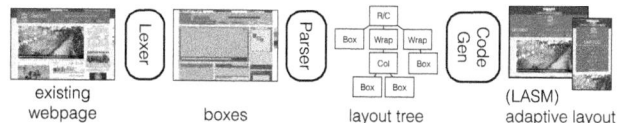

Figure 1. The ReMorph system design is loosely based on a compiler with lexer, parser and code generation stages.

Abandoning HTML/CSS

Lexing is responsible for extracting boxes from a webpage. Unlike most other systems that solve a similar problem, our lexer is designed for both analysis and synthesis; it ensures that we can independently reposition and resize the extracted boxes. First the lexer *embalms* the page to remove dynamic Javascript behavior, preserve the CSS-Rule-to-DOM-Node mapping (by rewriting the CSS selectors), and create CSS-style-closures. After embalming, the lexer determines which DOM Nodes have any visible effect on the page, (requires looking at over 10 independent CSS attributes) and which order boxes are drawn in, (by reimplementing the algorithm in Appendix E of the CSS 2.1 specification[2]) and finally re-roots all visible DOM nodes as immediate children of the BODY element, sequenced in the correct draw order.

Parsing Visual Design Using NLP Algorithms

Parsing is responsible for hierarchically organizing the boxes output by the lexer. It produces a layout tree annotated with parameter values. Parsing must address (i) ambiguity about how boxes on the page should be grouped (Figure 2) and (ii) ambiguity about how those groups should respond when given more or less space in the layout. We use a 2d adaptation of the well known CYK parsing algorithm[3] from Natural Language Processing to resolve these ambiguities.

Figure 2. This horizontal sequence of boxes should be grouped into three subgroups of 6, 2, and 3 elements respectively, rather than one group of 11 elements.

CYK (aka. Chart) Parsing uses dynamic programming to solve subproblems in bottom-up order. Each sub-rectangle of the logical grid (Figure 3) defines a parsing sub-problem. Within this algorithmic structure, a grammar defines the structure of valid parses, while a scoring function (equivalently probability distribution) specifies which of the valid parses is the best choice. To solve a sub-problem, a problem's box is decomposed along a grid line (horizontally or vertically) into two sub-problems; all applicable grammar rules are matched, and we keep the highest scoring parse for each type of symbol. (Our current vocabulary has three non-terminals: columns, rowcols, and wrappers) By leveraging features computed from the original webpage, the scoring function can bias the parse towards more desirable results. (Figure 4)

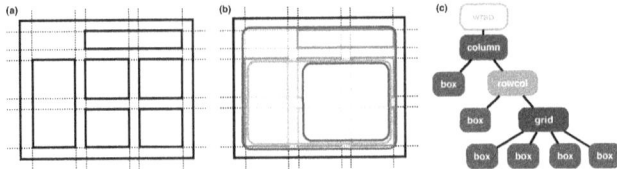

Figure 3. An example parsing problem, showing (a) the logical grid decomposition and one possible parse (b) in context and (c) abstractly.

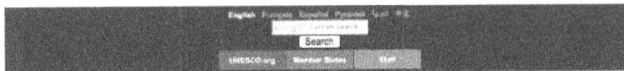

Figure 4. Using a simple feature (whether boxes come from the same HTML list) we can make desirable groupings more likely. As a result, the enclosing rowcol has switched to a column of 4 rows rather than a column of 11 items.

Generating Layout Assembly Code

Codegen is responsible for converting the layout tree from the parser into a layout program. Given a viewport width, this layout program sets the positions and sizes of all of the boxes on the page. We devised a small, easily implemented Layout Assembly (LASM) language in which to specify these programs. Each symbol in the layout tree is defined to expand into a particular chunk of LASM code. (Figure 6)

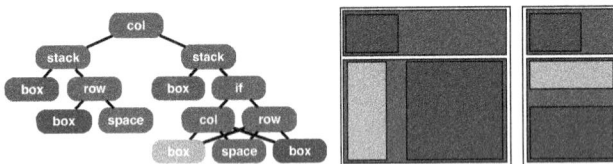

Figure 5. An example of a LASM program and the results of two executions with varying page widths

LASM programs execute (Figure 5) by recursively *placing* nodes by specifying a given input width; the resulting height is returned as output, along with the locations and sizes of all boxes in the sub-program. Row, Column, and Stack nodes sequence their child boxes horizontally, vertically, and in depth-order respectively. Box nodes cause a specific box to be positioned and sized, while Space nodes correspond to a visual no-op. Finally, If nodes choose which of their sub-trees to *place* depending on whether their input width is greater or less than a specified breakpoint.

LASM is deceptively simple. Formally, it is capable of encoding arbitrary piecewise-linear functions. This means it is capable of expressing layouts specified in most layout systems proposed to date, including sophisticated linear constraint systems such as the one proposed by Badros et al.[1]

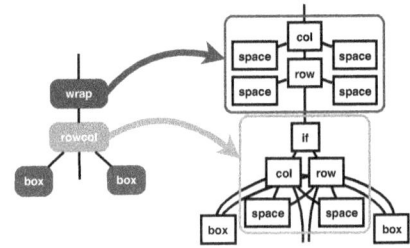

Figure 6. Code generation converts a layout tree into a LASM DAG by expanding nodes into chunks of LASM glued together using the same overall topology.

DESIGN TOOL OR AUTOMATION?

ReMorph can compute retargetings automatically, but we can also incorporate it into a design tool. To help explore this option, we conducted a preliminary study. We asked participants to retarget an existing website to a narrower width appropriate for mobile devices. While retargeting, our participants focused on the vertical order of page elements, while omitting elements they found less important. However our participants' decisions about the correct sequence or presence of page elements were mutually inconsistent. As a result, we are working on a design tool that (i) leverages ReMorph for a good starting proposal, (ii) makes re-sequencing & suppression of content easy, and (iii) relies on ReMorph to solve peripheral issues, like the setting of thousands of gutter, margin and other whitespace variables.

Currently the ReMorph system works on a limited set of test pages used for development. Moving forward, we plan to evaluate (a) how frequently ReMorph produces acceptable designs automatically, (b) how much effort is required of designers to edit the designs to their satisfaction, and (c) what kinds of designs are not addressed by ReMorph.

ACKNOWLEDGMENTS

Thanks to Pat Hanrahan and Ranjitha Kumar for their advice.

REFERENCES

1. Badros, G. J., Borning, A., Marriott, K., and Stuckey, P. Constraint cascading style sheets for the web. In *Proceedings of the 12th Annual ACM Symposium on User Interface Software and Technology*, UIST '99, ACM (New York, NY, USA, 1999), 73–82.

2. Bos, B., Çelik, T., Hickson, I., and Lie, H. W. Cascading style sheets level 2 revision 1 (css 2.1) specification. World Wide Web Consortium, Candidate Recommendation CR-CSS21-20070719, July 2007.

3. Jurafsky, D., and Martin, J. H. *Speech and Language Processing (2nd Edition) (Prentice Hall Series in Artificial Intelligence)*, 2 ed. Prentice Hall, 2008.

4. Marcotte, E. Responsive Web Design, May 2010. `http://alistapart.com/article/responsive-web-design`.

5. Zickuhr, K., and Smith, A. Digital Differences, April 2012. `http://pewinternet.org/Reports/2012/Digital-differences.aspx`.

bioPrint: An Automatic Deposition System
for Bacteria Spore Actuators

Jifei Ou[1]   **Lining Yao[1]**   **Clark Della Silva[1]**   **Wen Wang[2]**   **Hiroshi Ishii[1]**

1 MIT Media Lab
{jifei, liningy, clarkds, ishii}@media.mit.edu

2 MIT Chemical Engineering
wen.eve.wang@gmail.com

ABSTRACT

We propose an automatic deposition method of bacteria spores, which deform thin soft materials under environmental humidity change. We describe the process of two-dimensional printing the spore solution as well as a design application. This research intends to contribute to the understanding of the control and pre-programming the transformation of future interfaces.

INTRODUCTION

It has been shown in earlier work that the Bacillus Subtilis spore can be used to bend and release a thin sheet substrate, due to this spore's hygroscopic behavior. The resulting mechanism has a high energy density (10.6 MJ/m³) and is easy to assemble. Inspired by these results, we introduce a computer controllable system to deposit structures of spore solutions onto substrate geometries to achieve a wide variety of shape transformations. While most prior work focuses on programming the biological materials at nano and micro scales, we believe that this approach can also add to the programmability at the macro (human) scale, so that such materials can be used in the field of Human-Computer Interaction and Design.

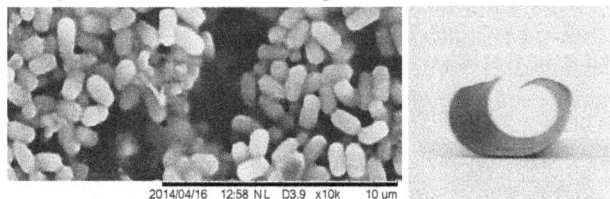

2014/04/16 12:58 NL D3.9 x10k   10 um

Figure 1: (a) SEM scanning of bacillus subtilis spores applied on a latex substrate (b) Bending of latex substrate material with spores as surface attachment.

RELATED WORK

Developing stimuli-responsive and "smart" materials, especially polymers [3], is a growing field in chemistry. A paper published by Nature Nanotechnology introduced Bacillus spores (originated from Bacillus bacteria) as a potential building block for humidity responsive materials [1]. The magic of actuation lies in the cortex of the Bacillus spore [2]. It absorbs water and swells when relative

humidity (RH) increases and releases water, returning to its original size when RH decreases.

BIO-PRINTER

In order to achieve a higher accuracy of shape-change driven by the spores, we built an automatic depositing system that can apply the spore on the substrate material.

Hardware Setup

The system consists of two parts: a printhead that can spray tiny droplets of spore solution and a desktop CNC milling machine that can move the printhead in three-axis (Figure 2).

Figure 2: Setup of bacteria spores printer.

Printing is accomplished using a small CNC router (available from zentoolworks.com) modified to accept the print head. We designed a customized printhead to hold the inkjet cartridge carrier in place, and stabilize two pneumatic tubing, which accelerates the drying process of the spore solution by constantly blowing gentle air onto the substrate while printing.

We used an Arduino InkShield (available from http://nicholasclewis.com) to control the deposition of the spore actuators. The InkShield uses HP C6602A cartridge, which has 12 nozzles that can be individually controlled. This attribute gives us the space to easily vary the density and the resolution of the spores for each print.

Customized Printing Path and G-code

For converting the printing pattern to machine toolpath, we used a free web-based software Makercam. The software converts an SVG file to G-code file for the milling machine to read. Since the generated CNC G-code contains spindle and Z-axis control, yet lacks of inkShield control, we have to customize the motor control board and the G-code to fit our system. The InkShield is controlled using the spindle head enable output of the motor control board. This output is connected to the arduino controlling the print head, and the print head is enabled when the spindle enable line goes high. The G-code is then modified to bring the spindle enable line high after the print head has moved to the

UIST'14 Adjunct, October 5–8, 2014, Honolulu, HI, USA.
ACM 978-1-4503-3068-8/14/10.
http://dx.doi.org/10.1145/2658779.2658806

correct height. In contrary, for a normal CNC router, the spindle enable is brought high and then the head is moved down to start cutting. By starting to print after the head is moved down, excess spray of the ink is prevented.

Printing Process

To replace the ink in the original cartridge with spore solution, we carefully cut out the top cap of the cartridge and rinsed both the cartridge and the sponge inside. After they completely dried, we pour 5 mL spore solution in the cartridge and soak the sponge in. The top cap needs to be taped back on the cartridge body so that the cartridge can be snapped into the carrier. An ultrasonic cleaner is also necessary as the nozzles of cartridge can be blocked by the impurities. Figure 3 shows the whole printing process.

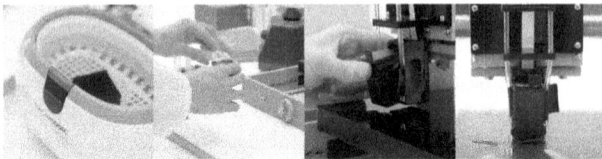

Figure 3: Printing Process

Flow Rate of Spore Deposition

We can calculate the speed of spore deposition from the equation:

$$S = S_n \times D, (1)$$

where S_n is the speed of nozzle jetting and D is the density of spore solution. The density of spore solution we use is 5.25×10^9 per milliliter. The speed of a single nozzle jetting is 0.24uL per second. Therefore in our test the actual speed of spore deposition is 1.26×10^6 per second.

Machine Feed Rate and Material Bending Angle

Based on our test experience, the optimum parameters to cover the surface nicely are with print head diameter (liquid drop) D as 0.5mm and step over p as 20%. Once these two parameters are set, feed rate v is directly related to the bending performance of the final sample.

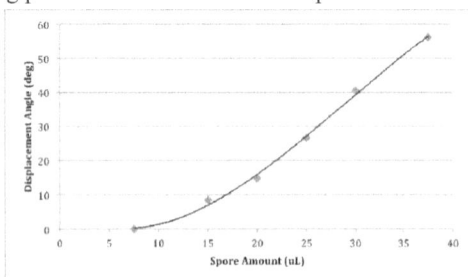

Table 1: Change of displacement angle with spore amount with a sample size of 5mm * 20mm

Table 1 shows that the displacement angle of a 5mm by 20mm material sample is directly related to the spore amount. The table holds true as long as the sample width to height ratio is 1:4. Based on table 1, a desired angle α corresponding to a spore volume V. The amount of spore we need for every square millimeter sample (ρ) can be calculated as

$$\rho = V / 20 \times 5 = 0.01V, (2)$$

For the feed rate v, since inkjet volume at certain amount of time t should equal to the desired volume of spore at the size covered by the same printing time:

$$S \times t = v \times D \times p \times t \times \rho, (3)$$

Machine feed rate v can be calculated based on (2) and (3):

$$v = S / (D \times p \times \rho) = 1.26 \times 10^9 / V. (4)$$

APPLICATION

We are inspired by the natural anisotropic structure of material composites, whose shape can be programmed into the materials' micro or larger structures, we print leaves with different shapes. Spore actuators follow the vein structure of certain leaves, which creates biomimetic transformation of the leaves that resemble the real natural organisms (Figure 4). Considering lots of natural leaves transform due to the gain and loss of water inside the veins, here spore actuators swell and shrink to create the similar effect.

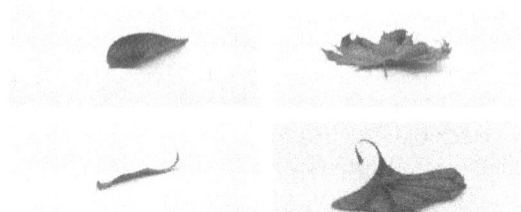

Figure 4: Spore actuators follows the vein structures of leaves to create biomimetic transformation.

We then apply the transformable leaves to the design of living tea bags. The leave on top of the tea bag curls up at the beginning. After pouring hot waters into the teacup, the curled leaves will slowly unwrap, to indicate the tea bag is fully soaked in the water. Once the tea is ready and the tea bag is pulled out of the cup, the leave will curl up again to hint the end of its life. (Figure 5)

Figure 5: Tealeaf unwraps to indicate the tea is ready, and curls up again after use.

REFERENCE

1. Chen, X., Mahadevan, L. Driks, A and Sahin O. Bacillus spores as building blocks for stimuli-responsive materials and nanogenerators. Nature Nanotechnology 2014, 9, 137–141.

2. McKenney, P.T., Driks, A., Eichenberger, P. The Bacillus subtilis endospore: assembly and functions of the multilayered coat, Nature Reviews Microbiology 2013, 11, 33-44 Meng, H., Li, G. Reversible switching transitions of stimuli-responsive shape changing polymers, J. Mater. Chem. A, 2013,1, 7838-7865.

3. Meng, H., Li, G. Reversible switching transitions of stimuli-responsive shape changing polymers, J. Mater. Chem. A, 2013,1, 7838-7865.

FatBelt: Motivating Behavior Change Through Isomorphic Feedback

Trevor Pels, Christina Kao, Saguna Goel
Human Computer Interaction (Computer Science), Stanford University
{tpels, chris18, sgoel1}@stanford.edu

ABSTRACT

The ultimate problem of systems facilitating long-term health and fitness goals is the disconnect between an action and its eventual consequence. As the long-term effects of behavior change are not immediately apparent, it can be hard to motivate the desired behavior over a long period of time. As such, we introduce a system that uses physical feedback through a wearable device that inflates around the stomach as a response to calorie overconsumption, simulating the long-term weight-gain associated with over-eating. We tested a version of this system with 12 users over a period of 2 days, and found a significant decrease in consumption over a baseline period of the same length, suggesting that through physical response, FatBelt moved calorie intake drastically closer to participants goals. Interviews with participants indicate that isomorphism to the long-term consequences was a large factor in the system's efficacy. In addition, the wearable, physical feedback was perceived as an extension of the user's body, an effect with great emotional consequences.

Author Keywords

Wearable computing; physical feedback; health and fitness.

ACM Classification Keywords

J.3 Life and Medical Sciences: Health

INTRODUCTION

Any long-term goal requiring short-term sacrifice must overcome the distance between the two. In particular, the medical solution for obesity has long been available: controlled calorie intake, proportionate to size and activity level [1]. Yet Americans are unable to maintain this portion control, leading to a widespread obesity crisis.

Past research has found that computational calorie tracking is already more effective than pencil-and-paper counting, and that feedback from a counselor is better still [2]. In addition, HCI research has found that physical feedback generally increases engagement and sense of realism [3]. This effect

should allow a more vivid and emotionally resonant simulation of long-term negative consequences.

In this paper, we explore a system using wearable computing and physical feedback to create short-term consequences simulating long-term results. This system, "FatBelt", operates under the hypothesis that making the consequences of users' actions short-term, *while maintaining isomorphism to the long-term consequences*, will result in greater behavior change. It uses a small inflatable pack worn across the user's stomach, beneath the shirt that automatically inflates when the user consumes greater than his or her daily calorie goal, simulating the long-term physical effects of overeating.

We conducted an evaluation with 12 users using a lightweight, manual version of the belt for 2 days, after a 2 day baseline. We found that calorie intake decreased significantly with the belt. We also conducted interviews with all participants, and with several others who used a more fully-featured belt for shorter periods of time. Users reported that belt inflation was a strong disincentive, for reasons relating to the mild physical sensations and the social pressures associated with overeating. And unexpectedly, physical feedback delivered through a wearable device was integrated into participants' physical conceptions of self, lending it the weight of a bodily response.

FATBELT SYSTEM

The FatBelt system consists of the following two components: a calorie-counting app and an inflatable belt worn around the waist. After having eaten lunch, John enters a description of the meal he took into his mobile device. The app detects how much he has exceeded his calorie limit and accordingly sends a Bluetooth signal to the FatBelt which inflates, making John aware of the consequences of overeating.

App

The calorie counting app: a simple iOS application allowing logging of caloric consumption. If users consume over half of their daily calorie goal before 3:00 PM or exceed their limit before the end of the day, the app displays a message and sends a Bluetooth signal to the belt.

Belt

The automatic belt: an inflatable tube, an electric pump, 2 batteries, an Arduino, and a Bluetooth shield. The inflatable tube is affixed to the inside of the user's shirt, over the stomach area; the remaining components hang from a separate belt

UIST'14 Adjunct, October 5–8, 2014, Honolulu, HI, USA.
ACM 978-1-4503-3068-8/14/10.
http://dx.doi.org/10.1145/2658779.2658807

around the waist. When the Bluetooth shield receives a signal from the app, it activates the Arduino, allowing the batteries to power the electric pump and inflate the belt.

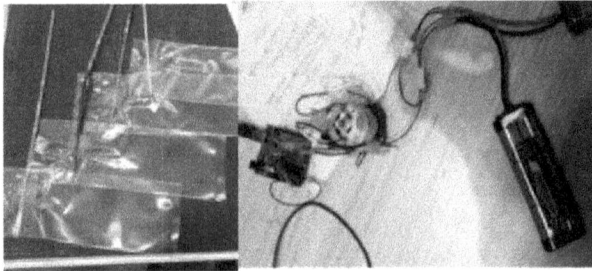

Figure 1. Inflatable pack (left) which is tied to the pump (right)

The lightweight version has no pump; instead, there is a straw which runs up the user's torso. When they overconsume, the app prompts them to blow into the straw, inflating the belt. We decided to use this model for testing since it is (a) unobtrusive, (b) easy to replicate in large quantities, and (c) less expensive, but the functionality is essentially the same.

EVALUATION
We completed two evaluations, each focusing on either quantitative or qualitative data.

Method
Our first study, after pilot testing, evaluated the underlying theory of the device on a feasible scale. We recruited 12 participants to use the app on its own for 2 days (with in-app feedback), then the app and the "light" belt for another 2 days. We tracked their consumption and conducted interviews with each afterwards. The second study tested the full belt as a subjective experience, on a smaller scale. Five participants spent between 1 and 3 meals using the heavy belt. This was to ensure there were no significant differences from the "light" version and to supplement the interview data from the primary study.

Results
Participants' calorie consumption was highly significantly lower while using the belt than without it ($p = 0.0027$). The mean calorie consumption for the baseline was 1779 (st. dev=512) and the experimental was 1374 (st. dev=442) per day. For the experimental phase,there was no significant difference between the first and second day during either period ($p = 0.3470$ and $p = 0.6940$), and in fact the mean increased slightly within each period. This suggests that these results are due to the presence of the belt rather than simply becoming accustomed to the system.

Participants said that inflating the belt was a strong disincentive, for two main reasons. First, many said that they were embarrassed to do so. This was most often because of the stigma associated with wearable computing devices. However, though several participants inflated their belts at crowded tables, none of the other diners noticed. The second reason was that the inflated belt made them "feel fat." This was distinct from embarrassment, in that it focused on their view of themselves rather than others' views of them.

DISCUSSION
The system provided a strong disincentive, but one which was mostly internal. Inflation was not painful or uncomfortable, and the social consequences were minimal. We explore why users were still strongly adverse to this.

Isomorphic Social Consequences
We initially expected the social pressures associated with inflating the belt to be great. However, after getting qualitative feedback about the way the belt was perceived, essentially no non-participants noticed the belt. It seems, therefore, that users' responses were due not to the inflation of the belt, but to its association with the long-term effects of overconsumption and the social norms against them. Their motivational power was effectively transferred to the short-term consequence of belt inflation which appears to answer our research question affirmatively.

Body Feedback
One unexpected result expressed by many users was the ability of physical feedback through the wearable device to impact their physical self-conception. It was not simply that the belt and its size represented weight gain; participants actually felt as if they had experienced growth. In our case, this mainly served to further associate inflation with the long-term effects. In general, the increase in impact when physical feedback occurs as a change to what the user perceives as his or her "self" could be a fruitful possibility for exploration.

CONCLUSION AND FUTURE WORK
In this paper, we explored the power of isomorphic short-term responses to harness the motivational power of long-term goals. FatBelt effectively moved calorie intake drastically closer to participants' goals with a simple physical response, along with a proportionally greater psychological impact of physical feedback that is integrated into the user's concept of self. In the future, we would like to verify the long-term resilience of this effect in a controlled study, and explore its application in other areas (exercise, quitting tobacco, budgeting, creative practice, etc.). The interpretation of wearable, physical feedback as a bodily response is also an exciting possibility for exploration.

REFERENCES
1. Jakicic, John M., et al. "American College of Sports Medicine position stand. Appropriate intervention strategies for weight loss and prevention of weight regain for adults." *Medicine and science in sports and exercise* 33.12 (2001): 2145-2156.

2. Tate, Deborah F., Elizabeth H. Jackvony, and Rena R. Wing. "A randomized trial comparing human e-mail counseling, computer-automated tailored counseling, and no counseling in an Internet weight loss program." *Archives of internal medicine*

3. Klasnja, Predrag, et al. "Using mobile personal sensing technologies to support health behavior change in everyday life: lessons learned." *American Medical Informatics Association, 2009 for Ubifit*

M-Gesture: Geometric Gesture Authoring Framework for Multi-Device Gestures Using Wearable Devices

Ju-Whan Kim[1], Tek-Jin Nam[2]

CIDR lab, Department of Industrial Design, KAIST

291 Daehak-ro, Yuseong-gu, Daejeon, 305-701, Republic of Korea

[1]juwhan.k@gmail.com, [2]tjnam@kaist.ac.kr

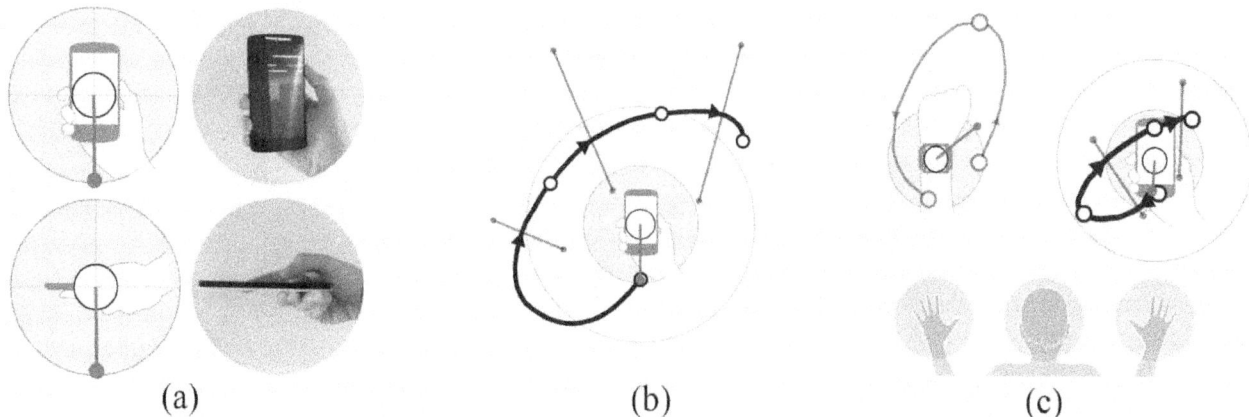

Figure 1. Screen images of the M-Gesture framework.

ABSTRACT

Wearable devices and mobile devices have great potential to detect various body motions as they are attached to different body parts. We present M-Gesture, a geometric gesture authoring framework using multiple wearable devices. We implemented physical metaphor, geometric gesture language, and continuity in spatial layout for easy and clear gesture authoring. M-Gesture demonstrates the use of geometric notation as an intuitive gesture language.

Author Keywords

Multi Device Gesture Authoring; Geometric Notation

ACM Classification Keywords

H.5.2. Information interfaces and presentation (e.g., HCI): User Interfaces – Interaction Styles

INTRODUCTION

As smart wearable devices are being increasingly used, the potential of multi-device gesture interface is also growing. Although wearable devices capture kinetic information of multiple body parts, the information is not processed in a unified manner. Recently, several attempts to create joint-gesture interfaces using multiple wearable devices have been made [1]. However, existing works are dependent on

UIST'14 Adjunct, October 5–8, 2014, Honolulu, HI, USA.
ACM 978-1-4503-3068-8/14/10.
http://dx.doi.org/10.1145/2658779.2658808

certain device combinations, applications, or contexts. Many HCI researchers and interface designers are relying on textual programming, which significantly hinders fast realization and interaction exploration. Moreover, end users who are not familiar with mobile programming have no means to utilize their smart watch as a gesture sensor. Our research goal is to propose a multi-device gesture authoring framework that researchers, interface designers, and even end users can use to intuitively develop their own gestures in the world of smart wearable devices.

RELATED WORK

There exist touchscreen-gesture and single-device spatial gesture authoring frameworks. The gesture authoring "language" arranges from a low-level programming language to a high-level natural language. One of the natural languages can be the user's demonstration. The *Programming-By-Demonstration* (PBD) approach [5, 6] makes computers infer the user's intention from the user's demonstration of the target gesture. One of the weaknesses of PBD is the appropriate selection of sensors and features, which frequently fails, even among expert programmers. Also PBD is a black box approach that is hard to analyze and correct mistakenly composed gestures. Low-level languages let the user directly describe the user's intention in a language that computers understand, such as GestureML [2] and Proton [4]. Although it allows clear communication between users and computers, significant learning and authoring effort are also required.

M-GESTURE

To overcome the black box problem and the laborious authoring issue, we present M-Gesture, a visually intuitive and easy *gesture authoring framework* for multi-device gestures. A gesture can be defined not only by its symbolic notation, but also by geometric parameters such as each component's position, length, and direction. M-Gesture contains three themes: *physical metaphor, geometric authoring language,* and *continuity in spatial layout.*

Physical Metaphor

M-Gesture geometrically displays raw sensor values *by physical metaphor of the pendulum.* 3-axis accelerometers are the most common and rich motion sensors that can detect orientation, motions, and some of rotations of devices. Although acceleration values convey valuable information about gesture motions, the raw sensor value often seems confusing to people who are not familiar with physics. We present acceleration values as a virtual pendulum (Fig. 1-a) to avoid confusion. The movement of a physical object dangling from the device follows the inertial force, which is in opposition to acceleration. We assume that the virtual metaphor makes the acceleration information acceptable and predictable to ordinary people.

Geometric Gesture Language

A geometric markup language called Hurdle metaphor [3] defines a gesture pattern (Fig. 1-b). As a device moves in real space, movement of the virtual pendulum creates an acceleration trajectory in the virtual space. A hurdle is a geometric line segment (the thin grey lines in Fig. 1-b) that detects the 2-D intersection by the acceleration trajectory. A gesture definition of M-Gesture is declared by a series of geometric hurdle-crosses of the acceleration values. A user directly draws the hurdle-crosses (the thick black curves in Fig. 1-b) on the touchscreen. A freeform drawing allows users to reflect their intention to the gesture representation. Geometric notation allows users to understand the gesture pattern by looking at it. This feature contrasts clearly with the symbolic notations that demand that users interpret and simulate the gesture behavior when they read the representations.

Continuity in Spatial Layout

The layout of M-Gesture is designed to show the continuity between the real-world and virtual-world configurations. The geometric sensor space for each device is located according to the body part it is attached to. The appearance of the device and the body part are displayed beneath the sensor space (Fig. 1-c) so that users can keep tracking which space represents which device and the real-world orientation of each device.

Implementation

The framework is implemented and tested on an Android platform. The host device collects each device's accelerometer values and passes them through a low-pass filter. The 3-D acceleration values are transformed into 2-D depending on how a user determines its viewing angle. The 2-D acceleration values form a trajectory that is displayed upon each device view. A state machine is built based on how a user draws hurdles and crossings. A cross of the next hurdle makes the state transits to the next, and a transition to the last state is regarded as the gesture detection. Geometric intersection is the only causal factor of a gesture detection for the current version.

CONCLUSION

This poster presents a gesture authoring framework for multiple handheld and wearable devices to capture rich body gestures. It allows users to intuitively compose multi-device body gestures using the geometric gesture authoring language of hurdle. Its geometric definition shows both low-level detail and high-level properties of a gesture (e.g., the position of the hurdle determines the sensor value level threshold, and the hurdle-crosses convey the outline shape of the gesture motion).

This system provides points of discussion for HCI and interface researchers' communities. It demonstrates the potential of geometric notation for intuitive and clear programming language in the right context. A physical metaphor can be applied to other interfaces as a way to deliver a confusing concept of physics or technology.

However, the use of accelerometers does not allow full range of motion. The gesture detection algorithm and its features can be further improved to reduce false-positive errors. A user study of intuitiveness and ease of use is expected to enhance the validity of this research.

ACKNOWLEDGEMENT

This paper is based on work supported by the ICT R&D program of MSIP/IITP. [10041313, UX-oriented Mobile SW Platform]

REFERENCES

1. Chen, X.A., Grossman, T., Wigdor, D.J., & Fitzmaurice, G. Duet: exploring joint interactions on a smart phone and a smart watch. *Proc. of CHI 14*, ACM Press (2014), 159-168.

2. IDEUM, GestureML, www.gestureml.org.

3. Kim, J.W. & Nam, T.J. EventHurdle: supporting designers' exploratory interaction prototyping with gesture-based sensors. *Proc. of CHI 13*, ACM Press (2013), 267-276.

4. Kin, K., Hartmann, B., Derose, T., & Agrawala, M. Proton: multitouch gestures as regular expressions. *Proc. of CHI 12*, ACM Press (2012), 2885-2894.

5. Li, Y. Gesture search: a tool for fast mobile data access. *Proc. of UIST 10*, ACM Press (2010), 87-96.

6. Lü, H. & Li, Y. Gesture coder: a tool for programming multi-touch gestures by demonstration. *Proc. of CHI 12*, ACM Press (2012), 2875-2884.

Eugenie: Gestural and Tangible Interaction with Active Tokens for Bio-Design

Casey Grote[1], Evan Segreto[1], Johanna Okerlund[1], Robert Kincaid[2], Orit Shaer[1]

Wellesley College[1]   Agilent Technologies[2]
oshaer@wellesley.edu   robert_kincaid@agilent.com

ABSTRACT

We present a case study of a tangible user interface that implements novel interaction techniques for the construction of complex queries in large data sets. Our interface, Eugenie, utilizes gestural interaction with active physical tokens and a multi-touch interactive surface to aid in the collaborative design process of synthetic biological circuits. We developed new interaction techniques for navigating large hierarchical data sets and for exploring a combinatorial design space. The goal of this research is to study the effect of gestural and tangible interaction with active tokens on sense-making throughout the bio-design process.

Author Keywords

Gestures; tabletop; multi-display environments; cross-device interaction; tangible tokens;

ACM Classification Keywords

H.5.2 [Information Interfaces and Presentation]: User Interfaces—input devices and strategies, interaction styles

INTRODUCTION

Multi-touch and tangible user interfaces offer unique opportunities for facilitating collaborative learning and discovery. However, existing interaction techniques have limitations when exploring large data sets [6]. For example, direct touch is a common multi-touch input method, but in data-intense applications, wherein data representations are often small, finger size and occlusion pose a challenge [1, 7]. In addition, WIMP-style control elements–such as scrollbars, sliders, and textfields–may not be effective in data-intense multi-touch interfaces, because they are often too small for accurate touch or consume expensive screen real-estate [1].

Recent studies have explored novel multi-touch interaction techniques that provide advantage over WIMP-style touch controls; e.g. [1, 7]. However, these techniques often suffer from low discoverability and lack of persistence [1]. Our goal is to define novel interaction techniques for multi-touch and tangible interfaces that support the construction of complex queries using large data sets. Our work draws upon Tangible Query Interfaces (TQI) [5], which introduced tangible interaction techniques for querying aggregated data using active

tokens. We also build upon research by Valdes et al. on user expectations regarding active tangible tokens combined with interactive surfaces [6].

In this abstract we present Eugenie, a tangible user interface that utilizes gestural interaction with active tokens and a multi-touch interactive surface. Active tokens are programmable physical objects with integrated display, sensing, or actuation technologies that allow users to dynamically modify the tokens' associations with datasets or controls [6]. We chose to examine the use of this technology within the application domain of synthetic biology by creating an interface that supports bio-design, the process of creating new biological constructs through the combination of well-defined genetic parts. Bio-design is an intricate multi-step process that, to date, has not been adequately supported by existing bioinformatics tools. For over three years, we have been collaborating closely with domain experts to address the need for novel user interfaces that make bio-design more tractable and accessible to a broad range of users [3, 4].

DESIGN AND CONCEPT

Eugenie is designed to support a top-down bio-design paradigm, a process in which users define increasingly specific design parameters with each iteration. The top-down approach typically consists of three stages: 1. *Research* - users search for information about the structure and function of existing biological constructs 2. *Specification* - users specify the desired functionality of their biological construct by constraining its structure and behavior. This process typically begins with general rules applied to generic parts. Currently, many synthetic biologists use Eugene [2], a domain-specific programming language, for specification; 3. *Exploration* - users explore concrete instantiations of their specification. Users then iterate on this paradigm, adding more rules until they reach the desired result.

Our application, Eugenie, is a tangible user interface that leverages the Eugene programming language's functionality for design specification. The interface consists of a tabletop multi-touch surface and a set of three to twelve active tangible tokens.

The system supports three main stages of the top-down design paradigm. The *research* stage is supported by both the surface interface and the tokens. The surface interface includes a search bar in which users can input keywords or specific part names in order to select existing biological constructs. The active tokens use a tree-like search functionality for browsing the MIT Registry, which contains over 3000 parts. Users

UIST'14, Oct 05-08 2014, Honolulu, HI, USA
ACM 978-1-4503-3068-8/14/10.
http://dx.doi.org/10.1145/2658779.2659765

neighbor the tokens vertically to traverse the tree; for example, when a token is neighbored below another that displays the generic biological part "promoter", sub-categories that exist within the class "promoter" are displayed (see Figure 1).

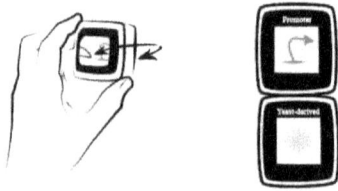

Figure 1. Tilting to scroll through categories and neighboring to display sub-categories

Both the surface and token interfaces support the *specification* stage. The surface interface implements three horizontally sliding panels that update simultaneously as users enter information (see Figure 2). The Structure View panel allows users to specify *structure* (e.g. "x BEFORE y" or "x AND y"). We created a visual language that maps manipulation of visual parts to Eugene functions. To add parts to the Structure View, users "stamp" the tokens onto the surface. Structure may also be defined using the tokens alone. Users may collapse or expand biological parts displayed by the token into one biological construct by stacking: simpler constructs stacked atop more complex constructs collapses, while the opposite expands.

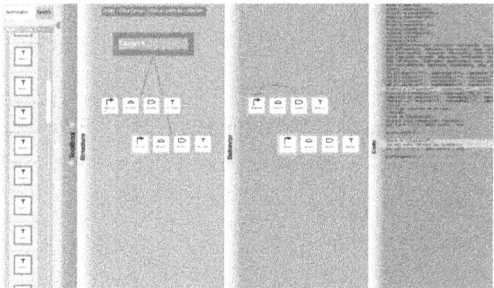

Figure 2. The tabletop interface

The Behavior View panel allows users to specify *relationships* between structures. For example, x INDUCES y is expressed by dragging from x to y and choosing "induces" from a pop-up menu. This relationship is expressed on the surface using standard synthetic biology notation. Users may also use our token-based language for behavior specification. For example, NOT x is expressed by clicking the token; clicking again undoes the operation. The Code View panel automatically generates Eugene code as the user inputs information in the Structure and Behavior Views. When users select a part in the Structure or Behavior Views, the relevant Eugene code pertaining to the part is highlighted. Eugenie supports the final paradigm stage, *exploration*, using the surface interface. Results that adhere to the specified structural and behavioral constraints are populated in a fourth panel, the Results View. The design process outlined here is repeated until a suitable list of results has been generated.

IMPLEMENTATION

Eugenie uses Sifteo cubes ver. 2.0: commercially available, clickable 1.7-inch block micro-computers that can interact with each other. We programmed the cubes using the Sifteo SDK and C++. The tabletop application is implemented on the SUR40 device using the Microsoft Surface 2.0 SDK and written in C#. Synthetic biological circuits are created using the domain-specific programming language, Eugene [2]. We implemented Client-Server communication between the SUR40 and Sifteo applications using PyUSB, a Python module that supports USB access.

CONCLUSION AND FUTURE WORK

We presented Eugenie, a tangible user interface for collaborative bio-design that utilizes gestural interaction with active tokens and a multi-touch interactive surface. We developed new interaction techniques for navigating large hierarchical data sets and for exploring a combinatorial design space. Future work includes evaluating the interface with users, as well as further expanding and implementing our gestural language.

ACKNOWLEDGMENTS

We thank Traci Haddock, Swapnil Bhatia, Ernst Oberortner, and Doug Densmore. This work was partially funded by NSF Grant No. IIS-1149530 and by a grant from Agilent Technologies.

REFERENCES

1. Drucker, S., Fisher, D., Sadana, R., Herron, J., and Schraefel, M. Touchvix: A case study comparing two interfaces for data analytics on tablets. In *Proc. CHI 2013*, ACM Press (2013).

2. Huang, H., Oberortner, E., Densmore, D., and Kuchinsky, A. Eugene's enriched set of features to design synthetic biological devices. In *Proc. IWBDA 2013* (2013).

3. Shaer, O., Valdes, C., Liu, S., Lu, K., Chang, K., Xu, W., Haddock, T. L., Bhatia, S., Densmore, D., and Kincaid, R. Designing reality-based interfaces for experiential bio-design. *Personal and Ubiquitous Computing* (November 2013).

4. Shaer, O., Valdes, C., Liu, S., Lu, K., Haddock, T. L., Bhatia, S., Densmore, D., and Kincaid, R. Moclo planner: Interactive visualization for modular cloning bio-design. In *Proc. Symposium on Biological Data Visualization 2013*, IEEE (2013).

5. Ullmer, B., Ishii, H., and Jacob, R. J. Tangible query interfaces: Physically constrained tokens for manipulating database queries. In *Proc. Interact 2003* (2003).

6. Valdes, C., Eastman, D., Grote, C., Thatte, S., Shaer, O., Mazalek, A., Ullmer, B., and Konkel, M. Exploring the design space of gestural interaction with active tokens through user-defined gestures. In *Proc. CHI 2014*, ACM Press (2014).

7. Voida, S., Tobiasz, M., Stromer, J., Isenberg, P., and Carpendale, S. Getting practical with interactive tabletop displays: Designing for dense data, fat fingers, diverse interactions, and face-to-face collaboration. In *Proc. the ITS 2009*, ACM Press (2009).

OverCode: Visualizing Variation in Student Solutions to Programming Problems at Scale

Elena L. Glassman
MIT CSAIL
elg@mit.edu

Jeremy Scott
MIT CSAIL
jks@mit.edu

Rishabh Singh
MIT CSAIL
rishabh@csail.mit.edu

Philip Guo
MIT CSAIL,
University of Rochester
pg@cs.rochester.edu

Robert C. Miller
MIT CSAIL
rcm@mit.edu

ABSTRACT

In MOOCs, a single programming exercise may produce thousands of solutions from learners. Understanding solution variation is important for providing appropriate feedback to students at scale. The wide variation among these solutions can be a source of pedagogically valuable examples, and can be used to refine the autograder for the exercise by exposing corner cases. We present OverCode, a system for visualizing and exploring thousands of programming solutions. OverCode uses both static and dynamic analysis to cluster similar solutions, and lets instructors further filter and cluster solutions based on different criteria. We evaluated OverCode against a non-clustering baseline in a within-subjects study with 24 teaching assistants, and found that the OverCode interface allows teachers to more quickly develop a high-level view of students' understanding and misconceptions, and to provide feedback that is relevant to more students.

Author Keywords

Data mining; programming exercises; MOOC

ACM Classification Keywords

H.5.2. Information Interfaces and Presentation: Graphical user interfaces

INTRODUCTION

Intelligent tutoring systems (ITSes), Massive Open Online Courses (MOOCs), and websites like Khan Academy and Codecademy are now used to teach programming courses at a massive scale. In these courses, a single programming exercise may produce thousands of solutions from learners, which presents both an opportunity and a challenge. For teachers, the wide variation among these solutions can be a source of pedagogically valuable examples [4], and understanding this variation is important for providing appropriate, tailored feedback to students [1, 3]. The variation can also be useful for

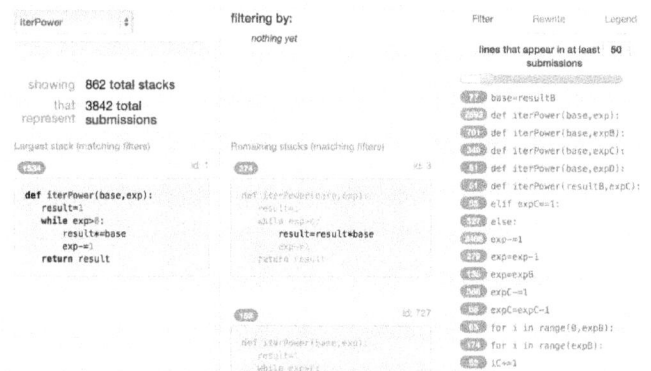

Figure 1. OverCode user interface.

refining evaluation rubrics, since it can expose corner cases in automatic grading tests.

Sifting through thousands of solutions to understand their variation and find pedagogically valuable examples is a daunting task, even if the programming exercises are simple and the solutions are only tens of lines of code long. Without tool support, a teacher may not read more than 50-100 of them before growing frustrated with the tedium of the task. Given this small sample size, teachers cannot be expected to develop a thorough understanding of the variety of strategies used to solve the problem, or produce instructive feedback that is relevant to a large proportion of learners, or find unexpected interesting solutions.

An information visualization approach would enable teachers to explore the variation in solutions at scale. Existing techniques [2, 3, 5] use a combination of clustering to group solutions that are semantically similar, and graph visualization to show the variation between these clusters. These clustering algorithms perform pairwise comparisons that are quadratic in both the number of solutions and in the size of each solution, which scales poorly to thousands of solutions. Graph visualization also struggles with how to label the graph node for a cluster, because it has been formed by a complex combination of code features. Without meaningful labels for clusters in the graph, the rich information of the learners' solutions is lost and the teacher's ability to understand variation is weakened.

In this poster we present OverCode, a system for visualizing and exploring the variation in thousands of programming solutions. OverCode is designed to visualize correct solutions, in the sense that they pass the automatic grading tests typically used in a programming class at scale. OverCode uses a novel clustering technique that creates clusters of identical cleaned code, is time linear in both the number of solutions and the size of each solution. The cleaned code is readable, executable, and describes every solution in that cluster. The cleaned code is shown in a visualization that puts code front-and-center (Figure 1). In OverCode, the teacher reads through code solutions that each represent an entire cluster of solutions that look and act the same. The differences between clusters are highlighted to help instructors discover and understand the variations among submitted solutions. Clusters can be filtered by the lines of code within them. Clusters can also be merged together with *rewrite rules* that collapse variations that the teacher decides are unimportant.

A cluster in OverCode is a set of solutions that perform the same computations, but may use different variable names or statement order. OverCode uses a lightweight dynamic analysis to generate clusters, which scales linearly with the number of solutions. It clusters solutions whose variables take the same sequence of values when executed on test inputs and whose set of constituent lines of code are syntactically the same. An important component of this analysis is to rename variables that behave the same across different solutions. The renaming of variables serves three main purposes. First, it lets teachers create a mental mapping between variable names and their behavior which is consistent across the entire set of solutions. This may reduce the cognitive load for a teacher to understand different solutions. Second, it helps clustering by reducing variation between similar solutions. Finally, it also helps make the remaining differences between different solutions more salient.

In two user studies with a total of 24 participants, we compared the OverCode interface with a baseline interface that showed original unclustered solutions. When using Over-Code, participants felt that they were able to develop a better high-level view of the students' understandings and misconceptions. While participants did not necessarily read more lines of code in the OverCode interface than in the baseline, the code they did read came from clusters containing a greater percentage of all the submitted solutions. Participants also drafted mock class forum posts about common good and bad solutions that were relevant to more solutions (and the students who wrote them) when using OverCode as compared to the baseline.

The main contributions of this work are:

- a novel visualization that shows similarity and variation among thousands of solutions, with cleaned code shown for each variant.

- an algorithm that uses the behavior of variables to help cluster solutions and generate the cleaned code for each cluster of solutions.

- two user studies that show this visualization is useful for giving instructors a bird's-eye view of thousands of students' solutions.

SUMMARY
We have designed the OverCode system for visualizing thousands of Python programming solutions to help instructors explore the variations among them. Unlike previous approaches, OverCode uses a lightweight static and dynamic analysis to generate stacks of similar solutions and uses variable renaming to present cleaned solutions for each stack in an interactive user interface. It allows instructors to filter stacks by line occurrence and to further merge different stacks by composing rewrite rules. Based on two user studies with 24 current and potential teaching assistants, we found Over-Code allowed instructors to more quickly develop a high-level view of students' understanding and misconceptions, and provide feedback that is relevant to more students. We believe an information visualization approach is necessary for instructors to explore the variations among solutions at the scale of MOOCs, and OverCode is an important step towards that goal.

ACKNOWLEDGMENTS
This material is based, in part, upon work supported by the National Science Foundation Graduate Research Fellowship (grant 1122374), the Microsoft Research Fellowship, the Bose Foundation Fellowship, and by Quanta Computer as part of the Qmulus Project. Any opinions, findings, conclusions, or recommendations in this paper are the authors', and do not necessarily reflect the views of the sponsors.

REFERENCES
1. Basu, S., Jacobs, C., and Vanderwende, L. Powergrading: a clustering approach to amplify human effort for short answer grading. *TACL 1* (2013), 391–402.

2. Gaudencio, M., Dantas, A., and Guerrero, D. D. Can computers compare student code solutions as well as teachers? In *Proceedings of the 45th ACM Technical Symposium on Computer Science Education*, SIGCSE '14, ACM (New York, NY, USA, 2014), 21–26.

3. Huang, J., Piech, C., Nguyen, A., and Guibas, L. J. Syntactic and functional variability of a million code submissions in a machine learning mooc. In *AIED Workshops* (2013).

4. Marton, F., Tsui, A., Chik, P., Ko, P., and Lo, M. *Classroom Discourse and the Space of Learning.* Taylor & Francis, 2013.

5. Nguyen, A., Piech, C., Huang, J., and Guibas, L. J. Codewebs: scalable homework search for massive open online programming courses. In *WWW* (2014), 491–502.

Author Index

www.ingramcontent.com/pod-product-compliance
Lightning Source LLC
Chambersburg PA
CBHW082034230326
41598CB00081B/6508